Mc<

500 Financial Accounting and Reporting Questions

for the CPA Exam

Frimette Kass-Shraibman, PhD, CPA; Vijay Sampath, DPS, MBA, CPA;
Denise M. Stefano, CPA, CGMA, MBA; and
Darrel Surett, CPA

Mc
Graw
Hill
Education

New York Chicago San Francisco Athens London Madrid
Mexico City Milan New Delhi Singapore Sydney Toronto

1 2 3 4 5 6 7 8 9 10   QFR/QFR   1 0 9 8 7 6 5 4

ISBN   978-0-07-180707-4
MHID   0-07-180707-1

e-ISBN   978-0-07-180708-1
e-MHID   0-07-180708-X

Library of Congress Control Number 2014939550

McGraw-Hill Education products are available at special quantity discounts to use as premiums and sales promotions or for use in corporate training programs. To contact a representative, please visit the Contact Us pages at www.mhprofessional.com.

CONTENTS

INTRODUCTION

Congratulations! You've taken a big step toward CPA exam success by purchasing *McGraw-Hill Education: 500 Financial Accounting and Reporting Questions for the CPA Exam.* This book gives you 500 multiple-choice questions that cover all of the most essential material for the Financial Accounting and Reporting section of the CPA exam. Each question is clearly explained in the answer key. The questions will give you valuable independent practice to supplement your other studies.

You might be the kind of student who needs extra study a few weeks before the exam for a final review. Or you might be the kind of student who puts off preparing until the last minute before the exam. No matter what your preparation style, you will benefit from reviewing these 500 questions, which closely parallel the content, format, and degree of difficulty of the questions on the actual CPA exam. These questions and the explanations in the answer key are the ideal last-minute study tool for those final weeks before the test.

If you practice with all the questions and answers in this book, we are certain you will build the skills and confidence needed to excel on the CPA exam. Good luck!

—*Editors of McGraw-Hill Education*

McGraw-Hill Education

500
Financial
Accounting
and Reporting
Questions

for the CPA Exam

CHAPTER 1

Accounting Theory and Conceptual Understanding

1. Which of the following are included in the Accounting Standards Codification?
   I. Financial Accounting Standards Board (FASB) statements of financial accounting standards
   II. International Financial Reporting Standards (IFRS)
   (A) I only
   (B) II only
   (C) both I and II
   (D) neither I nor II

2. According to the FASB and International Accounting Standards Board (IASB) conceptual framework, for financial information to be useful, it must be
   I. relevant
   II. faithfully represented
   (A) I only
   (B) II only
   (C) both I and II
   (D) neither I nor II

3. According to the FASB and IASB conceptual framework, relevance includes which of the following qualitative characteristics?
   I. predictive value
   II. confirming value
   (A) I only
   (B) II only
   (C) both I and II
   (D) neither I nor II

4. According to the FASB and IASB conceptual framework, in the category of faithful representation, which of the following describes information that is free from bias in selection or presentation?
   I. relevance
   II. neutrality
   (A) I only
   (B) II only
   (C) both I and II
   (D) neither I nor II

5. Which of the following is a fundamental qualitative characteristic of financial reporting?
   I. relevance
   II. faithful representation
   (A) I only
   (B) II only
   (C) both I and II
   (D) neither I nor II

6. According to the FASB and IASB conceptual framework, which of the following is an enhancing (rather than fundamental) qualitative characteristic of financial reporting?
   I. comparability
   II. verifiability
   (A) I only
   (B) II only
   (C) both I and II
   (D) neither I nor II

7. According to the FASB and IASB conceptual framework, both timeliness and understandability are
   (A) enhancing qualitative characteristics of useful financial information
   (B) fundamental qualitative characteristics of useful financial information
   (C) characteristics of relevance
   (D) characteristics of faithful representation

8. According to the Accounting Conceptual Framework, the net realizable value method is generally used to measure which of the following?
   I. property plant and equipment
   II. accounts receivable
   III. inventory
   (A) II and III
   (B) I and II
   (C) I, II, and III
   (D) II only

9. Which of the following correctly describes the difference between accrual accounting and cash basis accounting as it relates to revenue?
   I. Under accrual accounting, if the earnings process is not complete, revenue is nevertheless recorded if the cash has already been received.
   II. Under the cash basis, if cash has been collected, revenue can be recorded even if the earnings process is not complete.
   (A) I only
   (B) II only
   (C) both I and II
   (D) neither I nor II

10. Accrual accounting adheres to which of the following principles of accounting with regard to revenue and expense recognition?
    I. matching principle
    II. historical cost principle
    (A) I only
    (B) II only
    (C) both I and II
    (D) neither I nor II

11. According to the FASB conceptual framework, when selecting accounting principles in accordance with US generally accepted accounting principles (GAAP), and when in doubt, the method that is less likely to overstate assets and understate liabilities should be chosen according to which rule or assumption?
    (A) full disclosure
    (B) periodicity
    (C) going concern
    (D) conservatism

12. Which of the following elements of the financial statements includes all differences between beginning and ending equity other than transactions between a firm and its owners?

    (A) retained earnings
    (B) net income
    (C) paid in capital in excess of par
    (D) comprehensive income

13. Under US GAAP, the effect of a material transaction that is infrequent in occurrence but not unusual in nature should be presented separately as a component of income from continuing operations when the transaction results in a

    I. gain
    II. loss

    (A) I only
    (B) II only
    (C) both I and II
    (D) neither I nor II

Use the following facts to answer questions 14–15:

During January of Year 3, Durka Corp agreed to sell the assets and product line of its Arelco division. The sale was completed on January 15, Year 4, and resulted in a gain on disposal of $900,000. Arelco's operating losses were $600,000 for Year 3 and $50,000 for the period January 1 through January 15, Year 4.

14. If the tax rate is 30%, what amount of net gain (loss) should be reported in Durka's Year 3 income statement under US GAAP?

    (A) $420,000
    (B) ($420,000)
    (C) ($600,000)
    (D) -0-

15. Assuming a 30% tax rate, what amount of net gain (loss) should be reported in Durka's Year 4 income statement under US GAAP?

    (A) $850,000
    (B) $900,000
    (C) $595,000
    (D) $255,000

16. The Pastorini Corporation reported the following items on the income statement. Which of the following items would be reported as income from continuing operations under the IFRS?
  I. large loss from a foreign currency transaction
  II. a union strike that shuts down operations for three months
  III. a foreign government taking possession of a company's only plant
  IV. damage to a factory from a flood in an area that never had flood damage before

(A) III only
(B) III and IV
(C) II, III, and IV
(D) I, II, III, and IV

17. Which of the following accounting changes is treated as a change in accounting estimate?
  I. change in depreciation method
  II. change in useful life of an asset

(A) I only
(B) II only
(C) both I and II
(D) neither I nor II

18. Which of the following accounting changes is treated as a change in accounting principle?
  I. a change from First In-First Out inventory valuation to average cost
  II. a change from the direct write-off method of recognizing bad debt expense to the allowance method

(A) I only
(B) II only
(C) both I and II
(D) neither I nor II

19. On January 1, Year 8, Ashbrook Corp changed from one IFRS method to another. The change in principle better presents the financial information of Ashbrook Corp. Under the old method the pretax accounting income was $600,000. Had Ashbrook Corp been using the new method, pretax accounting income would have been $900,000. Ashbrook Corp's effective tax rate is 30%. How should Ashbroook Corp report the cumulative effect of a change in accounting principle for Year 8?

(A) $300,000 additional income on the income statement
(B) $210,000 additional income on the income statement
(C) $300,000 increase to beginning retained earnings balance
(D) $210,000 increase to beginning retained earnings balance

20. A change in inventory methods that would be handled prospectively as a change in estimate rather than a change in accounting principle would include
    I. a change from FIFO to LIFO
    II. a change from LIFO to FIFO
    (A) I only
    (B) II only
    (C) both I and II
    (D) neither I nor II

21. Which of the following are reported as adjustments to the beginning balance of retained earnings for the earliest period presented?
    I. correction of an error in a period that is not being presented
    II. cumulative effect of a change in inventory from FIFO to weighted average
    (A) I only
    (B) II only
    (C) both I and II
    (D) neither I nor II

22. Rex Corp changed from straight line depreciation to double declining balance, resulting in an additional expense of $20,000 after tax for Year 5. Also in Year 5, Rex Corp failed to accrue bad debt expense of $30,000 (after tax) in its income statement. What amount should Rex Corp report as a prior period adjustment in Year 5?
    (A) $20,000
    (B) $30,000
    (C) $50,000
    (D) -0-

23. Financial statements of all prior periods presented should be restated when there is a change in reporting entity. Which of the following would be considered a change in entity?
    I. a change in companies included as subsidiaries when reporting consolidated financial statements in both years
    II. when consolidated financial statements are issued in the current year and individual financial statements were issued in the prior year
    (A) I only
    (B) II only
    (C) both I and II
    (D) neither I nor II

24. The cumulative effect of which of the following accounting changes would be presented as an adjustment to the beginning balance of retained earnings for the earliest period presented?

   I. a change in the amount of mineral expected to be recoverable from an underground mine

  II. a change in the expected useful life of a machine from 7 years to 4 years

(A) I only
(B) II only
(C) both I and II
(D) neither I nor II

25. On October 31, Year 8, Kingman Corp decided to change from the completed contract method to the percentage of completion method. Kingman Corp is a calendar year corporation and used US GAAP. If comparative financial statements are NOT being presented, the cumulative effect of this change is

(A) shown as of October 31, Year 9
(B) shown as of January 1, Year 9
(C) not shown
(D) shown as of December 31, Year 9

26. Which of the following is correct regarding the reporting of comprehensive income?

   I. Comprehensive income can be presented together with the income statement as a single financial statement.

  II. Comprehensive income may be shown separately on its own financial statement.

(A) I only
(B) II only
(C) both I and II
(D) neither I nor II

27. Which of the following standard setting bodies requires that a description of significant policies be included as an integral part of the financial statements?

   I. US GAAP

  II. IFRS

(A) I only
(B) II only
(C) both I and II
(D) neither I nor II

28. Which of the following should be disclosed in a footnote called "summary of significant accounting policies"?
  I. basis of profit recognition on long-term construction contracts
  II. criteria for measuring cash equivalents
  (A) I only
  (B) II only
  (C) both I and II
  (D) neither I nor II

29. Footnote disclosure of significant judgments and estimates is a requirement under which of the following standards?
  I. US GAAP
  II. IFRS
  (A) I only
  (B) II only
  (C) both I and II
  (D) neither I nor II

30. Which of the following is correct regarding interim reporting?
  I. Comprehensive income is NOT reported.
  II. Each statement must be marked "unaudited."
  (A) I only
  (B) II only
  (C) both I and II
  (D) neither I nor II

31. Which of the following accounting standards requires a statement in the footnotes that financial statements are presented in accordance with the reporting framework?
  I. US GAAP
  II. IFRS
  (A) I only
  (B) II only
  (C) both I and II
  (D) neither I nor II

32. Disclosures involving which of the following would be included as part of the "summary of significant accounting policies"?
   I. maturity dates associated with long-term debt
   II. subsequent events

   (A) I only
   (B) II only
   (C) both I and II
   (D) neither I nor II

33. Which is correct regarding interim financial reporting?
   I. Interim financial reporting is required under both GAAP and IFRS.
   II. Permanent inventory declines should NOT be recorded in the interim period of decline but rather at year end.

   (A) I only
   (B) II only
   (C) both I and II
   (D) neither I nor II

34. Which of the following is correct regarding the US Securities and Exchange Commission (SEC) reporting standards for a large accelerated filer?
   I. Form 10-K must be filed within 90 days of the close of the fiscal year.
   II. Form 10-Q must be filed within 40 days of the close of the first three fiscal quarters.

   (A) I only
   (B) II only
   (C) both I and II
   (D) neither I nor II

35. Which of the following is correct regarding forms 10-K and 10-Q for US registered companies?
   (A) They must be prepared using US GAAP.
   (B) Form 10-Q must be prepared using US GAAP, but Form 10-K can be prepared using US GAAP or IFRS.
   (C) They can be prepared using either US GAAP or IFRS.
   (D) Form 10-K must be prepared using US GAAP, but Form 10-Q may be prepared using IFRS.

36. Privately held companies are exempt from reporting which of the following?
  I. earnings per share (EPS)
  II. business segment information
  (A) I only
  (B) II only
  (C) both I and II
  (D) neither I nor II

The following information pertains to Cricket Corp's segments for Year 13:

Segment	Sales to Unaffiliated Customers	Intercompany Sales	Total Revenue
Travis	$6,000	$4,000	$10,000
Bass	$9,000	$5,000	$14,000
Lead	$4,000	$1,000	$5,000
Capo	$45,000	$18,000	$63,000
Combined	$64,000	$28,000	$92,000
Elimination		$28,000	$28,000
Consolidated	$64,000		$64,000

37. If Cricket uses the revenue test to determine reportable segments, which of the following is correct?
  I. Bass would NOT be a reportable segment in Year 13, since its revenue from sales to unaffiliated customers of $9,000 is less than 10% of $92,000.
  II. Lead would NOT be a reportable segment in Year 13, since its combined revenue of $5,000 is less than 10% of $92,000.
  (A) I only
  (B) II only
  (C) both I and II
  (D) neither I nor II

38. Wershing Corp, a publicly held corporation, is subject to the requirements of segment reporting. In its income statement for December 31, Year 12, Wershing Corp reported revenues of $60,000,000, operating expenses of $58,000,000, and net income of $2,000,000. $40,000,000 of Wershing Corp sales were to external customers. External revenues reported by operating segments must be at least how much for Year 12?

   (A) $45,000,000
   (B) $6,000,000
   (C) $4,000,000
   (D) $30,000,000

39. Eagle Hardware is a development stage enterprise, had no revenue, and incurred only the following three costs in Year 13, its first year of operations:

Legal fees to incorporate	$50,000
Underwriters' fees for IPO	$32,000
Land acquired to become future corporate headquarters	$100,000

   Eagle Hardware should charge how much to organization expense in Year 13?

   (A) -0-
   (B) $50,000
   (C) $82,000
   (D) $150,000

40. Which of the following is a required disclosure for a development stage enterprise?

   I. identification of the financial statements as those of a development stage enterprise
   II. number of shares of stock issued and dates of issuance

   (A) I only
   (B) II only
   (C) both I and II
   (D) neither I nor II

CHAPTER 2

Revenue and Expense Recognition

41. Which of the following requirements must be met for revenue to be recognized under US generally accepted accounting principles (GAAP)?
  I. There must exist persuasive evidence of an arrangement or contract.
  II. Services have been rendered or delivery of goods has occurred.
  III. At least 10% of the cash consideration must be received.

  (A) I only
  (B) I and II
  (C) I, II, and III
  (D) II only

42. Advantage Voice and Data LLC develops hardware and software for the telecom industry. On September 22, Year 2, Advantage signs a multiple element arrangement with Voicenext LLC, where Advantage will sell a phone system to Voicenext, train Voicenext staff, and offer post-sales customer support to Voicenext staff through December 31 of Year 3. The total value of the contract is $250,000. The phone system is installed on December 1 of Year 2; the employees' training is completed as of December 31 of Year 2. Although the contract is not substantially complete, Advantage would like to recognize revenue in Year 2 for the elements of the contract that have been completed thus far, including the installation of the system and training of the staff. Which of the following is a condition that must exist for Advantage to recognize revenue from separate elements of this contract prior to the completion of the entire agreement?
  I. The element has value on a stand-alone basis.
  II. The element can be sold separately.

  (A) I only
  (B) II only
  (C) both I and II
  (D) neither I nor II

43. According to the concept of accrual accounting, which of the following describes a deferral?
    I. Deferral of revenues will occur when cash is received but is NOT recognizable for financial statement purposes.
    II. Deferral typically results in the recognition of a liability or prepaid expense.
    (A) I only
    (B) II only
    (C) both I and II
    (D) neither I nor II

44. An example of a deferral would NOT include
    I. cash collected in advance of services being rendered
    II. cash paid up front for a 1-year insurance policy
    (A) I only
    (B) II only
    (C) both I and II
    (D) neither I nor II

45. Brace Inc. prepaid an annual insurance policy in advance on August 1, Year 10, in the amount of $3,000. The entry to adjust the prepaid expense account at December 31, Year 10, would include
    (A) credit of $1,250 to prepaid insurance
    (B) debit of $1,750 to insurance expense
    (C) credit of $1,750 to prepaid insurance
    (D) debit of $1,250 to prepaid insurance

46. Perry's Gift Shop, a retail store, sold gift certificates that are redeemable in merchandise. On November 1, Year 12, a customer buys $6,000 of gift certificates from Perry's Gift Shop. The gift certificates lapse 1 year after the date of issuance. Which of the following is correct?
    (A) On November 1, Year 12, Perry would record a credit to revenue for $6,000.
    (B) On November 1, Year 12, Perry would record a credit to deferred revenue for $6,000.
    (C) On December 31, Year 12, Perry would record a credit to revenue for the months of November and December in the amount of $1,000.
    (D) On November 1, Year 12, Perry would record a debit to prepaid expense for $6,000.

47. With regard to cash received in advance for gift certificates, the deferred revenue account would decrease by which of the following?
    I. lapse or expiration of certificates
    II. redemption of certificates
    (A) I only
    (B) II only
    (C) both I and II
    (D) neither I nor II

48. Which of the following is correct regarding cash basis and accrual basis revenue as related to accounts receivable?
    I. A decrease in accounts receivable from the beginning of the year to the end of the year generally represents cash collections.
    II. Under the cash basis, revenue is recognized when the receivable is initially recorded.
    (A) I only
    (B) II only
    (C) both I and II
    (D) neither I nor II

49. When adjusting service revenue from cash basis to accrual basis, which of the following items would be added to cash fees collected?
    I. the ending balance of accounts receivable
    II. the beginning balance of accounts receivable
    (A) I only
    (B) II only
    (C) both I and II
    (D) neither I nor II

50. Compared to an accrual, a deferral is a transaction that impacts
    (A) cash and the income statement at the same time
    (B) the income statement before impacting cash
    (C) cash before impacting the income statement
    (D) none of the above

51. The ending balance of unearned fees represents
    I. cash received in advance and NOT yet earned during the period
    II. the decrease in accounts receivable for the period
    (A) I only
    (B) II only
    (C) both I and II
    (D) neither I nor II

52. Which of the following would increase cash basis revenue in Year 1 compared to accrual basis revenue in Year 1?
  I. collecting cash in Year 1 for services to be performed in Year 2
  II. earning revenue in Year 1; cash to be collected in Year 2
(A) I only
(B) II only
(C) both I and II
(D) neither I nor II

53. Which of the following would increase accrual basis revenue in Year 1 compared to cash basis revenue in Year 1?
  I. collecting cash in year 1 for services to be performed in Year 2
  II. earning revenue in Year 1; cash had already been collected in Year 0
(A) I only
(B) II only
(C) both I and II
(D) neither I nor II

54. When adjusting service revenue from cash basis to accrual basis, which of the following items would be added to cash fees collected?
  I. beginning unearned fees
  II. ending unearned fees
(A) I only
(B) II only
(C) both I and II
(D) neither I nor II

55. Moss, a consultant keeps her accounting records on a cash basis. During Year 10 she collected $100,000 in fees from clients. At December 31, Year 9, she had accounts receivable of $40,000. At December 31, Year 10, she had accounts receivable of $60,000 and unearned fees of $4,000. On the accrual basis, what was her service revenue for Year 10?
(A) $120,000
(B) $180,000
(C) $116,000
(D) $124,000

56. Storage Inc. owns a warehouse and leases space under a variety of agreements. Some customers pay in advance, and others fall behind on their rent. Storage Inc.'s financial records contained the following data:

	Year 1	Year 2
Rent receivable	$7,600	$8,200
Unearned rent	$28,000	$21,000

During Year 2, Storage Inc. received $60,000 cash from tenants. What amount of rental revenue should Storage Inc. record for Year 2?

(A) $60,000
(B) $67,600
(C) $52,400
(D) $68,240

Use the following facts to answer questions 57–58:

Millet Inc. uses the percentage of completion method to account for long-term construction contracts. On January 3, Year 12, Millet signed a 3-year contract with the state of New Jersey to build a road. The contract was for $2,000,000. Costs incurred in Year 12 amounted to $300,000, and total costs remaining on the contract were expected to be $1,200,000. Millet collected $200,000 from the state in advance at the time the contract was signed and another $150,000 at the end of Year 12. In Year 13, another $900,000 was spent, and it was estimated that an additional $400,000 of costs would be spent in Year 14.

57. How much profit from the contract should Millet Inc. recognize in Year 12?

(A) -0-
(B) $100,000
(C) $350,000
(D) $500,000

58. How much profit from the contract should Millet Inc. recognize in Year 13?

(A) $300,000
(B) $400,000
(C) $100,000
(D) $200,000

59. For a long-term construction contract being accounted for using the percentage of completion method, the construction in progress account is debited for

    I. construction costs incurred

   II. profit from the construction contract recognized to date

  (A) I only

  (B) II only

  (C) both I and II

  (D) neither I nor II

60. Everlast Construction Inc. uses the percentage of completion method to account for long-term construction contracts. The account "progress billings" is credited by Everlast Construction Inc. when

  (A) bills that have been sent to customers are returned with payment

  (B) construction costs are paid

  (C) profit is recorded

  (D) bills are mailed to customers

61. With regard to profit recognition from long-term construction contracts accounted for on the percentage of completion method,

  (A) progress billings impact profit, but cash collections do not

  (B) cash collections impact profit, but progress billings do not

  (C) both cash collections and progress billings impact profit recognition

  (D) neither cash collections nor progress billings impact profit recognition

62. The completed contract method of accounting for long-term construction projects

  (A) is no longer permitted under US GAAP

  (B) is to be used when the degree of completion can be determined with reasonable accuracy

  (C) recognizes losses in the year they are apparent even if the project is not substantially completed

  (D) is essentially a cash basis rather than accrual basis method

63. Olney Contracting is hired by the state of Arizona on January 1, Year 13, to build a section of a new highway. The contract will take several years to complete. The sales price is $50 million, and the company estimates that the work will cost $44 million. During Year 13, $11 million is spent. During Year 14, another $20 million is spent, and engineers expect that the project will require additional costs of $15 million after Year 14. Olney Corp must use the percentage of completion method to account for this contract if the buyer has the ability to fulfill its obligations and Olney has the ability to

    I. estimate the degree of completion with reasonable accuracy

   II. complete the job

(A) I only

(B) II only

(C) both I and II

(D) neither I nor II

Use the following facts to answer questions 64–65:

The Buxton Corp sold an asset on March 1 of Year 13 for the amount of $100,000. The cost of the asset was $60,000. Buxton was unable to estimate how much of the $100,000 they may collect; therefore, they chose to account for the sale under the installment method. In Year 13, $20,000 was collected in connection with this sale, and in Year 14, $10,000 more was collected.

64. How much gross profit from the sale should be realized by Buxton Corp on the December 31, Year 13, income statement?

(A) -0-

(B) $8,000

(C) $6,667

(D) $40,000

65. How much gross profit from the sale should be deferred by Buxton Corp on December 31, Year 13?

(A) $32,000

(B) $60,000

(C) $40,000

(D) $92,000

66. Which of the following is considered a cash basis rather than an accrual basis method of revenue recognition?
    I. percentage of completion
    II. completed contract
    III. installment method
    (A) II and III
    (B) III only
    (C) II only
    (D) I only

Use the following facts to answer questions 67–69:

In Year 13, Russell Inc. uses the cost recovery method to account for a $5,000 sale with a total cost of $2,500. During Year 13, Russell collects $2,000 and then collects $3,000 in Year 14.

67. Using the cost recovery method, how much will Russell report as gross profit in Year 13?
    (A) $2,500
    (B) $1,000
    (C) $500
    (D) -0-

68. Using the cost recovery method, how much will Russell report as gross profit in Year 14?
    (A) $500
    (B) $2,500
    (C) $1,500
    (D) -0-

69. If Russell Inc. had used the installment method rather than cost recovery, how much gross profit would have been realized in Year 13?
    (A) -0-
    (B) $2,000
    (C) $2,500
    (D) $1,000

Use the following facts to answer questions 70–71:

The payroll for the month ended July 31 is summarized as follows for Stanley's Sportland Inc.:

Total wages	$100,000
Federal income tax withheld	$700

All wages paid were subject to FICA. FICA tax rates were 7% each for employee and employer. Stanley's Sportland Inc. remits payroll taxes on the 15th of the following month.

70. In its financial statements for the month ended July 31, what amounts should Stanley's Sportland Inc. report as total payroll tax liability?
    (A) $7,000
    (B) $14,000
    (C) $7,700
    (D) $14,700

71. In its financial statements for the month ended July 31, what amounts should Stanley's Sportland Inc. report as total payroll tax expense?
    (A) $7,000
    (B) $14,000
    (C) $7,700
    (D) $14,700

72. Dartam Publishing created a board game called "Visit New York" and sold it to Parker Brothers for royalties of 10% of sales. Royalties are payable semiannually on March 31 (for July through December sales of the previous year) and on September 30 (for January through June sales of the same year). On September 30, Year 4, Dartam Publishing received their first royalty check from Parker Brothers in the amount of $10,000. On March 31, Year 5, Dartam Publishing received a royalty check in the amount of $20,000. On September 30, Year 5, Dartam Publishing received a royalty check for $30,000. Dartam Publishing estimated that board game sales of "Visit New York" would total $180,000 for the second half of Year 5. How much royalty revenue should Dartam Publishing report for the year ended December 31, Year 5?
    (A) $48,000
    (B) $68,000
    (C) $21,000
    (D) $50,000

73. Which of the following is correct regarding patent costs under US GAAP?
   I. Fees to acquire a patent from a third party are expensed.
   II. Most costs incurred to internally generate a patent are capitalized.

(A) I only
(B) II only
(C) both I and II
(D) neither I nor II

74. Under US GAAP, which of the following is correct regarding patent costs?
   I. Costs associated with a successful patent defense should be capitalized.
   II. Costs associated with an unsuccessful patent defense should be expensed.

(A) I only
(B) II only
(C) both I and II
(D) neither I nor II

75. All research and development costs are expensed as incurred under which of the following accounting standards?
   I. US GAAP
   II. International Financial Reporting Standards (IFRS)

(A) I only
(B) II only
(C) both I and II
(D) neither I nor II

76. Which of the following is correct regarding costs associated with goodwill?
   I. Costs of developing and maintaining goodwill are NOT capitalized.
   II. Goodwill is capitalized when incurred in the purchase of another entity and then amortized using the straight line method.

(A) I only
(B) II only
(C) both I and II
(D) neither I nor II

77. Which of the following is correct regarding capitalization and amortization of intangible assets under US GAAP?
    I. Intangible assets with infinite lives such as goodwill should be capitalized but NOT amortized.
    II. Intangible assets with finite lives such as patents, franchises, and covenants not to compete should be capitalized and amortized.
    (A) I only
    (B) II only
    (C) both I and II
    (D) neither I nor II

78. Intangible assets may be reported under the revaluation model (fair value) rather than the cost model under which of the following standards?
    I. US GAAP
    II. IFRS
    (A) I only
    (B) II only
    (C) both I and II
    (D) neither I nor II

79. During Year 1, Guidry Co. incurred $300,000 of research and development costs in its laboratory to develop a product for which a patent was granted on July 1, Year 1. Legal fees and other costs associated with the patent totaled $72,000. The estimated economic life of the patent is 12 years. What amount should Guidry capitalize for the patent on July 1, Year 1, under US GAAP?
    (A) $72,000
    (B) $300,000
    (C) $372,000
    (D) -0-

80. If a company incurs costs to develop computer software, the company will expense all costs rather than capitalize them if the software is developed for
    I. internal use only
    II. sale to customers
    (A) I only
    (B) II only
    (C) both I and II
    (D) neither I nor II

81. In Year 13, Gigabyte Logic incurred the following computer software costs for the development and sale of computer software programs:

Planning costs	$40,000
Design of software	$120,000
Substantial testing of the project's initial stages	$64,000
Production and packaging costs for the first month's sales	$72,000
Producing product masters after technological feasibility was established	$180,000

What amount of these software costs should NOT be expensed by Gigabyte Logic as research and development?

(A) -0-
(B) $180,000
(C) $252,000
(D) $224,000

82. Costello Corp produces software for sale and also for internal uses. During the current year, Costello Corp incurred the following costs:

Research and development costs contracted out to third parties	$40,000
Design production and testing of preproduction prototypes	$120,000
Testing in search for new products	$25,000
Quality control	$13,000

In the current year income statement, what amount should Costello Corp expense as research and development under US GAAP?

(A) $198,000
(B) $160,000
(C) $65,000
(D) $185,000

83. On January 2, Year 13, Scotti purchased a Subway franchise with a useful life of 20 years for $90,000. An additional franchise fee of 4% of sales must be paid each year to Subway World headquarters. Sales in Year 13 for Scotti's new Subway amounted to $300,000. In its December 31, Year 13, balance sheet, what amount should Scotti report as an intangible asset franchise?

(A) $4,500
(B) $85,500
(C) $16,500
(D) $90,000

84. On December 31, Benning Inc. analyzed a patent with a net carrying value of $500,000 for impairment. The entity determined the following:

Fair value	$485,000
Undiscounted future cash flows	$498,000

What is the impairment loss that will be reported on the December 31 income statement under US GAAP?

(A) $15,000
(B) $2,000
(C) $17,000
(D) -0-

85. On December 31, Desi Corp analyzed a trademark with a net carrying value of $320,000 for impairment. The entity determined the following:

Fair value	$280,000
Undiscounted future cash flows	$333,000

What is the impairment loss that will be reported on the December 31 income statement under US GAAP?

(A) $40,000
(B) $13,000
(C) -0-
(D) $55,000

86. When testing for impairment of assets with a finite life, which of the following is correct?
   I. Comparing fair value (rather than undiscounted cash flows) to the asset's carrying amount will result in a smaller impairment loss.
   II. No impairment is recorded if the undiscounted cash flows exceed the asset's carrying amount.

(A) I only
(B) II only
(C) both I and II
(D) neither I nor II

87. When testing an asset for impairment that is held for disposal as a part of a discontinued operation rather than held for use,
  I. the asset's carrying amount is first compared to the undiscounted cash flows to see if any impairment has occurred
  II. if an impairment has occurred, the discounted cash flows (asset's fair value) is compared to the asset's carrying amount

(A) I only
(B) II only
(C) both I and II
(D) neither I nor II

88. Under US GAAP, no restoration of impairment loss is permitted even if the asset recovers in value when the asset is
  I. held for disposal
  II. held for use

(A) I only
(B) II only
(C) both I and II
(D) neither I nor II

89. For fixed assets, no reversal of an impairment loss is permitted when the asset is held for use under
  I. US GAAP
  II. IFRS

(A) I only
(B) II only
(C) both I and II
(D) neither I nor II

CHAPTER 3

Marketable Securities

90. Under US generally accepted accounting principles (GAAP), investment securities should be classified into categories based on the intent of the purchaser. Which of the following is one of the acceptable classifications?

   I. available for sale
  II. mark to market
 III. trading
 IV. held to maturity

  (A) I, II, III, and IV
  (B) I and III
  (C) I, III, and IV
  (D) III and IV

91. According to US GAAP, both debt and equity securities may be classified as

   I. available for sale
  II. trading
 III. held to maturity

  (A) I and III
  (B) I and II
  (C) II only
  (D) II and III

92. Management can choose to classify which of the following securities as "available for sale" or "held to maturity"?

   I. debt securities
  II. equity securities that are NOT classified as "trading"

  (A) I only
  (B) II only
  (C) both I and II
  (D) neither I nor II

93. On January 1 of the current year, Fords Co. paid $800,000 to purchase 2-year, 7%, $1,000,000 face value bonds that were issued by another publicly traded corporation. Fords Co. plans to sell the bonds in the first quarter of the following year. The fair value of the bonds at the end of the current year was $1,030,000. At what amount should Fords report the bonds in its balance sheet at the end of the current year?

(A) $1,000,000
(B) $1,030,000
(C) $870,000
(D) $800,000

94. Which is correct regarding unrealized gains and losses on marketable securities held for investment?

I. Unrealized gains on trading securities should NOT be reported on the income statement if the security has not been sold.
II. Unrealized losses on available-for-sale securities should NOT be reported on the income statement unless the loss is considered "other than temporary."

(A) I only
(B) II only
(C) both I and II
(D) neither I nor II

Use the following facts to answer questions 95–96:

Azur Corp purchases marketable securities in Green Corp during Year 1. At the end of Year 1, the fair value of Green Corp stock has dropped below its cost. Azur Corp considered the decline in value to be temporary as of December 31, Year 1. The security is classified as an available-for-sale asset.

95. What should be the effect on Azur Corp's financial statements at December 31, Year 1?

(A) decrease in available-for-sale assets and decrease in net income
(B) no effect on available-for-sale assets and decrease in net income
(C) no effect on net income and decrease on available-for-sale assets
(D) decrease in available-for-sale assets and decrease in other comprehensive income

96. Assume in Year 2 that the value of the security has not changed, but Azur Corp now considers the drop to be permanent. What should be the effects of the determination that the decline was other than temporary on Azur's Year 2 net available-for-sale assets and net income?

    (A) decrease in net available-for-sale assets and no effect on net income
    (B) no effect on net available-for-sale assets and decrease in net income
    (C) no effect on both net available-for-sale assets and net income
    (D) decrease in both net available-for-sale assets and net income

97. With regard to marketable securities held as available-for-sale, which of the following are reported in comprehensive income?
    I. unrealized temporary losses
    II. unrealized losses considered other than temporary
    III. unrealized gains

    (A) I and II
    (B) I and III
    (C) II and III
    (D) I, II, and III

98. Trixie Corp had the following items in the current year:

Loss on early extinguishment of bonds	$4,000
Realized gain on sale of available-for-sale securities	$31,000
Unrealized loss on available-for-sale securities	$16,000

    Which of the following amounts would the statement of comprehensive income report as other comprehensive income or loss?

    (A) $15,000 other comprehensive income
    (B) $20,000 other comprehensive loss
    (C) $11,000 other comprehensive loss
    (D) $16,000 other comprehensive loss

99. With regard to investments in securities, which of the following is correct regarding the cost (fair value) method?
    I. The investment in investee account is adjusted for investee earnings.
    II. The investment in investee is adjusted to fair value at the end of the reporting period.

    (A) I only
    (B) II only
    (C) both I and II
    (D) neither I nor II

100. Under the cost method, the investment in investee account is reduced for
    I. cash dividends received that are NOT in excess of investee earnings
    II. ordinary losses incurred by the investee

(A) I only
(B) II only
(C) both I and II
(D) neither I nor II

101. Which of the following if received from the investee will affect the income reported by an investor, using the equity method?
    I. cash dividend
    II. stock dividend

(A) I only
(B) II only
(C) both I and II
(D) neither I nor II

102. Woodley Inc. became a 4% owner of Jensen Inc. by purchasing 5,000 shares of Jensen Inc.'s stock on March 1, Year 13. Woodley Inc. received a stock dividend of 1,000 shares on September 1, Year 13, when the market value of Jensen Inc. was $20 per share. Jensen Inc. paid a cash dividend of $3 per share on November 1, Year 13, to shareholders of record on October 1, Year 13. In its Year 13 income statement, what amount would Woodley Inc. report as dividend income?

(A) $15,000
(B) $18,000
(C) $25,000
(D) $32,000

103. Rochelle Corp acquired 40% of Clark Inc.'s voting common stock on January 2, Year 13, for $400,000. The carrying amount of Clark's net assets at the purchase date totaled $900,000. Fair values equaled carrying amounts for all items except equipment, for which fair values exceeded carrying amounts by $100,000. The equipment has a 5-year life. During Year 13, Clark reported net income of $150,000. What amount of income from this investment should Rochelle Corp report in its Year 13 income statement?

(A) $56,000
(B) $60,000
(C) $52,000
(D) $68,000

104. Singer Co. uses the equity method to account for its January 1, Year 1, purchase of Kaufman Inc.'s common stock. On January 1, Year 1, the fair values of Kaufman's FIFO inventory and land exceeded their carrying amounts. Which of these excesses of fair values over carrying amounts will reduce Singer's reported equity in Kaufman's Year 1 earnings?

  I. inventory excess

 II. land excess

(A) I only

(B) II only

(C) both I and II

(D) neither I nor II

CHAPTER 4

Stockholders' Equity

105. A corporation has common stock with a $10 par value. A new share of this stock is issued for $13 to an investor. Which of the following is correct?
  I. The company will debit common stock for the par value of $10.
  II. The company will debit cash for $13 and credit gain on sale of stock for $3 if the purchaser of the stock was already a stockholder and is simply buying additional shares.

 (A) I only
 (B) II only
 (C) both I and II
 (D) neither I nor II

106. A company has common stock with a $10 par value and fair market value of $15. The company exchanges 1,000 shares of this common stock for an acre of land.
  I. The land will be debited for $10,000.
  II. The common stock account will be credited for $10,000 and no additional paid-in capital will be recorded.

 (A) I only
 (B) II only
 (C) both I and II
 (D) neither I nor II

107. A company was organized in January Year 6 with authorized capital of $10 par value common stock. On February 1, Year 6, 2 shares were issued at par for cash. On March 1, Year 6, the company's attorney accepted 5,000 shares of the common stock in settlement for legal services with a fair value of $60,000. Additional paid-in capital would increase on
   I. February 1, Year 6
   II. March 1, Year 6

   (A) I only
   (B) II only
   (C) both I and II
   (D) neither I nor II

108. Yoko Corp issues 2,000 shares of its $5 par value common stock to Klein as compensation for 500 hours of trust services performed. Klein usually bills $180 per hour for similar services. On the date of issuance the Yoko Corp stock was traded on a public exchange at $100 per share. The journal entry to record the stock issued to Klein would include a
   I. credit to common stock for $10,000
   II. credit to additional paid-in capital for $190,000

   (A) I only
   (B) II only
   (C) both I and II
   (D) neither I nor II

109. Mr. A subscribes to buy 1,000 shares of the common stock of Company Z for $22 per share, although the par value is only $10 per share. He pays $4 per share immediately and will pay the remaining $18 per share later. Which of the following is correct?
   I. Additional paid-in capital is increased at the time of the subscription by $4,000.
   II. On the day of the subscription, a common stock subscribed account is increased for the $10 par value of the stock.

   (A) I only
   (B) II only
   (C) both I and II
   (D) neither I nor II

110. Which is correct regarding the rights of common and preferred stockholders?
  I. Preferred stock has no set rights; the rights must be defined in the stock certificate.
  II. All common stocks issued by companies incorporated within a state typically will have the same legal rights because they are established by the laws of that state.
  (A) I only
  (B) II only
  (C) both I and II
  (D) neither I nor II

111. Which is correct regarding cumulative preferred stock?
  I. *Cumulative* means that if the preferred stock dividend is not declared, it will have to be paid before holders of common stock can receive any dividend payment.
  II. The issuing company reports a liability on the balance sheet for the dividends that are in arrears.
  (A) I only
  (B) II only
  (C) both I and II
  (D) neither I nor II

Use the following facts to answer questions 112–113:

On February 1, Year 13, Matte Corp issued 5,000 shares of $100 par convertible preferred stock for $110 per share. One share of preferred stock can be converted into 2 shares of Matte Corp's $10 par value common stock at the option of the preferred shareholder. On December 31, Year 14, when the market value was $40 per share, all of the preferred stock was converted.

112. What amount should be credited to additional paid-in capital-preferred stock on February 1, Year 13?
  (A) $500,000
  (B) $125,000
  (C) 50,000
  (D) -0-

113. How much should be credited to additional paid-in capital from common stock as a result of the conversion on December 31, Year 14?
  (A) -0-
  (B) $100,000
  (C) $350,000
  (D) $450,000

114. Nickki Corp purchased equipment by making a down payment of $2,000 and issuing a note payable for $16,000. A payment of $4,000 is to be made at the end of each year for 4 years. The applicable rate of interest is 7%. The present value of an ordinary annuity factor for 4 years at 7% is 4.18, and the present value for the future amount of a single sum of 1 dollar for 4 years at 7% is 0.645. Installation charges were $1,000. What is the capitalized cost of the equipment?

(A) $18,720
(B) $19,720
(C) $12,255
(D) $11,255

115. With regard to dividends paid from one corporation to another, retained earnings of the corporation paying the dividend is debited on which of the following dates?

(A) date of declaration and the date of record
(B) date of declaration and the date of payment
(C) date of declaration only
(D) end of the fiscal year

116. With regard to dividends, which of the following result in a reduction of retained earnings at the date of declaration?
  I. property dividends
  II. cash dividends

(A) I only
(B) II only
(C) both I and II
(D) neither I nor II

Use the following facts to answer questions 117–119:

Stefano Inc. was organized on January 2, Year 13, with $50,000 authorized shares of $5 par common stock. During Year 13, the company had the following capital transactions:

January 14	issued 20,000 shares at $11 per share
July 28	repurchased 5,000 shares at $16 per share
December 5	reissued the 5,000 shares held in treasury for $19 per share

117. Under US generally accepted accounting principles (GAAP), how much additional paid-in capital is recorded by Stefano Inc. on January 14?

(A) $550,000
(B) $220,000
(C) $100,000
(D) $120,000

118. Assuming Stefano Inc. uses the cost method to account for its treasury stock transactions, under US GAAP, how much is recorded for treasury stock on July 28, Year 13?
   (A) $80,000 credit
   (B) $80,000 debit
   (C) $25,000 credit
   (D) $25,000 debit

119. Assume Stefano Inc. uses the cost method to account for its treasury stock transactions. Under US GAAP, the entry to record the reissuance of the 5,000 treasury shares on December 5, Year 13, would include a credit to
   (A) gain on sale in the amount of $15,000
   (B) retained earnings in the amount of $15,000
   (C) additional paid-in capital in the amount of 15,000
   (D) treasury stock in the amount of $95,000

Use the following facts to answer questions 120–126:

Handy Inc. was organized on January 2, Year 13, with 40,000 authorized shares of $10 par value common stock. During Year 13, Handy Inc. had the following capital transactions:

January 2, Year 13	issued 20,000 shares at $15 per share
June 7, Year 13	repurchased 5,000 shares at $18
December 29, Year 13	reissued the 5,000 shares held in treasury for $30 per share

120. How much additional paid-in capital was recorded on January 2, Year 13?
   (A) $300,000
   (B) $150,000
   (C) $200,000
   (D) $100,000

121. Assume Handy Inc. uses the par value method of accounting for treasury stock transactions. Under US GAAP, how much is recorded for treasury stock on June 7, Year 13?
   (A) $50,000
   (B) $90,000
   (C) $25,000
   (D) $40,000

122. Assume Handy Inc. uses the par value method to account for treasury stock transactions. Under US GAAP, how much is recorded for additional paid-in capital on June 7, Year 13?

(A) -0-
(B) $40,000 debit
(C) $25,000 debit
(D) $50,000 debit

123. Assume Handy Inc. uses the par value method to account for treasury stock transactions. Under US GAAP, the journal entry on June 7, Year 13, would impact retained earnings in which of the following ways?

(A) no effect
(B) debit of $15,000
(C) debit of $40,000
(D) credit of $15,000

124. Assume Handy Inc. uses the par value method to account for treasury stock transactions. Under US GAAP, the journal entry on December 29, Year 13, would impact treasury stock in the amount of

(A) $150,000 debit
(B) $150,000 credit
(C) $50,000 debit
(D) $50,000 credit

125. Assume Handy Inc. uses the par value method to account for treasury stock transactions. Under US GAAP, the journal entry on December 29, Year 13, to reissue the treasury stock would impact additional paid-in capital in the amount of

(A) $100,000
(B) $150,000
(C) $50,000
(D) -0-

126. Assuming Handy Inc. uses the par value method to account for treasury stock transactions, how much is the ending balance of additional paid-in capital on December 31, Year 13?

(A) $100,000
(B) $150,000
(C) $175,000
(D) $200,000

127. On January 6, Year 13, Theo Corp issues a stock dividend to investors of record on February 3, Year 13. When determining how to account for this stock dividend, which of the following factors is the most important factor to Theo Corp?

(A) the par value of the shares
(B) the market value of the shares
(C) the number of shares authorized
(D) the size of the stock dividend

Use the following facts to answer questions 128–129:

The Reisig Corporation has 200,000 shares of $10 par value common stock outstanding on December 31, Year 12. On January 2, Year 13, they declare a stock dividend of 10,000 shares when the fair market value is $18. On the date of record, February 3, Year 13, the share price is $15. The shares are issued on March 1, Year 13, when the market value of the shares is $25.

128. When Reisig Corporation records the journal entry for the stock dividend, retained earnings will be debited for the number of new shares multiplied by which of the following amounts?

(A) par value of the shares
(B) market value of the shares on January 2, Year 13
(C) market value of the shares on February 3, Year 13
(D) market value of the shares on March 1, Year 13

129. When recording the journal entry to distribute the stock dividend, Reisig Corporation will credit additional paid-in capital for

(A) $80,000
(B) $100,000
(C) $50,000
(D) $150,000

Use the following facts to answer questions 130–132:

On June 25, Year 13, Allegra Corp issues a 30% stock dividend on its 200,000 shares of $10 par value common stock. The shares will be issued on July 8, Year 13. The market price of Allegra Corp stock is $15 per share on June 25, and on the date the shares are distributed, the stock is selling for $12 per share.

130. The journal entry to record the declaration of the stock dividend on June 25, Year 13, will include a
    (A) debit to retained earnings for $600,000
    (B) debit to retained earnings for $900,000
    (C) credit to additional paid-in capital for $300,000
    (D) credit to additional paid-in capital for $200,000

131. The journal entry on June 25, Year 13, will include a credit to common stock distributable in the amount of
    (A) $200,000
    (B) $300,000
    (C) $600,000
    (D) $900,000

132. On July 8, Year 13, the additional paid-in capital account is credited for
    (A) $300,000
    (B) $200,000
    (C) $600,000
    (D) -0-

133. Which of the following dividends will result in a decrease to total stockholders' equity?
    I. large stock dividend
    II. cash dividend
    III. small stock dividend
    (A) I, II, and III
    (B) II and III
    (C) II only
    (D) III only

134. The Toro Corporation is splitting its 10,000 shares of $20 par value common stock 2:1. Common stock is currently $200,000, additional paid-in capital is $500,000, and retained earnings is $1,000,000. In connection with a stock split, the Toro Corporation will
    (A) increase total stockholders' equity
    (B) decrease total stockholders' equity
    (C) decrease retained earnings
    (D) make no journal entry

135. Which of the following is a corporation likely to attempt to reduce its number of shares outstanding and increase its market price and par value of its stock?
    I. stock dividend of 20% or less
    II. stock split
    III. reverse stock split
    (A) I, II, and III
    (B) II and III
    (C) III only
    (D) I and III

136. When issuing stock options to employees, which of the following factors is most relevant in determining the accounting treatment under US GAAP?
    (A) the par value of the shares issued
    (B) the market value of the shares issued
    (C) the authorized number of shares
    (D) whether the stock options are issued in lieu of salary

137. Under a compensatory stock option plan, the expense to the corporation is
    (A) not booked until the options are exercised
    (B) booked on the date the options are granted to employees
    (C) determined on the date the options are granted to employees
    (D) equal to the cash paid for the shares by the employee upon exercise

138. When accounting for the expense related to compensatory stock options, which of the following is decreased?
    I. net income
    II. retained earnings
    III. total stockholders' equity
    (A) I, II, and III
    (B) I and II
    (C) I only
    (D) I and III

139. When accounting for compensatory stock options, when the employees exercise their options and purchase the shares for an amount above par but below the market price, the journal entry will include a

(A) credit to additional paid-in capital-stock options
(B) debit to additional paid-in capital-common stock
(C) credit to common stock for the difference between the strike price and the market price
(D) debit to additional paid-in capital-stock options

140. Losses due to write-downs of assets under a quasi-reorganization would affect which of the following under US GAAP?

   I. retained earnings
  II. income statement

(A) I only
(B) II only
(C) both I and II
(D) neither I nor II

CHAPTER 5

Fixed Assets

141. Lavroff Corp is purchasing an asset for use in its meat packaging business. Which of the following costs associated with the machine's purchase needs to be capitalized rather than expensed?

   I. cost of shipping the machine to Lavroff's plant

  II. cost of readying the machine for its intended use

(A) I only

(B) II only

(C) both I and II

(D) neither I nor II

142. At the end of Year 1, Buck Inc. had a class of assets with a carrying value of $1,200,000 and recorded a revaluation gain of $150,000. On December 31, Year 2, the assets had a carrying value of $900,000 and a recoverable amount of $720,000. Under the International Financial Reporting Standards (IFRS), what amount of impairment loss will Buck Inc. report on its December 31, Year 2, income statement?

(A) $190,000

(B) $150,000

(C) $40,000

(D) $30,000

143. A company has a parcel of land to be used for a future production facility. The company applies the revaluation model under IFRS to this class of assets. In Year 3, the company acquired the land for $80,000. At the end of Year 3, the carrying amount was reduced to $70,000, which represented the fair value at that date. At the end of Year 4, the land was revalued and the fair value increased to $85,000. How should the company account for the Year 4 change in fair value?

(A) by recognizing $15,000 in other comprehensive income
(B) by recognizing $10,000 on the income statement and $5,000 in other comprehensive income
(C) by recognizing $15,000 on the income statement
(D) by recognizing $10,000 in other comprehensive income

144. Fixed assets can be revalued upward from the asset's carrying amount if the reporting framework is
  I. US generally accepted accounting principles (GAAP)
  II. IFRS

(A) I only
(B) II only
(C) both I and II
(D) neither I nor II

145. When replacing an asset in which the cost of the old asset is known,
  I. replace the old carrying value with the capitalized cost of the new asset
  II. reduce accumulated depreciation of the asset class to increase book value

(A) I only
(B) II only
(C) both I and II
(D) neither I nor II

146. If an old asset's life is extended but not improved, and the carrying value of the specific old asset is NOT known, what happens to the amount spent to extend the life of the old asset?
  I. reduces accumulated depreciation of the asset class
  II. gets capitalized

(A) I only
(B) II only
(C) both I and II
(D) neither I nor II

147. Under US GAAP, if a hurricane causes damage to property, and extraordinary repairs are made that result in extending the life of the old property but not improving the old property,

   I. the cost should be recorded as an asset

  II. accumulated depreciation of the old asset should be reduced

(A) I only

(B) II only

(C) both I and II

(D) neither I nor II

148. Baker Corp purchases land for use as a future plant site. An old building on the site needs to be razed and the scrap materials will be sold. Legal fees will need to be paid to record ownership, and title insurance will need to be acquired. Which of the following should be capitalized rather than expensed in connection with the acquisition?

   I. title insurance

  II. legal fees for recording ownership

 III. razing of old building less proceeds from sale of scrap

(A) I and II

(B) II and III

(C) III only

(D) I, II, and III

149. Which of the following costs would NOT be capitalized to the land account?

   I. filling in dirt to level the property prior to excavation

  II. excavating costs

(A) I only

(B) II only

(C) both I and II

(D) neither I nor II

150. Which of the following is correct regarding land improvements?

   I. Costs incurred to construct sidewalks and fences would be capitalized to land improvements rather than to land.

  II. Land improvements can be depreciated.

(A) I only

(B) II Only

(C) both I and II

(D) neither I nor II

151. Vijay Fitness Inc. purchased land with the intention of building its new administrative headquarters on the site. Assuming the following can be debited to either land, land improvement, or building, which of the following should be charged to land improvements?

   I. clearing of trees and grading
   II. architect's fee
  III. installation of a septic system

  (A) I, II, and III
  (B) II and III
  (C) I and III
  (D) III only

152. Van Horn Inc. owns several parcels of land. Which of the following should be charged to land improvements?

   I. special assessment for a sewer system on Parcel #627; the sewer system will be owned by the township
   II. cost of a sewer system on Parcel #381; the sewer system will be owned by Van Horn Inc.

  (A) I only
  (B) II only
  (C) both I and II
  (D) neither I nor II

153. The Fleer Corporation spends $100,000 for land and building. The land was recently appraised for $20,000, but the building was appraised for $120,000. If only $100,000 is spent, how much is allocated to the land?

  (A) $14,280
  (B) $16,160
  (C) $20,000
  (D) $15,840

154. Downey Co. purchased an office building and the land on which it is located for $800,000 cash and an existing $200,000 mortgage. For realty tax purposes, the property is assessed at $944,000, 65% of which is allocated to the building. At what amount should Downey record the building?

  (A) $944,000
  (B) $613,600
  (C) $520,000
  (D) $650,000

155. Under IFRS, assets are classified as investment property on the balance sheet if they are
    I. held for rental income
    II. to be sold for a quick profit
    (A) I only
    (B) II only
    (C) both I and II
    (D) neither I nor II

156. LaRue Corp is a Canadian corporation that uses IFRS. LaRue Corp has the following account balances as of December 31, Year 5:

Land used in manufacturing operations	$11,000,000
Land held for rental income	$4,000,000
Buildings used in manufacturing operations	$10,500,000
Goods held for resale	$2,500,000
Buildings held for capital appreciation	$3,000,000

    Under IFRS, what will LaRue Corp report as investment property on its December 31, Year 5, balance sheet?
    (A) $4,000,000
    (B) $7,000,000
    (C) $28,500,000
    (D) $18,000,000

157. Which of the following statements regarding the accounting for investment property under IFRS is correct?
    I. If the entity elects the fair value method, no depreciation expense will be taken.
    II. Gains and losses from fair value adjustments on investment property are reported on the income statement.
    (A) I only
    (B) II only
    (C) both I and II
    (D) neither I nor II

158. Under IFRS, revaluation gains are reported on the income statement when the asset is classified as
    I. investment property
    II. property plant and equipment
    (A) I only
    (B) II only
    (C) both I and II
    (D) neither I nor II

159. Medina Corp is constructing a warehouse for use in manufacturing operations. The capitalization of interest cost is appropriate during a construction delay that is

   I. intentional
  II. related to permit processing or inspections

(A) I only
(B) II only
(C) both I and II
(D) neither I nor II

160. During the current year, Hodge Corp constructed machinery for its own use and constructed machinery for sale to customers in the ordinary course of business. The Acme Credit Company financed these assets both during construction and after construction was complete. Hodge Corp should capitalize interest during construction rather than expense it if the interest related to the machinery built for which of the following?

   I. Hodge's own use
  II. sale to customers

(A) I only
(B) II only
(C) both I and II
(D) neither I nor II

161. Capitalization of interest cost is appropriate to finance the cost of items held for resale (inventory) if the assets are

   I. self-constructed
  II. acquired in the open market

(A) I only
(B) II only
(C) both I and II
(D) neither I nor II

162. Interest cost after construction is completed is capitalized if the asset being constructed is

   I. built to use
  II. built to sell

(A) I only
(B) II only
(C) both I and II
(D) neither I nor II

163. Frimette Fabricating Corp was constructing fixed assets that qualified for interest capitalization and had the following outstanding debt issuance during the entire year of construction:

$5,000,000 face value, 7% interest
$7,000,000 face value, 10% interest

None of the borrowings were specified for the construction of the qualified fixed asset. Average expenditures for the year were $800,000. What interest rate should Frimette Fabricating Corp use to calculate capitalized interest on the construction?

(A) 7%
(B) 8.7%
(C) 8.5%
(D) 10%

164. Which of the following is a required disclosure regarding interest cost?
　I. total interest cost incurred for the period
　II. total capitalized interest cost for the period, if any

(A) I only
(B) II only
(C) both I and II
(D) neither I nor II

165. Which of the following is correct regarding capitalized interest?
　I. Capitalized interest is reduced by income received on the unexpended portion of the construction loan.
　II. The amount of capitalized interest is the lower of actual interest cost incurred or computed capitalized interest.

(A) I only
(B) II only
(C) both I and II
(D) neither I nor II

166. Posner Inc. began constructing a building for its own use in January of Year 4. During Year 4, Posner incurred interest of $62,000 on specific construction debt related to this building and $22,000 on various other debt issued prior to Year 4. Interest computed based on the weighted average amount of accumulated expenditures for the building during the year was $37,000. Posner should capitalize what amount of interest in Year 4?

(A) $37,000
(B) $59,000
(C) $62,000
(D) $84,000

167. An asset is purchased April 1, Year 1, for $75,000 and has an estimated useful life of 7 years. The asset has a salvage value of $5,000. For tax purposes, the asset is being depreciated based on a 10-year life. For GAAP purposes, how much is straight line depreciation expense on the income statement dated December 31, Year 1?

(A) $10,000
(B) $7,500
(C) $7,000
(D) $5,250

Use the following facts to answer questions 168–169:

Chef Giant Inc. uses the sum of the year's digits depreciation. In early January of Year 12, Chef Giant Inc. purchased and began depreciating a machine that cost $50,000 and had an estimated salvage value of $5,000. The machine had an estimated life of 5 years.

168. How much depreciation expense should be taken on the December 31, Year 12, income statement?

(A) $16,667
(B) $15,000
(C) $7,500
(D) $12,000

169. How much is the carrying value of the machine on the balance sheet dated December 31, Year 13 (the asset's second year)?

(A) $50,000
(B) $35,000
(C) $27,000
(D) $23,000

170. When calculating an asset's net carrying value, the accumulated depreciation is subtracted from the asset's depreciable base when the method of depreciation is
  I. straight line
  II. sum of the years' digits

(A) I only
(B) II only
(C) both I and II
(D) neither I nor II

171. A depreciable asset has an estimated 10% salvage value. Under which of the following methods, properly applied, would the accumulated depreciation equal the original cost at the end of the asset's estimated useful life?
  I. sum of the years' digits
  II. double declining balance
  III. straight line
  (A) I and II
  (B) II and III
  (C) II only
  (D) not I, II, or III

172. Bruder Inc. bought a battery (plug-in) truck at a cost of $70,000 in January of Year 1, and it is being depreciated using the units of production method. The truck had an estimated useful life of 10 years and a battery with an estimated total capacity of 200,000 miles. In Year 1, the truck is driven 12,000 miles. The salvage value of the truck is $10,000. How much depreciation should be taken in Year 1 based on the units of production method?
  (A) $6,000
  (B) $3,600
  (C) $4,200
  (D) $7,000

173. A company uses cost depletion to allocate the cost of removing natural resources. Which of the following is correct?
  I. Depletion base is the cost to purchase the property minus the estimated net residual value.
  II. If the number of units produced exceeds the number of units sold, the depletion expense would be equal to the number of units produced.
  (A) I only
  (B) II only
  (C) both I and II
  (D) neither I nor II

174. Which of the following is correct regarding impairment losses under US GAAP?
  I. Impairment losses are typically reported before tax if the impairment loss is related to discontinued operations.
  II. Impairment losses reduce the carrying value of an asset due to a decline in book value below fair value.
  (A) I only
  (B) II only
  (C) both I and II
  (D) neither I nor II

CHAPTER **6**

Earnings per Share

175. According to US generally accepted accounting principles (GAAP), which of the following entities are NOT required to present earnings per share (EPS) on the face of the income statement?
  I. private entities that have yet to go public or make a filing for a public offering
  II. entities whose shares are traded on a US securities exchange
(A) I only
(B) II only
(C) both I and II
(D) neither I nor II

176. A company can report basic EPS and not have to report fully diluted EPS if they have
  I. common stock outstanding, no preferred stock, and options that are convertible into common stock
  II. common stock outstanding, no preferred stock, and bonds that are convertible into common stock
(A) I only
(B) II only
(C) both I and II
(D) neither I nor II

177. For purposes of calculating basic EPS, income available to common shareholders is determined by
  I. deducting dividends declared in the period on noncumulative preferred stock (regardless of whether they have been paid)
  II. deducting dividends accumulated in the period on cumulative preferred stock (regardless of whether they have been declared)
(A) I only
(B) II only
(C) both I and II
(D) neither I nor II

178. At December 31, Year 11 and Year 10, Baum Inc. had 60,000 shares of common stock and 10,000 shares of preferred stock outstanding. The preferred stock was 5% $100 par value cumulative preferred stock, and no dividends were paid on any class of stock for the past 5 years. Net income for Year 11 was $1,400,000. For 2011, basic EPS amounted to

(A) $23.33
(B) $22.50
(C) $25.50
(D) $31.90

179. When calculating the weighted average number of shares outstanding during the period, which of the following is treated as if it were outstanding since the beginning of the year?

   I. stock dividends declared in July and paid in September
  II. stock issued above par in August

(A) I only
(B) II only
(C) both I and II
(D) neither I nor II

180. A company paid both preferred dividends and common dividends to shareholders during the current year. Which of those dividends should be subtracted from net income to compute income available to common shareholders in the calculation of EPS?

   I. common dividends
  II. preferred dividends

(A) I only
(B) II only
(C) both I and II
(D) neither I nor II

181. When calculating basic EPS, which of the following is correct regarding the calculation of weighted average common shares outstanding?

   I. Include the convertible preferred shares that were converted during the period in the calculation of weighted average common shares outstanding, and time-weight them.
  II. Ignore convertible preferred shares unless they are converted.

(A) I only
(B) II only
(C) both I and II
(D) neither I nor II

182. How do dividends in arrears from Year 1 relate to a Year 2 basic EPS calculation when attempting to compute net income available to common shareholders?

    I. Year 1 dividends in arrears are subtracted from Year 2 net income along with Year 2 unpaid dividends if the preferred stock is cumulative.

    II. Year 1 dividends in arrears are added to a Year 2 net loss if the preferred stock is cumulative.

(A) I only

(B) II only

(C) both I and II

(D) neither I nor II

183. When calculating EPS, income available to common shareholders is determined by deducting the preferred dividends

    I. declared in the period if the preferred stock is noncumulative regardless of whether the dividend was paid

    II. accumulated in the current period on cumulative preferred stock regardless of whether the preferred dividend has been declared

(A) I only

(B) II only

(C) both I and II

(D) neither I nor II

184. Which of the following is correct regarding a net loss for the period as it related to net income available to the common shareholders, the numerator of the EPS calculation?

    I. In the event of a net loss for the period, declared dividends on noncumulative preferred stock are added to the net loss even if the dividend was not paid.

    II. In the event of a net loss for the period, current year dividends on cumulative preferred stock are added to the net loss regardless of whether the dividends have been declared.

(A) I only

(B) II only

(C) both I and II

(D) neither I nor II

185. Dilutive stock options would generally be used to calculate
    I. basic EPS
   II. fully diluted EPS

(A) I only
(B) II only
(C) both I and II
(D) neither I nor II

186. Debt that was converted into common shares during the period would be included in the denominator to calculate weighted average common shares outstanding for the computation of
    I. basic EPS
   II. fully diluted EPS

(A) I only
(B) II only
(C) both I and II
(D) neither I nor II

187. Lansing Corp had 60,000 shares of common stock outstanding at January 1, Year 13. On July 1, Year 13, it issued 10,000 additional shares of common stock. What is the number of shares that Lansing Corp should use to calculate Year 13 EPS?

(A) $60,000
(B) $70,000
(C) $65,000
(D) none of the above

188. On December 1 of the current year, Hackett Corp declared and issued a 3% stock dividend on its 70,000 shares of outstanding common stock. There was no other common stock activity during the year. Net income for the current year was $100,000. What number of shares should Hackett use in determining basic earnings per common share for the current year?

(A) 70,000
(B) 72,100
(C) 70,175
(D) none of the above

189. The following information pertains to Conover Inc.'s outstanding shares for Year 13:
Preferred stock $10 par 5% cumulative 1,000 shares outstanding 1/1/Year 13

Common stock $1 par value:
Shares outstanding 1/1/13	10,000
2:1 stock split 3/1/13	10,000
Shares issued 10/1/13	5,000

What are the weighted average number of shares that Conover Inc. should use to calculate Year 13 earnings per share?

(A) 25,000
(B) 23,333
(C) 21,250
(D) 19,583

190. Gordon Corp had 360,000 shares of common stock issued and outstanding at December 31, Year 12, and 100,000 shares of nonconvertible preferred stock. On January 2, Year 13, Gordon Corp issued 100,000 more shares of nonconvertible preferred stock. Gordon Corp declared and paid $45,000 cash dividends on the common stock and $20,000 on the preferred stock during Year 13. Net income for the year ended December 31, Year 13, was $290,000. What should be Gordon Corp's Year 13 earnings per common share?

(A) $0.75
(B) $0.81
(C) $0.63
(D) $0.59

Use the following facts to answer questions 191–193:

At December 31, Year 12, Chaucer Corp had 100,000 common shares outstanding along with 10,000 shares of preferred stock. Each share of preferred stock is convertible into 2 shares of Chaucer common stock. During Year 12, Chaucer Corp paid dividends of $30,000 on its preferred stock. Chaucer also had 1,000, 9% convertible bonds outstanding. Each bond is convertible into 30 shares of Chaucer common stock. Both the debt and the preferred stock would be potentially dilutive if converted. Net income for Year 12 is $750,000. Assume that the income tax rate is 30%.

191. The preferred dividend would be subtracted from Chaucer Corp's net income to calculate Year 12
    I. basic EPS
    II. fully diluted EPS
    (A) I only
    (B) II only
    (C) both I and II
    (D) neither I nor II

192. Calculate Chaucer Corp's basic EPS for Year 12.
    (A) $7.50
    (B) $7.80
    (C) $7.20
    (D) $7.02

193. Calculate Chaucer Corp's fully diluted EPS for Year 12.
    (A) $5.42
    (B) $5.00
    (C) $6.78
    (D) $5.77

CHAPTER 7

Accounting for Income Taxes

194. With regard to deferred taxes, using the installment sales method for tax purposes would typically result in a
 I. deferred tax asset
 II. deferred tax liability
 (A) I only
 (B) II only
 (C) both I and II
 (D) neither I nor II

195. Which of the following typically would result in a deferred tax liability?
 I. warranty expense
 II. bad debt expense
 (A) I only
 (B) II only
 (C) both I and II
 (D) neither I nor II

196. The Suretsky Corp was organized in Year 1 and had organization and start-up costs of $15,000. With respect to deferred taxes, organization costs and start-up expenditures result in a
 I. deferred tax asset
 II. deferred tax liability
 (A) I only
 (B) II only
 (C) both I and II
 (D) neither I nor II

197. Station Toy Train Co., a cash basis taxpayer, prepares accrual basis financial statements. In its Year 13 balance sheet, Station's deferred income tax liabilities increased compared to Year 12. Which of the following changes during Year 13 would cause this increase in deferred income tax liabilities?

   I. an increase in prepaid insurance
  II. an increase in rent receivable
 III. an increase in liability for warranty obligations

  (A) II and III
  (B) I only
  (C) I and II
  (D) III only

198. Which is correct regarding current and deferred income tax expense?

   I. Deferred income tax expense is equal to the change in deferred tax liability (or asset) on the balance sheet from the beginning of the year to the end of the year.
  II. Current income tax expense is equal to the income taxes payable on the corporate tax return, assuming no estimated tax payments were made.

  (A) I only
  (B) II only
  (C) both I and II
  (D) neither I nor II

199. The Ginger Corporation owes current and deferred income taxes in Year 11. Which of the following represents the change in the amount of taxes owed in future years at the end of Year 11 to the amount of taxes owed in future years at the end of year 12?

  (A) current income tax payable
  (B) deferred income tax payable
  (C) deferred income tax expense
  (D) current income tax expense

200. Which of the following is correct regarding the calculation of current income tax expense?
  I. Net income per the income statement multiplied by the current tax rate equals the current year income tax expense.
  II. Taxable income per the tax return multiplied by the tax rate equals the current year income tax expense.
  (A) I only
  (B) II only
  (C) both I and II
  (D) neither I nor II

Use the following facts to answer questions 201–204:

The Aragona Corporation reports net income on its Year 13 financial statements before income tax expense of $400,000. Aragona Corporation has been profitable in the past and expects to continue to be profitable. The company expensed warranty costs in Year 13 on the books for $35,000 that is expected to impact the tax return in Year 16. Aragona Inc. also had $60,000 in revenue that will not be taxed until Year 15. Aragona Corp has a tax rate for Year 13 of 30% and an enacted rate of 40% beyond Year 13. In addition, Aragona Corp made four estimated tax payments of $25,000 each in Year 13.

201. How much will Aragona Corp report as taxable income on its income statement for December 31, Year 13?
  (A) $375,000
  (B) $495,000
  (C) $425,000
  (D) $400,000

202. How much would Aragona Corp report as current year tax income tax expense on the December 31, Year 13, income statement?
  (A) $150,000
  (B) $112,500
  (C) $12,500
  (D) none of the above

203. How much would Aragona Corp report as deferred income tax expense on the December 31, Year 13, income statement?

(A) -0-
(B) $10,000
(C) $14,000
(D) $24,000

204. How much would Aragona Corp report as total income tax expense on the December 31, Year 13, income statement?

(A) $112,500
(B) $10,000
(C) $122,500
(D) none of the above

205. Bruford Corp, a newly organized company, reported pretax financial income of $100,000 for the current year. Among the items reported in Bruford's income statement are the following:

Premium on officer's life insurance with Bruford as owner and beneficiary	$5,000
Interest received on municipal bonds	$10,000

The enacted tax rate for the current year is 25% and 30% thereafter. In its December 31 balance sheet, Bruford should report a deferred income tax liability of

(A) $3,000
(B) $3,750
(C) $2,500
(D) -0-

Use the following facts to answer questions 206–209:

Pecorino Corp had pretax financial income of $125,000 in Year 13. To compute the provision for federal income taxes, the following information was provided:

Interest income received on state of Florida bonds	$18,000
Tax depreciation in excess of financial statement amount	$8,000
Rent received in advance	$14,000
Corporation tax rate	30% in Year 12
	35% in Year 13
	40% in Year 14
	45% in Year 15

Pecorino made four installments of corporate estimated tax in the amount of $9,000 each during Year 13.

206. How much permanent difference between book income and taxable income existed at December 31, Year 13?

(A) $26,000

(B) $18,000

(C) $40,000

(D) $14,000

207. What amount of taxable income should be reported for Pecorino in Year 13?

(A) $131,000

(B) $139,000

(C) $147,000

(D) $113,000

208. What amount of current income tax expense should be reported in Pecorino's December 31, Year 13, income statement?

(A) $39,550

(B) $45,200

(C) $50,850

(D) $33,900

209. What amount of current income tax payable should be reported in Pecorino's December 31, Year 13, balance sheet?

(A) -0-
(B) $39,550
(C) $36,000
(D) $3,550

210. The Shea Corporation has a temporary difference in Year 1 that is from a noncurrent liability and expected to reverse in Years 2, 3, and 4. In Year 1 the tax rate is 30%. In Years 2, 3, and 4, the enacted rate is 40%. Under US GAAP, the deferred tax liability is based on which of the following tax rates?

(A) tax rate for Year 1
(B) enacted rate for Years 1 and 2 divided by two
(C) enacted rate for Years 1, 2, 3, and 4 divided by four
(D) enacted rate for Years 2, 3, and 4

211. In Year 1, its first year of operations, Mack Industries has temporary differences resulting from the following two items. Which of the following differences should be reported as current deferred tax assets/liabilities on the Year 1 balance sheet?

   I. depreciation expense
  II. warranty expense

(A) I only
(B) II only
(C) both I and II
(D) neither I nor II

212. Under US GAAP, with regard to balance sheet reporting of deferred tax assets and liabilities, which of the following are netted?

   I. current deferred tax assets with current deferred tax liabilities
  II. current deferred tax assets with noncurrent deferred tax liabilities

(A) I only
(B) II only
(C) both I and II
(D) neither I nor II

213. Which of the following standards allow for deferred tax liabilities to be classified as either current or noncurrent?

    I. IFRS
    II. US GAAP

(A) I only
(B) II only
(C) both I and II
(D) neither I nor II

214. Among the items reported on Fisk Corp's income statement for Year 13 were the following:

Income	
Life insurance proceeds on death of officer	$500,000
Expenses	
Estimate for future warranty expense	$25,000
Estimate for bad debt expense	$18,000

How much are total temporary differences between book income and taxable income for Fisk Corp in Year 13?

(A) $543,000
(B) $500,000
(C) $43,000
(D) $18,000

CHAPTER 8

Accounting for Leases and Pensions

215. Which of the following criteria must be met for a lease to be accounted for as a capital lease?
   I. The lease contains a bargain purchase option.
  II. The lease transfers title to the lessee at the expiration of the lease.
 III. The lease term is 75% or greater than the life of the asset.
 IV. The present value of the lease payments is 90% or more of the fair value of the leased asset at the inception of the lease.

  (A) all four of the criteria
  (B) any three of the criteria
  (C) any two of the criteria
  (D) any one of the criteria

216. The ADTC Group leases an asset from Mahan Corp for 8 years. The life of the asset is expected to be 10 years. If the lease does NOT contain a bargain purchase option or a transfer of title, which of the following is correct?

  (A) The leased asset would be accounted for by the ADTC Group as an operating lease.
  (B) The leased asset would be depreciated by the ADTC Group over 8 years.
  (C) The leased asset would be depreciated by the ADTC Group over 10 years.
  (D) The leased asset would be depreciated using the same method for book purposes as for tax purposes.

217. An 8-year capital lease entered into on December 31, Year 1, specified equal minimum annual lease payments. Part of this payment represents interest and part represents a reduction in the net lease liability. The portion of the minimum lease payment in the 6th year applicable to the reduction of the net lease liability should be

(A) less than in the 5th year
(B) more than in the 5th year
(C) the same as in the 7th year
(D) more than in the 7th year

218. For a lessor, which of the following is correct regarding the difference between a direct financing lease and a sales type lease?

 I. The total amount of profit will be less if the lease is accounted for as a direct financing lease rather than a sales type lease, because in a direct financing lease the lessor recognizes only interest income.

 II. If the lessor is either a manufacturer or dealer, the lease would be recorded as a sales type lease rather than direct financing.

(A) I only
(B) II only
(C) both I and II
(D) neither I nor II

219. In Year 2, Messing Corp sold an asset for $1,000,000 to Susserman Corp and simultaneously leased it back for 3 years. The asset's remaining life was 34 years, and the carrying amount at the time of sale was $350,000. The annual lease payments were $150,000 per year. How much gain should be recognized by Messing Corp in Year 2?

(A) $650,000
(B) $500,000
(C) $200,000
(D) -0-

220. The following information pertains to a sale and leaseback of equipment by Brennan Co. on December 31, Year 2:

Sales price	$300,000
Carrying amount	$210,000
Monthly lease payment	$3,550
Present value of lease payments	$37,800
Estimated remaining life	20 years
Lease term	1 year
Implicit rate	10%

What amount of deferred gain on the sale should Brennan report at December 31, Year 2, under US generally accepted accounting principles (GAAP)?

(A) $90,000
(B) $9,000
(C) $52,200
(D) -0-

221. The East Jersey Finance Corp leased an asset to Mountainview Inc. on January 2, Year 13, for payments of $1,500 per month for 5 years. The lease included a provision that Mountainview Inc. would receive the first 6 months free. The lease is being accounted for as an operating lease. How much rent expense should Mountainview Inc. record in Year 13?

(A) $8,100
(B) $9,000
(C) $16,200
(D) $18,000

222. Diamonds Cardworld signs an operating lease to pay monthly rent at a fixed amount of $10,000 per month on the first $500,000 of monthly sales. The lease contains a contingent rent agreement that stipulates that Diamonds must pay additional rent of 2% of sales over $500,000 in any month. Which of the following is correct?

  I. If sales for the month were $800,000, rent expense for the month would be $16,000.
  II. If sales for the month were below $500,000, rent expense would NOT be less than $10,000.

(A) I only
(B) II only
(C) both I and II
(D) neither I nor II

223. Anita's Plaque Factory Inc. signed a 10-year operating lease for $80,000 per year on January 1, Year 1. The lease included a provision for contingent rent of 5% of annual sales in excess of $500,000. Sales for the year ended December 31, Year 1, were $600,000. Anita's Plaque Factory also paid a $20,000 bonus for the lease. Rent expense for the year ended December 31, Year 1, was

(A) $80,000
(B) $82,000
(C) $85,000
(D) $87,000

224. Which of the following would be evidence that a lease should be accounted for by the lessee as an operating lease rather than a capital lease?
  I. The lease contains a bargain purchase option.
  II. The lease is for 8 years, and the asset's estimated life is 10 years.

(A) I only
(B) II only
(C) both I and II
(D) neither I nor II

225. When accounting for a 10-year operating lease that began January 2, Year 1, which of the following is a required footnote disclosure on December 31, Year 3?
  I. the full amount of the remaining lease obligation
  II. the total annual obligation for each of the next 3 succeeding years

(A) I only
(B) II only
(C) both I and II
(D) neither I nor II

226. On January 1, Year 13, Bowman Inc. entered into a 12-year operating lease for a factory. The annual minimum lease payments are $23,000. In the December Year 13 balance sheet, how much liability should be shown for the lease obligation?

(A) $23,000
(B) $276,000
(C) $253,000
(D) -0-

227. Sherman Inc. is leasing a building from Crabtree Inc. The space was formerly a bank, and now Sherman Inc. needs to pay for improvements to convert the premises to an indoor sports training facility. These leasehold improvements will include the removal of drop ceilings and the installation of special flooring and new walls with safety padding. The costs of these improvements are capitalized if Sherman Inc. is accounting for the lease as

    I. an operating lease

    II. a capital lease

(A) I only

(B) II only

(C) both I and II

(D) neither I nor II

Use the following facts to answer questions 228–230:

On November 30, Year 11, Summit leased office space to Edison Inc. for 15 years at a monthly rental of $25,000. On the same date, Edison paid Summit Inc. the following amounts:

First month's rent	$25,000
Refundable security deposit	$63,000
Last month's rent	$25,000
Installation of drop ceiling	$20,000
Installation of new walls	$30,000
Installation of flooring and lighting	$10,000

The life of the leasehold improvements is estimated to be 20 years. Edison Inc. is a calendar year corporation and accounting for this lease as an operating lease. There is no option to renew the lease.

228. Which of the following is correct?

    I. Leasehold improvements will be capitalized for $60,000.

    II. On Edison Inc.'s Year 11 balance sheet, the account "leasehold improvements" is listed under prepaid expenses, current assets.

(A) I only

(B) II only

(C) both I and II

(D) neither I nor II

229. Using the same facts, which of the following is correct?
  I. Edison Inc. will amortize the leasehold improvements over 20 years.
  II. The $25,000 for last month's rent will NOT be expensed on Edison Inc.'s Year 11 income statement.
  (A) I only
  (B) II only
  (C) both I and II
  (D) neither I nor II

230. The total expense recorded by Edison Inc. for Year 11 as a result of this lease is
  (A) $25,333
  (B) $25,000
  (C) $29,000
  (D) none of the above

Use the following facts to answer questions 231–234:

On January 2, Year 13, Queen Corp signs a noncancelable lease agreement with King Corp. The lease was for 5 years and called for Queen Corp to make payments of $100,000 starting December 31, Year 13. The present value of the lease payments are $371,600 based on an interest of 10%.

231. If Queen Corp is accounting for this lease as a capital lease and the first lease payment is made December 31, Year 13, what amount should Queen record as interest expense at December 31, Year 13?
  (A) $10,000
  (B) $50,000
  (C) $27,160
  (D) $37,160

232. What is the balance of the lease obligation that should be recorded by Queen Corp on the December 31, Year 13, balance sheet?
  (A) $198,760
  (B) $371,600
  (C) $308,760
  (D) $334,440

233. If Queen Corp is accounting for this lease as a capital lease and the first lease payment is made January 2, Year 13, what amount should Queen record as interest expense at December 31, Year 13?
  (A) $37,160
  (B) $27,160
  (C) $10,000
  (D) $50,000

234. What is the balance of the lease obligation that should be recorded by Queen Corp on the December 31, Year 13, balance sheet?

(A) $198,760
(B) $371,600
(C) $308,760
(D) $334,440

Use the following facts to answer questions 235–236:

Advantage Corporation leases equipment for 5 years with the first payment due immediately to customers and records the transaction as a direct financing lease under US GAAP. Advantage structures the payment to earn 7% annually. On January 2, Year 13, Advantage enters into a lease with Bussell Corp for equipment with a fair value of $105,000. There is no bargain purchase option, and the equipment has no residual value at the end of the lease. Assume that the present value factors are as follows:

The present value of an annuity due for 5 years at 7% is 4.2.
The present value of an ordinary annuity for 5 years at 7% is 3.89.

235. How much are the annual lease payments to be received by Advantage?

(A) $25,000
(B) $26,993
(C) $21,000
(D) none of the above

236. How much interest revenue will Advantage Corporation earn over the life of the lease?

(A) $7,351
(B) $8,750
(C) $20,000
(D) none of the above

237. Golf Finance Corp leased equipment to Fair Oaks Country Club Inc. on January 1, Year 13, and properly recorded the sales type lease. The first of eight annual lease payments of $300,000 are due at the beginning of each year. Golf Finance Corp had purchased the equipment for $1,100,000 and had a list price of $1,480,000. The present value of the lease payments is $1,700,000. The imputed interest rate on the lease was 11%, and Fair Oaks Country Club Inc. had an incremental borrowing rate of 10%. What amount of profit on the sale should Golf Finance Corp report in its Year 1 income statement?

(A) $380,000
(B) $600,000
(C) $220,000
(D) none of the above

238. Which of the following methods of accounting for pension expense is considered generally accepted under US GAAP?
   I. pay-as-you-go method
   II. terminal funding method
   (A) I only
   (B) II only
   (C) both I and II
   (D) neither I nor II

239. Easy Corp amended its defined benefit pension plan on January 1, Year 13, granting a total credit of $64,000 to four employees for services rendered prior to the plan's adoption. The employees, Adam, Bridget, Chester, and Drudge, are expected to retire from the company as follows:

Adam will retire after 6 years.
Bridget will retire after 8 years.
Chester and Drudge will retire after 10 years.

What is the amount of prior service cost amortization for Easy Corp in Year 13 under US GAAP?
   (A) $8,000
   (B) $6,400
   (C) $16,000
   (D) $64,000

240. The following information pertains to American Bottle Co.'s pension plan:

Actuarial estimate of projected benefit obligation at beginning of Year 9	$93,000
Assumed discount rate	10%
Service costs	$11,000
Pension benefits paid during the year	$5,000

If no change in actuarial estimates occurred during the year, the projected benefit obligation at December 31, Year 9, is
   (A) $108,300
   (B) $99,000
   (C) $118,300
   (D) $104,000

241. Under US GAAP, the separate components of net periodic pension cost are presented in which of the following ways on the income statement?

(A) The separate components of net periodic pension cost must be shown separately on the income statement.

(B) The separate components of net periodic pension cost can be shown separately or aggregated and shown as one amount on the income statement.

(C) The separate components of net periodic pension cost can be aggregated on the income statement and shown as one amount if the pension plan is overfunded, but must be shown separately on the income statement if the plan is underfunded.

(D) The separate components of net periodic pension cost must be aggregated on the income statement and shown as one amount.

242. The Bollestro Corporation's pension plan began Year 5 with a fair value of plan assets of $1,000,000. The entity contributed $50,000 into the plan during the year. They paid benefits to retirees in the amount of $20,000 in Year 5, and the fair value of plan assets at December 31, Year 5, was $1,300,000. How much was the actual return on the plan assets in Year 5?

(A) $200,000
(B) $270,000
(C) $300,000
(D) $370,000

243. Lexington Corp established a defined benefit pension plan on January 1, Year 5. The following information was available at December 31, Year 7:

Accumulated benefit obligation	$14,000,000
Projected benefit obligation	$18,500,000
Unfunded accrued pension cost	$300,000
Plan assets at fair market value	$9,000,000
Unrecognized prior service cost	$2,658,000

If the expected return on plan assets is 7% and the discount rate is 5%, what amount represents the funded status of the pension plan at December 31, Year 7?

(A) $9,500,000 underfunded
(B) $9,500,000 overfunded
(C) $5,000,000 underfunded
(D) $2,252,000 underfunded

244. Under US GAAP, when calculating the present value of future retirement payments, which of the following is taken into consideration by the projected benefit obligation but NOT taken into consideration by the accumulated benefit obligation?

(A) current salary levels
(B) past salary levels
(C) past and current salary levels
(D) future salary levels

245. Which of the following is correct regarding net periodic pension cost?

    I. Under US GAAP, interest cost included in the net pension cost recognized for a period by an employer sponsoring a defined benefit pension plan represents the increase in the projected benefit obligation due to the passage of time.

    II. The increase in the projected benefit obligation resulting from employee services in the current period is known as the current service cost.

(A) I only
(B) II only
(C) both I and II
(D) neither I nor II

Use the following facts to answer questions 246–247:

Century Corp had service cost of $30,000 and interest cost of $20,000 related to its defined benefit pension plan for the year ended December 31, Year 13. The company's unrecognized prior service cost was $240,000 on December 31, Year 12, and the average remaining service life of employees was 15 years. Plan assets earned an expected and actual return of 12% in Year 13. The company made contributions to the plan of $35,000 and paid benefits of $40,000 in Year 13. Century Corp had assets with a fair value of $350,000 at December 31, Year 12. The pension benefit obligation was $410,000 at December 31, Year 12, and $450,000 at December 31, Year 13.

246. What is the funded status of Century Corp's pension plan at December 31, Year 13?

(A) $105,000 underfunded
(B) $63,000 overfunded
(C) $105,000 overfunded
(D) $63,000 underfunded

247. How much prior year service cost is amortized to pension expense in Year 13?

(A) $12,000
(B) $44,000
(C) $16,000
(D) $30,000

CHAPTER 9

Partnerships, Sole Proprietorships, and Fair Value Accounting

248. Person and Wolinsky formed a partnership, each contributing assets to the business. Mr. Person contributed equipment with a current market value in excess of its carrying amount. Mr. Wolinsky contributed land with a carrying amount in excess of its current market value. Which of the following should be recorded at fair value?

  I. equipment
 II. land

(A) I only
(B) II only
(C) both I and II
(D) neither I nor II

249. Dauber and Zuckerman formed the DZ partnership on November 13 and contributed the following: Dauber contributed cash of $40,000. Zuckerman contributed land with a fair market value of $60,000 subject to a mortgage of $25,000, which is assumed by the partnership. Zuckerman's basis in the land was $43,000. The partners agree to share profits and losses equally. Zuckerman's capital on November 13th would be

(A) $43,000
(B) $60,000
(C) $35,000
(D) $22,000

250. The partnership of Michael and Ivan has $180,000 worth of net assets. The partnership would like to add Tim as a partner with an exact one-fifth interest in capital. How much does Tim need to contribute to receive an exact one-fifth interest?
(A) $45,000
(B) $50,000
(C) $36,000
(D) $90,000

251. The partnership of Heaslip and Shapiro are considering adding Kenneth as a partner. When admitting Kenneth into the partnership, Kenneth's capital account equals the amount of his actual contribution under which of the following methods?
 I. bonus method
 II. goodwill method
(A) I only
(B) II only
(C) both I and II
(D) neither I nor II

252. Waldo, Weissman, and Broskie are partners in a partnership. Broskie wishes to retire. Which of the following methods of accounting for his retirement could increase the individual partner's capital accounts without changing total net assets of the partnership?
 I. goodwill method
 II. bonus method
(A) I only
(B) II only
(C) both I and II
(D) neither I nor II

253. Acquilino and Rudnick are partners in a partnership with capital balances of $45,000 and $35,000 respectively. They agree to admit Chu as a partner. After the assets of the partnership are revalued, Chu will have a 10% interest in capital and profits for an investment of $15,000. What amount should be recorded as goodwill to the original partners?
(A) -0-
(B) $65,000
(C) $15,000
(D) $55,000

254. Desimone and Jeffrey are partners in the Strat-o-Matic Partnership. During the current year, Desimone and Jeffrey maintained average capital balances in their partnership of $140,000 and $80,000 respectively. They share profit and loss equally, and each received interest of 5% on capital balances. Partnership profit before interest was $5,000. How much is ending capital for Desimone's partnership interest?

(A) $140,000
(B) $147,000
(C) $150,000
(D) $144,000

255. Barry and Saralee formed the Twin Brooks partnership in Year 13. The partnership agreement provides for annual salary allowances of $40,000 for Barry and $30,000 for Saralee. Barry and Saralee share profits equally, and they split losses 80/20. The partnership had earnings of $54,000 in Year 13 before any allowance to partners. What amount of earnings should be credited to Barry's capital account for Year 13?

(A) $26,800
(B) $27,200
(C) $27,000
(D) $28,300

Use the following facts to answer questions 256–257:

Rochelle and Bob form a partnership and contribute the assets as follows: Rochelle contributes cash of $80,000. Bob contributes land with a carrying amount of $10,000, a fair value of $70,000, and subject to a mortgage of $20,000. Rochelle and Bob agree to share profits and losses 60/40.

256. Rochelle's capital account on the date of formation is equal to

(A) $70,000
(B) $10,000
(C) $50,000
(D) $80,000

257. Bob's capital account on the date of formation is equal to

(A) $70,000
(B) $10,000
(C) $50,000
(D) $80,000

Use the following facts to answer questions 258–259:

Griffin and Owen are partners with capital balances of $50,000 and $30,000 respectively. Profits and losses are divided in the ratio of 60:40. Griffin and Owen decided to admit Tatum to the partnership, who invested equipment valued at $25,000 for a 30% capital interest in the new partnership. Tatum's cost of the equipment was $22,000. The partnership elected to use the bonus method to record the admission of Tatum into the partnership.

258. Tatum's capital account should be credited for
   (A) $31,500
   (B) $22,000
   (C) $25,000
   (D) none of the above

259. After Tatum's admission, the balance in Griffin's capital account is
   (A) $56,500
   (B) $53,900
   (C) $52,600
   (D) $46,100

260. Rukke and Murray share profits in the ratio of 70:30. On December 31, Year 13, they decide to liquidate the partnership. On that date, the partnership has assets of $420,000. Their only liabilities are accrued taxes of $100,000. Their capital accounts on the date of liquidation are as follows:

   Rukke $170,000
   Murray $150,000

   If the assets are sold for $360,000, what amount of the available cash should be distributed to Rukke?
   (A) $212,000
   (B) $182,000
   (C) $128,000
   (D) $132,000

Use the following facts to answer questions 261–264:

On November 1, Year 13, Chumley began a sole proprietorship with an initial cash investment of $3,000. The proprietorship provided $10,000 worth of services in November and received full payment in December. The proprietorship incurred expenses of $7,000 in December that were paid in January, Year 14. During December, Chumley withdrew $2,000 for personal use.

261. How much would Chumley's ending capital be on the cash basis at December 31, Year 13?

(A) $13,000
(B) $11,000
(C) $10,000
(D) $4,000

262. How much is the sole proprietorship's net income on the accrual basis for Year 13?

(A) $3,000
(B) $7,000
(C) $10,000
(D) $1,000

263. How much is the sole proprietorship's net income on the cash basis for Year 13?

(A) $3,000
(B) $13,000
(C) $10,000
(D) $11,000

264. How much is Chumley's ending capital on the accrual basis at December 31, Year 13?

(A) $3,000
(B) $6,000
(C) $7,000
(D) $4,000

265. With regard to fair value measurement, US GAAP regards fair value as
 I. the price to sell an asset
 II. the price to transfer a liability

(A) I only
(B) II only
(C) both I and II
(D) neither I nor II

266. Which of the following is correct regarding fair value measurement of an asset?
 I. It includes transportation costs if location is an attribute of the asset.
 II. Fair value is an entity-based measure rather than a market-based measure.

(A) I only
(B) II only
(C) both I and II
(D) neither I nor II

267. In fair value measurement of financial assets, the most advantageous market is the market with the

(A) greatest volume or level of activity
(B) best price without considering transaction costs
(C) lowest transaction costs
(D) best price after considering transaction costs

268. Under fair value reporting, when there is no principal market for a financial asset, which of the following is correct?
 I. Transaction costs are considered when determining the most advantageous market.
 II. Transaction costs are NOT included in the final fair value measurement.

(A) I only
(B) II only
(C) both I and II
(D) neither I nor II

269. Which of the following statements is correct regarding the inputs that can be used to measure fair value?

 I. A fair value measurement based on management assumptions only (no market data) would NOT be acceptable per US GAAP.

 II. Level 1 measurements are quoted prices in active markets for similar assets or liabilities.

(A) I only
(B) II only
(C) both I and II
(D) neither I nor II

270. Which of the following would be considered a level 2 input for a financial asset?

 I. quoted market price on a stock exchange for an identical asset
 II. historical performance and return on the investment
 III. quoted market prices available from a business broker for a similar asset

(A) I and II
(B) II and III
(C) III only
(D) I, II, and III

271. Which of the following would be considered a level 3 input?

 I. a warehouse whose price per square foot is derived from prices in observed transactions involving similar warehouses in similar locations

 II. a quoted stock price in an active market

(A) I only
(B) II only
(C) both I and II
(D) neither I nor II

272. Which of the following measures of fair value uses prices and other relevant information from identical or comparable transactions?

 I. market
 II. income

(A) I only
(B) II only
(C) both I and II
(D) neither I nor II

CHAPTER **10**

Current Liabilities and Contingencies

273. Current liabilities are obligations with maturities

(A) within 1 year
(B) within 1 year or one operating cycle, whichever is shorter
(C) within 1 year or one operating cycle, whichever is longer
(D) within one operating cycle

274. Dragon Corp is a calendar year corporation. Which of the following should be recorded as current liabilities at December 31, Year 5?
   I. dividends in arrears that the board of directors plans to declare in January of Year 6 and pay by March 15th of Year 6
  II. a bonus of $25,000 to a corporate executive expected to be paid February 5, Year 6

(A) I only
(B) II only
(C) both I and II
(D) neither I nor II

275. When recording trade accounts payable under the *net* method, which of the following is correct regarding the payment or settlement date?
   I. A purchase discount lost account would be credited if the payment date is after the discount period.
  II. A purchase discount would be debited if the buyer pays within the discount.

(A) I only
(B) II only
(C) both I and II
(D) neither I nor II

276. When purchases are made, the purchase is recorded as a credit to accounts payable
    (A) as if the discount is going to be taken, if using the gross method
    (B) without regard for the discount, if using the net method
    (C) as if the discount is going to be taken, if using the net method
    (D) as if the discount is going to be taken, using either the gross or net method

277. When recording accounts payable, a purchase discount is recorded
    (A) if using the net method
    (B) if using the gross method, but only if the payment is made during the discount period
    (C) if using the net method, provided the payment is made during the discount period
    (D) if using the gross method, but the purchase discounts are reduced by any purchase discounts lost

278. Under state law, Randolph pays 3% of eligible gross wages. Eligible gross wages are defined as the first $10,000 of gross wages paid to each employee. Randolph had three employees, each of whom earned $20,000 during the current year. In its December 31 balance sheet, what amount should Randolph report as accrued liability for unemployment?
    (A) $900
    (B) $300
    (C) $1,800
    (D) $600

279. On September 30, Graphnet Corp borrowed $1,000,000 on a 9% note payable. Graphnet Corp paid the first of four quarterly payments of $264,200 when due on December 30. How much of the first payment serves to reduce the principal?
    (A) $264,200
    (B) $90,000
    (C) $241,700
    (D) $758,300

280. Normally, interest is imputed when no, or an unreasonably low, rate is stated. An exception exists for receivables and payables arising from transactions with customers or suppliers in the normal course of business when the trade terms do NOT exceed

(A) 1 year

(B) 9 months

(C) 6 months

(D) 3 months

281. Which of the following is correct regarding the discount resulting from the determination of a note payable's present value?

I. The discount is NOT a separate account from the note payable account.

II. The note payable is reported on the balance sheet at the net of the note payable face value less the unamortized discount.

(A) I only

(B) II only

(C) both I and II

(D) neither I nor II

282. The New Era Bank operates a savings and loan division and also a mortgage division. When loans are made, origination fees are either deducted from the loan or collected up front. How are loan origination fees accounted for by a mortgage company or lending institution?

I. The amount collected up front is included in income in the year of receipt.

II. The amount deducted from the loan proceeds is deferred and recognized over the life of the loan as additional income.

(A) I only

(B) II only

(C) both I and II

(D) neither I nor II

283. Sundance Inc. borrowed $1,000,000 by selling bonds and had to sign a debt covenant. Which of the following is correct regarding the debt covenant?

I. A debt covenant may restrict Sundance Inc. from doing whatever it chooses with the proceeds of the bond issuance.

II. The debt covenant may require Sundance Inc. to maintain a certain minimum working capital.

(A) I only

(B) II only

(C) both I and II

(D) neither I nor II

284. Which of the following is correct regarding a typical debt covenant associated with a loan agreement?

    I. A typical debt covenant may restrict companies from disposing of certain assets, but it cannot restrict the payment of dividends to stockholders, since only the board of directors can make decisions with regard to dividend declaration.

    II. Violation of a debt covenant results in technical default of the loan, and the lender could call the entire loan due and payable immediately.

    (A) I only
    (B) II only
    (C) both I and II
    (D) neither I nor II

285. Brewer Inc. is a manufacturer of solar panels. Brewer should record a liability for warranty in the year of sale if the liability

    I. is probable
    II. can be reasonably estimated

    (A) I only
    (B) II only
    (C) both I and II
    (D) neither I nor II

286. Mack Inc. sells equipment service contracts that cover a 2-year period. The sales price of each contract is $500. Mack's past experience is that of the total dollars spent for repairs on service contracts, 30% is incurred evenly during the first contract year and 70% evenly during the second contract year. Mack sold 700 contracts evenly throughout the current year. How much is considered earned revenue for Mack at December 31, Year 1?

    (A) $297,500
    (B) $105,000
    (C) $245,000
    (D) $52,500

287. For financial accounting purposes, which of the following are recognized on the cash basis rather than the accrual basis?

    I. warranty expense
    II. service contract revenue

    (A) I only
    (B) II only
    (C) both I and II
    (D) neither I nor II

288. Under the International Financial Reporting Standards (IFRS), which of the following classifications of loss contingency is defined as "more likely than not" to occur?

(A) probable
(B) remote
(C) reasonably probable
(D) possible

289. With regard to loss contingencies under US GAAP, which of the following defines a remote chance of expropriation of assets by a foreign government?

(A) less than likely
(B) less than possible
(C) slight
(D) reasonably possible

290. Regarding loss contingencies, which of the following standards defines possible as "may but probably will NOT occur"?

  I. US GAAP
  II. IFRS

(A) I only
(B) II only
(C) both I and II
(D) neither I nor II

291. Under US GAAP, provision for a loss contingency relating to pending or threatened litigation is recorded if the

  I. loss is considered reasonably possible
  II. amount can be reasonably estimated

(A) I only
(B) II only
(C) both I and II
(D) neither I nor II

292. The Dodo Corporation has guaranteed the indebtedness of the Squonk Corporation. The Dodo Corporation can reasonably estimate the loss amount within a range of between $50,000 and $150,000. Which of the following is correct?

    I. US GAAP requires that the best estimate of the loss be accrued.

    II. If no estimated amount is considered better than any other, $150,000, the maximum amount in the range, should be accrued.

(A) I only
(B) II only
(C) both I and II
(D) neither I nor II

293. Minte Corp is determining whether to record a contingent loss from claims and assessments. Minte will record a contingent liability if the loss is probable and the amount can be reasonably estimated under

    I. US GAAP

    II. IFRS

(A) I only
(B) II only
(C) both I and II
(D) neither I nor II

294. Ulacia Corp is obligated to repurchase receivables that have been sold and needs to record a loss contingency. Ulacia Corp has estimated a range of losses between $75,000 and $150,000. Which of the following is correct?

    I. Under US GAAP, if no amount in the range is a better estimate than any other amount, the minimum amount, $75,000, should be accrued as the contingent loss.

    II. Under IFRS, the maximum amount of the range, $150,000, should be recorded.

(A) I only
(B) II only
(C) both I and II
(D) neither I nor II

295. During Year 4, Denny Corp became involved in a tax dispute with the Internal Revenue Service (IRS). At December 31, Year 4, Denny's tax advisor believed that an unfavorable outcome was probable. A reasonable estimate of additional taxes was $400,000, but could be as much as $500,000. After the Year 4 financial statements were issued, Denny Corp received and accepted an IRS settlement offer of $415,000. Under US GAAP, what amount of accrued liability should Denny Corp have reported in its December 31, Year 4, balance sheet?

    (A) $415,000
    (B) $400,000
    (C) $500,000
    (D) $450,000

296. Stabler Corp is discounting a note receivable at the First Alameda Bank. The contingent liability for this note receivable being discounted must be disclosed in the notes to the financial statements at its face amount if sold to the bank

    I. with recourse
    II. without recourse

    (A) I only
    (B) II only
    (C) both I and II
    (D) neither I nor II

297. Under US GAAP, an example of a loss contingency that would be recorded if probable would include

    I. a note discounted "with recourse"
    II. tax disputes with a state taxing agency

    (A) I only
    (B) II only
    (C) both I and II
    (D) neither I nor II

298. On February 19, Year 3, a Dunn Corp truck was in an accident with an auto driven by Aaron. On January 16, Year 4, Dunn received notice of a lawsuit seeking $500,000 in damages for personal injuries suffered by Aaron. Dunn Corp's counsel believes it is reasonably possible that Aaron will be awarded an estimated amount in the range between $150,000 and $300,000, and that $220,000 is a better estimate of potential liability than any other amount. Dunn's accounting year ends on December 31, and the Year 3 financial statements were issued on March 8, Year 4. What amount of loss should Dunn accrue at December 31, Year 3?

(A) $150,000
(B) $220,000
(C) $300,000
(D) -0-

299. Under US GAAP, a gain contingency
   I. should be disclosed in the notes unless the likelihood of the gain being realized is remote
   II. can be recorded as revenue but only if the likelihood of realization is probable

(A) I only
(B) II only
(C) both I and II
(D) neither I nor II

300. A potential gain contingency in the amount of $350,000 as of December 31, Year 2, is settled out of court on March 12, Year 3, for $275,000. The financial statements for Year 2 were issued on March 1, Year 3. Which of the following is correct regarding the gain contingency and its recognition and disclosure in Year 2?

(A) no disclosure in the footnotes, since gain contingencies are not recognized until realized
(B) loss of $75,000 should be recorded on the income statement since the settlement was for less than the contingency
(C) gain of $275,000 should be recorded in the Year 2 income statement
(D) footnote disclosure only in Year 2

301. Electric Motorcycles Inc. is currently involved in two lawsuits. One is a class-action suit in which consumers claim that one of Electric's best-selling bikes caused severe burn injuries. It is reasonably possible that Electric will lose the suit and have to pay $16 million in damages. Electric Motorcycles Inc. is suing another company for false claims against Electric. It is probable that Electric Motorcycles will win the suit and be awarded $4 million in damages. What amount should Electric report on its financial statements as a result of these two lawsuits?

(A) $4 million income
(B) -0-
(C) $12 million expense
(D) $16 million expense

302. Triano Corp settled litigation on February 22, Year 5, for an event that occurred during Year 4. An estimated liability was determined as of December 31, Year 4. This estimate was significantly less than the final settlement. The transaction is considered to be material. The financial statements for year-end Year 4 have not been issued. How should the settlement be reported in Triano's year-end Year 4 financial statements?

 I. disclosure
 II. accrual

(A) I only
(B) II only
(C) both I and II
(D) neither I nor II

CHAPTER **11**

Financial Instruments, Foreign Currency, Price Level Accounting, and Nonmonetary Exchanges

303. Which of the following is among the criteria that need to be met for a derivative to be designated a fair value hedge?
  I. There is formal documentation of the hedging relationship between the derivative and the hedged item.
  II. The hedged item is specifically identified.

  (A) I only
  (B) II only
  (C) both I and II
  (D) neither I nor II

304. Which of the following is among the criteria that need to be met for a derivative to be designated a fair value hedge?
  I. The hedge must be expected to be highly effective in offsetting changes in the fair value of the hedged item, and the effectiveness is assessed at least every 3 months.
  II. The hedged item presents exposure to changes in fair value that could affect income.

  (A) I only
  (B) II only
  (C) both I and II
  (D) neither I nor II

305. In a perfect hedge, which of the following would have NO possibility of occurrence?
    I. gain on the derivative instrument
    II. loss on the item being hedged
(A) I only
(B) II only
(C) both I and II
(D) neither I nor II

306. The risk that the other party to a financial instrument will NOT perform
    I. need NOT be disclosed unless the risk is considered above average
    II. is known as market risk
(A) I only
(B) II only
(C) both I and II
(D) neither I nor II

307. The risk of a significant number of unsecured accounts receivable with companies in the same industry is referred to as
    I. concentration of market risk
    II. concentration of credit risk
(A) I only
(B) II only
(C) both I and II
(D) neither I nor II

308. Which of the following is correct regarding a concentration of credit risk?
    I. risk that a counterparty will partially or completely fail to perform per the terms of the contract
    II. exists if a number of counterparties are engaged in similar activities and if the industry they are in experiences economic disaster or ceases to exist
(A) I only
(B) II only
(C) both I and II
(D) neither I nor II

309. Which of the following is correct regarding fair value hedges?
(A) Fair value hedge gains are recorded on the statement of comprehensive income.
(B) Fair value hedge losses are NOT recorded on the income statement.
(C) Fair value hedge gains are NOT recorded in the financial statements.
(D) Fair value hedge gains are recorded on the income statement.

310. Which of the following fair value hedge transactions are reported on the income statement?
  I. losses
  II. gains
  (A) I only
  (B) II only
  (C) both I and II
  (D) neither I nor II

311. Which of the following cash flow hedge transactions are reported on the income statement?
  I. gains, to the extent they are effective
  II. losses
  (A) I only
  (B) II only
  (C) both I and II
  (D) neither I nor II

312. A contract that conveys to a second entity a right to future collections on accounts receivable from a first entity is a
  I. financial instrument
  II. derivative instrument
  (A) I only
  (B) II only
  (C) both I and II
  (D) neither I nor II

313. With regard to foreign currency accounting, which of the following are included in the determination of net income for the period?
  I. remeasurement adjustments
  II. translation adjustments
  (A) I only
  (B) II only
  (C) both I and II
  (D) neither I nor II

314. Quirk Company's wholly owned subsidiary Larue Corp maintains its currency in euros. Because all of Larue's branch offices are in France, its functional currency is the euro. Translation of its financial statements resulted in a $3,300 gain. Remeasurement of Larue's Year 13 financial statements resulted in a gain of $10,500. What amount should Quirk report (parent company) as a foreign exchange gain in its income statement for the year ended December 31, Year 13?

(A) -0-
(B) $3,300
(C) $10,500
(D) $13,800

315. Su Industries has international subsidiaries in Asia. These subsidiaries enter into contracts in both the US dollar and local currencies. In Year 13, Su Industries experienced a remeasurement loss of $55,000 and a translation gain of $36,000. As a result of these conversions, Su Industries would show in accumulated other comprehensive income in Year 13

(A) -0-
(B) loss of $55,000
(C) loss of $19,000
(D) gain of $36,000

316. Salazar is a subsidiary of Padre Corp. If Salazar's functional currency is its local currency, Salazar's financial statements are
  I. *translated* to the reporting currency
  II. *remeasured* into the functional currency, the result of which is a gain or loss reported in the consolidated income statement

(A) I only
(B) II only
(C) both I and II
(D) neither I nor II

317. On October 5, Year 13, Griffin Corp purchased merchandise from an unaffiliated company in Taiwan for 20,000 Taiwan dollars when the spot rate was $0.65. Griffin Corp paid the bill in full in February of Year 14 when the spot rate was $0.74. The spot rate was $0.80 on December 31, Year 13. What amount should Griffin Corp report as a foreign currency transaction gain/loss in its income statement for the year ended December 31, Year 13?

(A) $3,000 gain
(B) $3,000 loss
(C) $1,800 loss
(D) -0-

318. Which of the following is considered monetary rather than nonmonetary?
   I. accounts receivable
   II. allowance for doubtful accounts

(A) I only
(B) II only
(C) both I and II
(D) neither I nor II

319. Which of the following is considered nonmonetary rather than monetary?
   I. equipment
   II. accumulated depreciation-equipment

(A) I only
(B) II only
(C) both I and II
(D) neither I nor II

320. Which of the following would result in a purchasing power decline?

(A) holding monetary assets in a period of deflation
(B) holding monetary assets in a period of inflation
(C) holding monetary liabilities in a period of inflation
(D) none of the above

321. Under US GAAP, certain large publicly held companies may disclose information concerning the effect of changing prices. Which of the following methods of measuring prices and price changes ignores asset appreciation but adjusts for changes in the purchasing power of the dollar?

(A) historical cost/constant dollar
(B) historical cost/nominal dollar
(C) current cost/nominal dollar
(D) current cost/constant dollar

322. Which of the following methods of measuring prices and the effects of price changes involve adjustments for both purchasing power and appreciation of assets?

(A) historical cost/constant dollar
(B) historical cost/nominal dollar
(C) current cost/nominal dollar
(D) current cost/constant dollar

323. Under US GAAP, a nonmonetary exchange is recognized at fair value of the assets exchanged unless

(A) exchange has commercial substance
(B) fair value is not determinable
(C) the assets are similar in nature
(D) the assets are dissimilar in nature

324. The Drexel Corporation exchanged equipment with an appraised value of $60,000 and an original cost of $52,000, and received from Dartmouth Corp equipment with a fair value of $64,000. Under US GAAP, how much is the gain on the exchange for Drexel Corporation, assuming that the transaction has commercial substance?

(A) -0-
(B) $8,000
(C) $4,000
(D) $12,000

325. On January 1, Year 9, Hayley Corp traded delivery trucks with Dylan Corp and paid $5,000 cash to Dylan Corp. Hayley Corp's truck had a fair value of $95,000 and accumulated depreciation of $75,000 on the date of exchange. Hayley Corp's asset had an original cost of $130,000. Hayley estimated that the value of Dylan Corp's truck was $90,000 on the date of exchange. The book value of Dylan Corp's asset on January 1, Year 9, was $70,000. The transaction had commercial substance. Under US GAAP, what amount of gain should be recorded by Hayley Corp?

(A) -0-
(B) $35,000
(C) $40,000
(D) $55,000

326. Under US GAAP, losses in connection with nonmonetary exchanges are deferred when the exchange is said to

   I. lack commercial substance
  II. have commercial substance

(A) I only
(B) II only
(C) both I and II
(D) neither I nor II

327. Under US GAAP, nonmonetary exchanges that lack commercial substance could possibly result in which of the following NOT being recognized immediately?

    I. losses

    II. gains

    (A) I only

    (B) II only

    (C) both I and II

    (D) neither I nor II

Use the following facts to answer questions 328–329:

Durant Corp exchanged equipment that cost $480,000 and had a fair value of $380,000 for a warehouse owned by Jordan Corp. Future cash flows will significantly change as a result of the exchange. On the date of exchange, the equipment had accumulated depreciation of $80,000, and Durant Corp had to pay $5,000 in cash.

328. How much gain or loss should be reported by Durant Corp?

    (A) -0-

    (B) $5,000 loss

    (C) $20,000 gain

    (D) $20,000 loss

329. After the exchange, how much is the basis of the warehouse to Durant Corp under US GAAP?

    (A) $480,000

    (B) $380,000

    (C) $385,000

    (D) $400,000

330. Under which of the following standards are nonmonetary exchanges characterized as exchanges of similar assets and exchanges of dissimilar assets?

    I. IFRS

    II. US GAAP

    (A) I only

    (B) II only

    (C) both I and II

    (D) neither I nor II

CHAPTER 12

Bonds and
Troubled Debt Restructuring

331. Zaran Corp issues bonds with a stated rate of 5%. If the market rate for comparable bonds is 6%, which of the following is correct?

(A) Zaran Corp will collect a premium.

(B) Zaran Corp will have to sell the bonds at a discount.

(C) Zaran Corp will sell the bonds at face value.

(D) The amount of interest paid by Zaran Corp to investors each period is based on the market rate of 6% rather than the stated rate of 5%.

332. Anna Inc. issues bonds with a stated rate of 5%. These bonds will sell at a premium if

  I. the market rate of interest was above 5%

 II. the bonds pay interest semiannually rather than annually

(A) I only

(B) II only

(C) both I and II

(D) neither I nor II

333. With regard to a 5-year $1,000 bond issued at 102 on January 1 Year 10 that pays interest semiannually on June 30 and December 31, the stated interest rate of 8% is used to calculate the

(A) amount of interest payment

(B) market price of the bond

(C) selling price of the bond

(D) actual amount of interest expense

334. On August 1, Year 4, Blue Corp purchased 500 of Karl Corp's 10% $1,000 bonds at 98 plus accrued interest. The bonds are dated May 1 and mature on May 1, Year 14. Interest is payable semiannually on May 1 and November 1. What amount did Karl Corp receive on the bond issuance?

(A) $502,500
(B) $496,250
(C) $500,000
(D) $483,750

Use the following facts to answer questions 335–336:

On January 2, Year 1, Brunner Corp issued 9% bonds with a face amount of $1,000,000 that mature on January 2, Year 7. The bonds pay interest semiannually on June 30 and December 31. The bonds were issued to yield 12%, which resulted in a discount of $140,000.

335. If Brunner uses the straight line method to amortize the discount, the amount of interest expense for the first interest payment date of June 30 Year 1 would be determined by

(A) subtracting the bond discount amortization for the period from the amount of cash interest paid
(B) adding the bond discount amortization for the period to the amount of cash interest paid
(C) multiplying the stated rate of interest by the par value of the bonds
(D) multiplying the market rate of interest by the par value of the bonds

336. If Brunner uses the effective interest method to amortize the discount, the amount of interest expense for the first interest payment date of June 30, Year 1, would be determined by

(A) subtracting the bond discount amortization for the period from the amount of cash interest paid
(B) multiplying the par value of the bonds by the stated rate of interest
(C) multiplying the carrying amount of the bonds by the market rate of interest
(D) multiplying the par value of the bonds by the market rate of interest

Use the following facts to answer questions 337–338:

On July 1, Year 1, Truncale Corp issued 8% bonds in the amount of $500,000, which mature on July 1, Year 11. The bonds were issued for $468,500 to yield 10%. Interest is payable annually on June 30. Truncale Corp uses the effective interest method to amortize the discount.

337. How much interest expense should Truncale Corp record on December 31, Year 1?

(A) $46,850
(B) $40,000
(C) $20,000
(D) $23,425

338. How much is the carrying value of the bonds on December 31, Year 1?

(A) $471,925
(B) $468,500
(C) $500,000
(D) $475,350

339. A bond is issued on May 1 of the current year and has interest payment dates of March 1 and September 1. The accrual for bond interest expense at December 31 would be for a period of

(A) 8 months
(B) 10 months
(C) 4 months
(D) 6 months

340. Reynolds Corp issued $200,000 worth of 11% bonds for par on January 31, Year 5. The bonds are dated December 31, Year 1, and pay interest semiannually on June 30 and December 31. What amount of accrued interest payable should Reynolds Corp report in its September 30, Year 5, balance sheet?

(A) $5,500
(B) $7,333
(C) $11,000
(D) $1,833

341. Which of the following describes unsecured bonds issued by a corporation that mature on different dates?

I. term bonds
II. serial bonds
III. debentures

(A) I and II
(B) I, II, and III
(C) I and III
(D) II and III

Use the following facts to answer questions 342–344:

On August 1, Year 13, Tucker Corp issued $800,000 worth of 7% bonds at par with interest payment dates of June 1 and December 1.

342. How much accrued interest should be recorded on August 1, Year 13?

(A) -0-
(B) $4,667
(C) $9,333
(D) none of the above

343. How much accrued interest should be recorded at December 31, Year 13?

(A) -0-
(B) $4,667
(C) $9,333
(D) none of the above

344. In its income statement for the current year ended December 31, Year 13, what amount of total interest expense should Tucker Corp report?

(A) $4,667
(B) $23,333
(C) $9,333
(D) $32,667

Use the following facts to answer questions 345–346:

The Holden Corporation issued 10-year bonds at 102 with a maturity value of $1,000,000. The bonds pay interest semiannually. The stated interest rate of the bonds was 6%.

345. The entry the Holden Corporation uses to record the original issue should include which of the following?

(A) credit to bond premium for $2,000
(B) credit to bonds payable for $1,020,000
(C) debit to cash for $1,000,000
(D) credit to bond premium for $20,000

346. The amortization of the bond premium each period would impact the financial statements in which of the following ways?

(A) interest expense being greater than the amount of cash paid for interest

(B) cash paid for interest being greater than interest expense

(C) interest expense and cash paid being equal if the premium were being amortized using the straight line method

(D) none of the above

347. Which of the following is correct regarding convertible bonds at issuance?

    I. Under US generally accepted accounting principles (GAAP), no value is assigned to the conversion feature.

    II. Under the International Financial Reporting Standards (IFRS), both a liability and an equity component should be recognized when the bonds are issued.

(A) I only

(B) II only

(C) both I and II

(D) neither I nor II

348. All costs associated with the issuance of a bond are

(A) expensed in the period incurred

(B) capitalized but NOT amortized

(C) capitalized and amortized over the outstanding term of the bonds

(D) capitalized and amortized over 5 years

349. The Thunder Corporation issues bonds and warrants simultaneously for $1,000,000 at par. Thunder Corporation would be required to account for the value of the warrants separately on the date the bonds are originally issued if the warrants are

    I. nondetachable

    II. detachable

(A) I only

(B) II only

(C) both I and II

(D) neither I nor II

350. On March 1, Year 1, Marco Corp issued $500,000 worth of 10% nonconvertible bonds at 102, due on February 28, Year 21. Each $1,000 bond was issued with 20 detachable stock warrants, each of which entitled the holder to purchase, for $60, one share of Marco's $10 par common stock. On March 1, Year 1, the market price of each warrant was $5. By what amount should the bond issue proceeds increase stockholders' equity?

(A) -0-
(B) $10,000
(C) $100,000
(D) $50,000

351. Which of the following is correct regarding a bond sinking fund?
I. Sinking fund accounts that are considered to offset current bond liabilities can be included within current assets.
II. A bond sinking fund is an example of an appropriation of retained earnings.

(A) I only
(B) II only
(C) both I and II
(D) neither I nor II

352. Which of the following is correct regarding troubled debt restructuring?
I. For the creditor, the objective is to minimize the recovery of the investment.
II. Concessions made by the creditor normally include reduced interest rates.

(A) I only
(B) II only
(C) both I and II
(D) neither I nor II

353. With regard to troubled debt restructuring, creditors typically make which of the following concessions to minimize the risk of bad debt write-off?
I. extension of maturity dates
II. reduction of accrued interest

(A) I only
(B) II only
(C) both I and II
(D) neither I nor II

Use these facts to answer questions 354–355:

Livingston Corp transferred land to Vette Corp pursuant to a troubled debt restructuring (considered to be both unusual and infrequent for Livingston Corp). The transfer was made in full liquidation of Livingston's liability to Vette Corp. Information pertaining to the land is as follows:

Carrying amount of land transferred	$140,000
Fair value of land transferred	$80,000
Carrying amount of liability liquidated	$165,000

354. What amount should Livingston report as ordinary gain (loss) on transfer of land?

(A) ($60,000)
(B) -0-
(C) ($85,000)
(D) $60,000

355. What amount should Livingston report as a pretax extraordinary gain (loss) on restructuring of payables under US GAAP?

(A) $25,000
(B) -0-
(C) $60,000
(D) $85,000

CHAPTER 13

Working Capital Components

Use the following facts to answer questions 356–358:

The Romanoff Company offers trade discounts of 30% and a sales discount of 2/10 net 30 on its sales. A customer bought items with a list price of $70,000 on April 1.

356. If all the preceding terms apply and Romanoff uses the gross method, which of the following is correct regarding the entry made on 4/1?

    (A) Sales will be credited for $70,000.
    (B) Accounts receivable will be debited for $49,000.
    (C) Trade discounts will be debited for $21,000.
    (D) Cash discounts taken will be debited for $980.

357. If all of the preceding terms apply, and assuming the buyer pays within the discount period, the journal entry to record the collection would include a

    (A) credit to accounts receivable for $48,020
    (B) credit to sales discounts taken for $980
    (C) debit to sales discounts taken for $980
    (D) debit to cash for $49,000

358. If the buyer paid after the 10-day discount period, which of the following is correct?

    (A) Sales discounts not taken would be credited for $980.
    (B) Sales discounts not taken would be debited for $980.
    (C) Accounts receivable would be credited for $49,000.
    (D) Cash would be debited for $48,020.

359. For financial statement reporting purposes, which of the following methods of recognizing bad debts is consistent with US GAAP since it provides for matching of revenues with expenses incurred to generate those revenues in the same accounting period?

    I. direct write-off method

    II. allowance method

(A) I only

(B) II only

(C) both I and II

(D) neither I nor II

360. Working capital can be defined as

(A) current assets divided by current liabilities

(B) cash plus net receivables plus marketable securities divided by current liabilities

(C) current assets minus current liabilities

(D) all of the above

361. Current assets are assets that are reasonably expected to convert into cash, be sold, or consumed

(A) within 1 year

(B) within 1 year or one operating cycle, whichever is shorter

(C) within one operating cycle

(D) within 1 year or one operating cycle, whichever is longer

362. If a current liability is expected to be refinanced on a long-term basis, the liability may be reclassified as long term on the balance sheet under which of the following standards?

    I. US GAAP

    II. IFRS

(A) I only

(B) II only

(C) both I and II

(D) neither I nor II

363. Besides cash, demand deposits, and money market accounts, highly liquid investments that are readily convertible into cash can be shown on the balance sheet as cash or cash equivalent if the investments have a maturity of 90 days or less

    I. from the date the investment is acquired

    II. from the balance sheet date

(A) I only

(B) II only

(C) both I and II

(D) neither I nor II

364. Which of the following could NOT be reported as cash or cash equivalents?

(A) money market accounts
(B) demand deposits
(C) US treasury bills with an original maturity of 60 days from date purchased
(D) legally restricted deposits held as compensating balances against borrowing arrangements with a lending institution

365. Turner has two items in the safe on December 31, Year 13. Which of these items should be included in Turner Corporation's cash or cash equivalents on December 31, Year 13?

 I. a check payable to Turner Corp in the amount of $600 dated January 2, Year 14, that Turner has on hand December 31 waiting to be deposited

 II. a US Treasury bill in the amount of $1,000 purchased December 1, Year 13, that matures February 15th, Year 14

(A) I only
(B) II only
(C) both I and II
(D) neither I nor II

366. The Early Corporation had a cash balance in the ledger at December 31, Year 13, of $15,000. Included in the $15,000 balance were the following two items:

 I. A check in the amount of $1,800 that was written to Snell Corporation. The check was dated December 31, Year 13, but was not mailed out to Snell Corporation until January 7, Year 14.

 II. A check payable to Early Corporation from a customer was deposited December 24, Year 13, and was returned for insufficient funds. The check was for $500 and was redeposited by Early Corporation January 2, Year 14, and cleared January 7, Year 14.

How much cash should Early report in December 31, Year 13, balance sheet?

(A) $15,000
(B) $13,200
(C) $14,500
(D) $12,700

367. A receives cash of $250,000 as a result of factoring its receivables "without recourse" to B. Which of the following best describes the transaction?
    I. The risk of uncollectible receivables remains with A.
    II. A has, in effect, obtained a loan from B for $250,000.
    (A) I only
    (B) II only
    (C) both I and II
    (D) neither I nor II

368. At January 1, Year 6, Edgar Co. had a credit balance of $250,000 in its allowance for uncollectible accounts. Based on past experience, 2% of Edgar's credit sales have been uncollectible. During Year 6, Edgar wrote off $315,000 of uncollectible accounts. Credit sales for Year 6 were $8,000,000. In its December 31, Year 6, balance sheet, what amount should Edgar report as allowance for uncollectible accounts?
    (A) $160,000
    (B) $315,000
    (C) $250,000
    (D) $95,000

Use the following facts to answer questions 369–370:

Costas Corp is an accrual based taxpayer and had written off $15,000 from a customer regarding a receivable deemed worthless in Year 12. In Year 13, Costas Corp recovers 40% of the receivable from the customer's bankruptcy trustee.

369. The entry in Year 12 to record the write-off of the $15,000 considered worthless
    I. increases the allowance for uncollectible accounts
    II. decreases net income
    III. decreases accounts receivable
    (A) I, II, and III
    (B) I and III
    (C) III only
    (D) II and II

370. In Year 13 when Costas Corp recovers 40% of the receivable from the bankruptcy trustee, this results in
    I. an increase in net income
    II. an increase in the allowance for doubtful accounts
    (A) I only
    (B) II only
    (C) both I and II
    (D) neither I nor II

Use the following facts to answer questions 371–372:

Hondo received from a customer a 1-year $400,000 note bearing annual interest of 10%. After holding the note for 6 months, Hondo discounted the note at Second Republic Bank at an effective interest rate of 13%.

371. How much is the maturity value of the note?
- (A) $440,000
- (B) $452,000
- (C) $497,200
- (D) $400,000

372. How much cash did Hondo receive from the bank?
- (A) $440,000
- (B) $402,800
- (C) $371,400
- (D) $411,400

Use the following facts to answer questions 373–376:

On December 31, Year 5, the Hackett Corp had a credit balance of $700 in its allowance for doubtful accounts prior to consideration of the following aging schedule that was prepared at year end.

Age	Amount	Estimated Uncollectible
0–30 days	$50,000	3%
31–60 days	$10,000	6%
Over 60 days	$5,000	$2,500

373. What amount should Hackett Corp report as the ending balance in the allowance account at December 31, Year 5?
- (A) $4,600 credit
- (B) $4,600 debit
- (C) $3,900 credit
- (D) $5,300 credit

374. How much should Hackett Corp record for bad debt expense in Year 5?
- (A) $4,600
- (B) $3,900
- (C) $5,300
- (D) $700

375. Assuming the allowance account had a previous balance prior to adjustment of $500 debit balance rather than $700 credit, how much should Hackett Corp record for the ending allowance account balance at December 31, Year 5?

(A) $4,100
(B) $4,600
(C) $5,100
(D) -0-

376. Assuming the allowance account had a previous balance prior to adjustment of $500 debit balance rather than $700 credit, how much should Hackett Corp record for bad debt expense in Year 5?

(A) $4,100
(B) $4,600
(C) $5,100
(D) -0-

377. At year end, when using the balance sheet approach to estimating bad debt expense, the previous balance in the allowance account is ignored for purposes of determining

  I. bad debt expense
  II. the ending balance in the allowance account

(A) I only
(B) II only
(C) both I and II
(D) neither I nor II

378. Miller Corporation adjusted its allowance for doubtful accounts at December 31, Year 11. The general ledger balances for accounts receivable and the related allowance account were $2,000,000 and $75,000 respectively. In addition, sales on credit for Year 11 were $3,000,000. Miller uses a balance sheet approach to estimate its bad debt expense, and for Year 11 estimates that 4% of accounts receivable will be uncollectible. What amount should Miller record as an adjustment to its allowance for doubtful accounts at December 31, Year 11?

(A) $5,000
(B) $45,000
(C) $120,000
(D) $3,000

379. The Lubrano Corporation uses the income statement approach to estimating bad debt expense. In Year 13, sales on credit amounted to $2,000,000. Sales returns and allowances were $200,000. Lubrano Corporation estimates that 2% of net credit sales will be uncollectible. The allowance for doubtful accounts had a balance at the beginning of Year 13 of $25,000. How much should Lubrano Corp charge to bad debt expense in Year 13?

(A) $40,000
(B) $36,000
(C) $11,000
(D) $15,000

380. At year end, the previous balance in the allowance account is ignored for purposes of determining bad debt expense when using the
  I. income statement (percent of sales) approach
  II. balance sheet approach (percent of receivables) approach

(A) I only
(B) II only
(C) both I and II
(D) neither I nor II

381. The following facts apply to Kaput Corporation in Year 13. If the allowance for doubtful accounts had a beginning balance of $55,000 and an ending balance of $45,000 and during the year, $15,000 of accounts receivable were written off as worthless, what amount should be recorded as bad debt expense for Year 13 under US GAAP?

(A) $10,000
(B) $15,000
(C) $5,000
(D) $25,000

382. In December of Year 13, Carpenter Inc. had a note payable scheduled to mature on February 23, Year 14. On December 30, Year 13, Carpenter Inc. signed a binding agreement with Summit Bank to refinance the existing note, and the refinancing commenced on January 2, Year 13. The financial statements were issued on February 15, Year 14. Under US GAAP, how should Carpenter Inc. report the note payable in its December 31, Year 13, income statement?

(A) long-term liability
(B) short-term liability
(C) short-term note receivable
(D) long-term note receivable

383. Simone Corp reported the following liabilities at December 31, Year 4:

Accounts payable	$500,000
Mortgage payable (current portion, $150,000)	$2,000,000
Bank loan (matures May 31, Year 5)	$800,000

The $800,000 bank loan was refinanced with a 10-year loan on January 9, Year 5, with the first principal payment due in the amount of $100,000 on January 2, Year 6. Simone Corp's Year 4 audited financial statements were issued February 26, Year 5. What amount should Simone Corp report as current liabilities at December 31, Year 4?

(A) $650,000
(B) $750,000
(C) $1,450,000
(D) $3,300,000

384. Which of the following is included within the category known as cash and cash equivalents?
   I. cash in checking accounts
   II. petty cash
  III. cash in bond sinking fund

(A) I, II, and III
(B) I and III
(C) I and II
(D) I only

385. Cone Corp is a calendar year corporation. Within the category of cash and cash equivalents is a postdated check received from one of Cone's customers dated 7 days after the balance sheet date. Cone has possession of the check as of December 31 and should classify the check as
   I. cash
   II. cash equivalent

(A) I only
(B) II only
(C) both I and II
(D) neither I nor II

386. The quick ratio includes which of the following in the numerator?
    I. net receivables
   II. short-term marketable securities
  III. inventory
  IV. prepaid rent

  (A) I, II, and III
  (B) I, II, III, and IV
  (C) I and II
  (D) I, II, and IV

387. Total current liabilities is used as the denominator in which of the following ratios?
    I. current ratio
   II. quick ratio

  (A) I only
  (B) II only
  (C) both I and II
  (D) neither I nor II

388. Which of the following is treated as a sale of receivables?
    I. factoring without recourse in exchange for cash
   II. pledging receivables in exchange for a loan

  (A) I only
  (B) II only
  (C) both I and II
  (D) neither I nor II

389. On June 1, Year 13, the Barnes Corporation factored $100,000 of its accounts receivable without recourse to the Rohn Corporation. Rohn Corporation retained 15% of the accounts receivable as an allowance for sales returns and charged a 5% commission on the gross amount of factored receivables. How much cash did Barnes Corporation receive from factoring the receivables?

  (A) $85,000
  (B) $95,000
  (C) $100,000
  (D) $80,000

CHAPTER 14

Accounting for Business Combinations

390. On December 30, Year 4, Policastro Inc. paid $960,000 for all of the issued and outstanding common stock of Salva Corp. On that date, the book value of Salva's assets and liabilities were $900,000 and $280,000 respectively. The fair values of Salva's assets and liabilities were $940,000 and $240,000 respectively. On Policastro's December 31, Year 4, balance sheet, what amount should be recorded as goodwill?

(A) $340,000
(B) $260,000
(C) $80,000
(D) none of the above

391. When a subsidiary is acquired with an acquisition cost that is less than the fair value of the underlying assets, which of the following is correct?
  I. The balance sheet is adjusted to fair value.
  II. Negative goodwill is recorded.

(A) I only
(B) II only
(C) both I and II
(D) neither I nor II

392. In a business combination accounted for properly as an acquisition, which of the following costs should be expensed in the period incurred by the combined corporation?
  I. registration and issuance costs
  II. consulting fees

(A) I only
(B) II only
(C) both I and II
(D) neither I nor II

393. On February 14, Year 11, Heart Corporation acquired 25% of Flower Corporation's common stock. On October 1, Year 13, Heart acquires 65% of Flower's outstanding common stock. Flower Inc. continues in existence as Heart's subsidiary. How much of Flower's Year 13 net income should be reported as accruing to Heart?

(A) 90% of Flower's net income

(B) 25% of Flower's net income from January 1 to September 30, and then all of Flower Inc.'s net income from October 1 through December 31

(C) all of Flower's net income

(D) 25% of Flower's net income from January 1 to September 30 and then 95% of Flower Inc.'s net income from October 1 through December 31

Use the following facts to answer questions 394–395:

Corporation A buys 80% of B Corporation for $500,000 on December 31, Year 1. The fair value of B Corporation's assets is $400,000. The fair value of B Corporation's liabilities is $50,000, and the book value of the net assets of B Corporation is $300,000 on December 31, Year 1.

394. How much is the implied value of B Corporation based on purchase price?

(A) $350,000

(B) $400,000

(C) $500,000

(D) $625,000

395. How much goodwill should be recorded by Corporation A on the consolidated financial statements dated December 31, Year 1?

(A) $150,000

(B) $275,000

(C) $200,000

(D) $50,000

Use the following facts to answer questions 396–397:

On December 31, Year 11, Platinum Corp buys 80% ownership in Steel Corp by purchasing 80,000 of Steel Corp's 100,000 voting common shares for $800,000 cash. Steel Corp had net assets with a book value of $400,000 and a fair value of $700,000 at the date of acquisition.

396. What is the implied fair value of Steel Corp based on purchase price?

(A) $800,000

(B) $1,000,000

(C) $700,000

(D) $300,000

397. Under US GAAP, the consolidated balance sheet of Platinum Corp and Steel Corp dated December 31, Year 11, would report goodwill in the amount of

(A) -0-
(B) $100,000
(C) $300,000
(D) $400,000

398. Salas Inc. is a publicly traded US corporation in the food industry. Salas Corp is the majority stockholder (owning 50% or more) of many other corporations, domestic and foreign. Some of the affiliated corporations are in the food industry, others are not. Which of the following subsidiaries should be included in consolidated financial statements for Salas?

   I. domestic
  II. foreign
 III. similar
  IV. dissimilar

(A) I only
(B) I and II
(C) I, III, and IV
(D) I, II, III, and IV

Use the following facts to answer questions 399–401:

On January 1, Year 1, Poplar Corp acquired 80% of Sienna Corp's 100,000 outstanding common shares for $2,800,000. On the date of acquisition, the book value of Sienna Corp's net assets was $2,750,000. Book value equaled fair value for all assets and liabilities of Sienna Corp, except land that had a fair value of $100,000 greater than book value and furniture and fixtures that had a fair value greater than book value of $50,000. On January 1, Year 1, Sienna Corp had an intangible asset, unpatented technology, with a fair value of $525,000.

399. How much is the implied value of Sienna Corp based on purchase price?

(A) $2,800,000
(B) $3,500,000
(C) $2,750,000
(D) $3,425,000

400. What is the goodwill to be reported on Poplar Corp's December 31, Year 1, balance sheet under US GAAP?

(A) -0-
(B) $75,000
(C) $600,000
(D) $750,000

401. In the eliminating journal entry made just after the acquisition, how would noncontrolling interest be recorded?

(A) debit of $560,000
(B) credit of 560,000
(C) credit of $700,000
(D) debit of $700,000

Use the following facts to answer questions 402–404:

On January 1, Year 13, Peyton Corp acquired 90% of Shore Corp's outstanding common stock for $180,000. On that date, the carrying value of Shore Corp's assets and liabilities approximated their fair values. During Year 13, Shore earned $18,000 of net income and paid $4,000 cash dividends to its stockholders.

402. Using the acquisition method, calculate the amount of noncontrolling interest at the date of acquisition on January 1, Year 13.

(A) -0-
(B) $20,000
(C) $18,000
(D) $14,000

403. Calculate the noncontrolling interest at December 31, Year 13.

(A) $20,000
(B) $18,600
(C) $21,400
(D) $22,200

404. On the December 31, Year 13, consolidated balance sheet, stockholders equity is equal to Peyton Corp's stockholders equity

(A) plus Shore Corp's stockholders equity
(B) plus Shore Corp's stockholders equity plus the fair value of the noncontrolling interest
(C) plus the fair value of the noncontrolling interest
(D) less the fair value of the noncontrolling interest

Use the following facts to answer questions 405–406:

On January 1, Year 12, Parsons Corporation acquired 100% of Stines Corporation by issuing 20,000 shares of Parsons Corporation common stock. The acquisition was announced on April 30, Year 12, when Parsons Corporation stock was selling for $35 per share and finalized on September 22, Year 12, when Parsons stock was selling for $40 per share. During Year 12, Parsons stock had an average selling price of $36 per share and a par value of $10 per share.

405. How much is the debit to investment in subsidiary on September 22, Year 12?

(A) $800,000
(B) $700,000
(C) $720,000
(D) $200,000

406. The journal entry to record the investment in subsidiary would include a credit to

(A) common stock for $800,000
(B) additional paid-in capital for $600,000
(C) common stock for $600,000
(D) additional paid-in capital for $200,000

407. On November 1, Year 3, Plato Corp acquired 100% of Socrates Corp for $375,000. The carrying value of Socrates assets were $550,000, and the fair value was $750,000 at the date of acquisition. The book and fair value of Socrates liabilities on November 1, Year 3, was $300,000. Additionally, Socrates had identifiable intangible assets at the date of acquisition with a fair value of $165,000. How much goodwill or gain is to be reported on Plato's December 31, Year 3, consolidated income statement?

(A) $75,000 gain
(B) $75,000 goodwill
(C) $240,000 goodwill
(D) $240,000 gain

Use the following facts to answer questions 408–410:

Prince Corp issues $100,000 shares of its $1 par value common stock to acquire Simmons Inc. in a business combination accounted for as an acquisition. The market value of Prince's common stock is $14 per share. Legal and consulting fees incurred in relationship to the purchase are $80,000. Registration and issuance costs for the common stock are $15,000.

408. How much should be expensed immediately in connection with this combination?

(A) -0-
(B) $15,000
(C) $80,000
(D) $95,000

409. What should be recorded in Prince Corp's additional paid-in capital for this business combination?

(A) $1,315,000
(B) $1,300,000
(C) $1,400,000
(D) $1,285,000

410. The journal entry to record the business combination would include a debit to investment in subsidiary in the amount of

(A) $1,400,000
(B) $1,305,000
(C) $1,385,000
(D) $1,320,000

411. Pie Corp buys 80% of Slice Corp stock in a business combination accounted for as an acquisition on January 2, Year 1. At the date of acquisition, Pie Corp's common stock is $140,000 and Slice Corp common stock is $30,000. Both Pie and Slice have additional paid-in capital of $120,000. Slice Corp has retained earnings of $50,000 at the date of acquisition. Which of the following is correct?

I. 80% of Slice's total equity is eliminated as of the date of acquisition.
II. Consolidated common stock will be $140,000.

(A) I only
(B) II only
(C) both I and II
(D) neither I nor II

412. In a business combination accounted for as an acquisition, which of the following is correct assuming the subsidiary is 80% owned by the parent?

I. A cash dividend paid by the subsidiary would decrease consolidated retained earnings.
II. A cash dividend paid by the subsidiary would increase the noncontrolling interest on the consolidated balance sheet.

(A) I only
(B) II only
(C) both I and II
(D) neither I nor II

Use the following facts to answer questions 413–414:

On December 31, Year 13, Potomac Corp acquired a 100% interest in Seltzer Corp by exchanging 25,000 shares of its common stock for 200,000 shares of Seltzer Corp's common stock. The fair value of Potomac's common stock on the date of acquisition was $10 per share, and the fair value of Seltzer Corp's common stock was $1.50 per share. Seltzer Corp had current assets with a book and fair value of $150,000, and property plant and equipment with a book value of $175,000 and a fair value of $250,000. Potomac Corp's property plant and equipment had a book value of $1,200,000 and a fair value of $1,400,000.

413. On the consolidated financial statements dated December 31, Year 13, consolidated property plant and equipment would be reported at

(A) $1,450,000
(B) $1,200,000
(C) $1,375,000
(D) $1,650,000

414. How much goodwill or gain should be recorded by Potomac Corp on the consolidated financial statements dated December 31, Year 13?

(A) goodwill of $250,000
(B) goodwill of $150,000
(C) gain of $250,000
(D) gain of $150,000

CHAPTER 15

Statement of Cash Flows

415. Required disclosures of a statement of cash flows prepared using the direct method under US GAAP includes a reconciliation of net income to net cash flow from
  I. operating activities
  II. financing activities
  III. investment activities

(A) I only
(B) both I and II
(C) both I and III
(D) I, II, and III

416. Under US GAAP, a reconciliation is needed from ending retained earnings to cash flows from operating activities when preparing the statement of cash flows using which of the following methods?
  I. direct method
  II. indirect method

(A) I only
(B) II only
(C) both I and II
(D) neither I nor II

417. Under US GAAP, which method of preparing the operating section of the statement of cash flows would include "cash paid to suppliers"?
  I. direct method
  II. indirect method

(A) I only
(B) II only
(C) both I and II
(D) neither I nor II

418. Which of the following would be included in the investing activities section of a statement of cash flows?
   I. borrowing money
   II. repaying amounts borrowed (the principal)
   (A) I only
   (B) II only
   (C) both I and II
   (D) neither I nor II

419. Which of the following would be included in the investing activities section of a statement of cash flows?
   I. making loans
   II. collecting loans
   (A) I only
   (B) II only
   (C) both I and II
   (D) neither I nor II

420. Cash flow per share is a required disclosure when preparing the statement of cash flows using which of the following methods?
   I. direct method
   II. indirect method
   (A) I only
   (B) II only
   (C) both I and II
   (D) neither I nor II

421. The direct method will provide a larger amount of net cash provided from operating activities compared to the indirect method when
   I. accelerated depreciation is used for book purposes rather than straight line
   II. bonds were issued at par rather than at a discount or premium
   (A) I only
   (B) II only
   (C) both I and II
   (D) neither I nor II

422. The statement of cash flows provides relevant information about which of the following?

    I. the cash receipts and disbursements of an enterprise during an accounting period

    II. a company's ability to meet cash operating needs in the future

(A) I only
(B) II only
(C) both I and II
(D) neither I nor II

423. Jenkins Inc. is preparing its statement of cash flows for Year 5. The following information pertains.

	12/31/Yr5	1/1/Yr5
Accounts receivable	$28,000	$21,000
Allowance for doubtful accts	$1,200	$700
Prepaid insurance	$10,000	$13,000
Payroll taxes payable	$9,600	$7,000

Net income for Year 5 is $190,000.

What amount should Jenkins Inc. include as net cash provided by operating activities using the indirect method?

(A) $190,000
(B) $189,100
(C) $190,900
(D) $183,900

424. Which of the following is correct regarding the statement of cash flows prepared using the indirect method?

    I. A loss from the sale of used equipment should be reported as a decrease to net income in the operating activities section.

    II. The entire amount of cash proceeds from the sale of equipment (including the loss) should be shown in the investing section of the statement of cash flows.

(A) I only
(B) II only
(C) both I and II
(D) neither I nor II

425. Which of the following items is included in the financing activities section of the statement of cash flows?
  I. cash effects of acquiring and disposing of property, plant, and equipment
  II. cash effects of transactions obtaining resources from owners and providing them with a return on their investment

  (A) I only
  (B) II only
  (C) both I and II
  (D) neither I nor II

426. During Year 13, Gulbin Corp had the following activities related to its financial operations:

Payment for the early extinguishment of debt (carrying amount, $400,000)	$425,000
Payment of Year 13 dividend, declared in Year 12	$50,000
Purchase of fixed assets	$30,000
Proceeds from the sale of treasury stock	$20,000

Under US GAAP, how much should Gulbin Corp report its net cash used in financing activities?

  (A) $495,000
  (B) $475,000
  (C) $425,000
  (D) $455,000

427. Under IFRS, dividends paid may be reported in which section of the statement of cash flows?

  (A) financing
  (B) operating
  (C) operating or financing
  (D) investing, financing, or operating

428. Under IFRS, interest paid may be reported as an outflow in which section of the statement of cash flows?

  (A) operating or financing
  (B) operating or investing
  (C) investing or financing
  (D) operating

429. In the statement of cash flows, paying interest and dividends may be reported as financing outflows under
   I. US GAAP
   II. IFRS

(A) I only
(B) II only
(C) both I and II
(D) neither I nor II

430. Dividends received may be reported as an investing or operating activity on the statement of cash flows under which of the following standards?
   I. US GAAP
   II. IFRS

(A) I only
(B) II only
(C) both I and II
(D) neither I nor II

431. Interest received may only be reported as an operating activity on the statement of cash flows under which of the following standards?
   I. US GAAP
   II. IFRS

(A) I only
(B) II only
(C) both I and II
(D) neither I nor II

432. Dividends received and interest paid may both be reported as an operating activity on the statement of cash flows under which of the following standards?
   I. US GAAP
   II. IFRS

(A) I only
(B) II only
(C) both I and II
(D) neither I nor II

433. If a debt repayment includes both principal and interest, how are the payments reported in a statement of cash flows prepared under US GAAP?

(A) Entire payment is presented as a financing outflow.
(B) Entire payment is presented as an operating outflow.
(C) The interest portion is presented as an operating outflow and the principal portion as an investing outflow.
(D) The interest portion is presented as an operating outflow and the principal portion as a financing outflow.

434. Under the indirect method, which of the following would be added back to net income to arrive at net cash flows from operating activities?
  I. bond discount amortization
  II. bond premium amortization

(A) I only
(B) II only
(C) both I and II
(D) neither I nor II

435. Dickinson Corp prepares its statement of cash flows using the indirect method. Dickinson's unamortized bond premium account decreased by $18,000 during Year 10. How should Dickinson Corp report the change in unamortized bond premium in its statement of cash flows for Year 10?

(A) financing cash outflow
(B) not an increase or decrease in net income to arrive at net cash flows from operating activities
(C) decrease to net income in arriving at net cash flows from operating activities
(D) increase to net income in arriving at net cash flows from operating activities

436. In its current year income statement, Micki Corp reported cost of goods sold of $350,000. Changes occurred for the year in certain current asset and current liability accounts as follows:

Accounts payable	$20,000 decrease
Inventory	$100,000 decrease

What amount should Micki Corp report as cash paid to suppliers in its current year cash flow statement prepared under the direct method?

(A) $350,000
(B) $470,000
(C) $430,000
(D) $270,000

437. Salinger Corporation prepared its statement of cash flows at December 31, Year 13, using the direct method. The following amounts were used in the computation of cash flows from operating activities:

Beginning inventory	$300,000
Ending inventory	$250,000
Cost of goods sold	$1,000,000
Beginning accounts payable	$200,000
Ending accounts payable	$100,000

What amount should Salinger Corp report as cash paid to suppliers?

(A) $850,000
(B) $1,000,000
(C) $1,150,000
(D) $1,050,000

438. Pry Corp prepares its statement of cash flows under the direct method. For Year 13, Pry Corp had revenue under accrual accounting of $200,000. Additional information is as follows from beginning to the end of Year 13:

Accounts receivable	increased by $8,000
Unearned fees	decreased by $6,000

How much is cash received from customers for Year 13?

(A) $214,000
(B) $186,000
(C) $202,000
(D) $198,000

439. Calhoun Corp had a beginning cash balance in Year 12 of $20,000. They had net cash provided by operating activities of $320,000 for Year 12, net cash used by investing activities of $402,000, and cash provided by financing activities of $262,000. During the year, there was a sale of a fixed asset that resulted in a loss of $10,000 and proceeds of $42,000 were received from the sale. What was Calhoun Corp's cash balance at the end of Year 12?

(A) $200,000
(B) $232,000
(C) $168,000
(D) $148,000

440. Traficante Corp had the following equity transactions at December 31, Year 8:

Cash proceeds from the sale of Price Corp stock (carrying amount $30,000)	$25,000
Dividends received on common stock of Aragona Corp	$8,500
Common stock purchased from Wingnut Corp	$13,000
Interest income received on County of Union Bonds	$2,000

What amount should Traficante Corp recognize as net cash from investing activities in its statement of cash flows dated December 31, Year 8:
(A) $25,000
(B) $12,000
(C) $14,000
(D) none of the above

441. Which of the following items is included in the financing activities section of the statement of cash flows?
  I. cash effects of acquiring and disposing of property, plant, and equipment
  II. cash effects of transactions obtaining resources from owners and providing them with a return on their investment
(A) I only
(B) II only
(C) both I and II
(D) neither I nor II

CHAPTER 16

Inventory Valuation Methods

442. In a period of falling prices, which of the following inventory valuation methods would show the highest net income?

(A) First In–First Out (FIFI)
(B) Last In–First Out (LIFO)
(C) weighted average
(D) All would be the same.

443. In a period of inflation, which of the following would be higher under LIFO rather than FIFO?

  I. cost of goods sold
 II. net income

(A) I only
(B) II only
(C) both I and II
(D) neither I nor II

Use the following information to answer questions 444–445:

Olympic Fascination Corp has inventory with a cost of $16,730, ceiling of $16,850, replacement cost of $16,490, and a market floor of $16,545.

444. How much is ending inventory under US generally accepted accounting principles (GAAP)?

(A) $16,730
(B) $16,850
(C) $16,490
(D) $16,545

445. How much is ending inventory under International Financial Reporting Standards (IFRS)?

(A) $16,730
(B) $16,850
(C) $16,490
(D) $16,545

446. For Year 13, the Franklin Corporation has beginning inventory of $41,875 and ending inventory of $32,109. Purchase returns and freight in are $20,200 and $24,360 respectively. Purchases are $112,800 and freight out is $5,733. How much is cost of goods sold for Year 13?

(A) $126,726
(B) $158,835
(C) $134,475
(D) $118,406

447. If LIFO is being used to account for ending inventory and cost of goods sold for tax purposes, which of the following accounting standards would then require LIFO to be used for financial statement purposes under what is known as the LIFO conformity rule?

   I. US GAAP
  II. IFRS

(A) I only
(B) II only
(C) both I and II
(D) neither I nor II

Use the following facts to answer questions 448–455:

Atlantic Corp had beginning inventory in January of Year 13 of 10,000 units costing $1 each. On February 10, 11,200 units were purchased costing $3 each. On March 20, 11,800 units were sold. On December 30, 11,600 more units were purchased at $6 each.

448. How much is the cost of goods available for sale on December 31, Year 13, using FIFO, assuming Atlantic Corp uses a periodic inventory system?

(A) $69,600
(B) $113,200
(C) $70,200
(D) $34,200

449. Under FIFO, what amount should Atlantic Corp report as cost of goods sold, assuming they use a periodic inventory system?

(A) $15,400
(B) $43,000
(C) $70,200
(D) $97,800

450. Under FIFO, what amount should Atlantic Corp report as ending inventory, assuming they use a periodic inventory system?

(A) $15,400
(B) $43,000
(C) $70,200
(D) $97,800

451. How much is cost of goods available for sale on December 31, Year 13, using LIFO, assuming Atlantic Corp uses a periodic inventory system?

(A) $113,200
(B) $43,000
(C) $79,000
(D) $34,200

452. Under LIFO, what amount should Atlantic Corp report as cost of goods sold, assuming they use a periodic inventory system?

(A) $43,000
(B) $70,200
(C) $34,200
(D) $79,000

453. Under LIFO, what amount should Atlantic Corp report as inventory at December 31, Year 13, assuming Atlantic uses a periodic inventory system?

(A) $79,000
(B) $43,000
(C) $70,200
(D) $34,200

454. Under LIFO, what amount should Atlantic Corp report as cost of goods sold at December 31, Year 13, assuming Atlantic uses a perpetual inventory system?

(A) $70,200
(B) $43,000
(C) $34,200
(D) $79,000

455. Under LIFO, what amount should Atlantic Corp report as ending inventory at December 31, Year 13, assuming they use a perpetual inventory?

(A) $34,200
(B) $79,000
(C) $43,000
(D) $70,400

Use the following facts to answer questions 456–458:

Lesnik Corp had beginning inventory in January of Year 13 of 10,000 units costing $1 each. On January 14, 4,000 units were purchased costing $3 each. On March 20, 8,000 units were sold. On December 22, 6,000 more units were purchased at $6 each.

456. If Lesnik Corp uses a periodic inventory system, how much is the average cost per unit for Lesnik Corp under the weighted average inventory valuation method?

(A) $2.90
(B) $2.00
(C) $3.33
(D) $4.00

457. If Lesnik Corp uses a periodic system, Lesnik Corp would report cost of goods sold using the weighted average method in the amount of

(A) $8,000
(B) $34,800
(C) $42,000
(D) $23,200

458. If Lesnik Corp uses a periodic system, Lesnik Corp would report ending inventory using the weighted average method in the amount of

(A) $23,200
(B) $34,800
(C) $54,000
(D) $16,000

459. In the calculation of ending inventory for Shula Corp at December 31, Year 13, which of the following should be included?

    I. Goods sold to Langer Corp on December 28, Year 13 terms FOB shipping point, still in transit at December 31, Year 13.

    II. Goods purchased from Mandich Corp December 29, Year 13, terms FOB destination, arrived January 2, Year 14.

(A) I only
(B) II only
(C) both I and II
(D) neither I nor II

460. Regarding goods on consignment, which of the following is correct about inventory rights and obligations at year end?

(A) The consignor, not the consignee, of the goods should include the goods in ending inventory.
(B) The consignee, not the consignor, of the goods should include the goods in ending inventory.
(C) The consignee and consignor should agree as to which party should include the goods in ending inventory.
(D) A seller of inventory should include goods held on consignment as inventory but exclude goods shipped on consignment.

461. Beginning inventory for Frozen Foods Inc. is incorrectly stated at $13,000, and ending inventory is incorrectly stated as $10,000. Assuming purchases for the year are correctly stated at $5,000, which of the following inventory errors would result in an understatement of cost of goods sold?

    I. Beginning inventory is understated by $1,000.

    II. Ending inventory is overstated by $2,000.

(A) I only
(B) II only
(C) both I and II
(D) neither I nor II

462. Which of the following correctly describes an inventory system where quantity is updated for each purchase and sale as they occur?

(A) LIFO
(B) FIFO
(C) perpetual
(D) periodic

Use the following facts to answer questions 463–464:

Musical Box Inc. uses a periodic inventory system. The following are inventory transactions for the month of January:

1/1	Beginning inventory	5,000 units at $4
1/9	Purchase	5,000 units at $6
1/19	Purchase	6,000 units at $7
1/22	Sale	9,000 units at $10

463. Using the average cost method of inventory valuation, what amount should Musical Box report for cost of goods sold?

(A) $40,250
(B) $39,667
(C) $51,750
(D) $50,100

464. Using the average cost method of inventory valuation, what amount should Musical Box report for ending inventory?

(A) $51,750
(B) $42,000
(C) $40,250
(D) $39,690

Use the following facts to answer questions 465–466:

The Sanchez Corporation had beginning inventory of 1,200 units in January 1, Year 10. The following information pertains to the month of January.

Inventory Units	Unit Cost	Total Cost	Units on Hand
1/1/10 1,200	$1	$1,200	1,200
1/11 Purchase 800	$3	$2,400	2,000
1/19 Sold 1,000			1,000
1/30 Purchase 600	$5	$3,000	1,600

465. Under the moving average method, what amount should Sanchez Corporation report as inventory under US GAAP at January 31?

(A) $3,600
(B) $3,000
(C) $4,200
(D) $4,800

466. Under the moving average method, Sanchez Corporation would price the next sale of inventory at which of the following costs?

(A) $1.80
(B) $3.00
(C) $5.00
(D) $3.45

467. In Year 12, a hurricane destroyed much of the inventory records of Sandy Corp, but the following information was rescued from the accounting department:

Sales for Year 12	$200,000
Beginning Inventory 1/1/12	$25,000
Ending Inventory 12/31/12	$10,000

If Sandy's gross margin normally is 20%, how much represents purchases for Year 12?

(A) $145,000
(B) $170,000
(C) $160,000
(D) $15,000

CHAPTER 17

Fund Accounting and Government-Wide Financial Statements

468. Under modified accrual accounting, which of the following is NOT correct regarding the general fund of a governmental unit?

(A) Budgetary accounting is emphasized in order to control spending.
(B) Encumbrance accounting is used to record purchase orders.
(C) Activity emphasizes flow of current financial resources.
(D) A statement of cash flows is prepared as part of the fund-based financial statements.

469. With regard to the dual objectives of governmental reporting, the idea that government agreement should be accountable to its public by demonstrating that resources allocated for a specific purpose are used for that purpose is described as

I. operational accountability
II. fiscal accountability

(A) I only
(B) II only
(C) both I and II
(D) neither I nor II

470. Which of the following is the most authoritative source for government accounting standards?

(A) Financial Accounting Standards Board (FASB)
(B) statements issued by the Governmental Accounting Standards Board (GASB)
(C) American Institute of CPAs (AICPA) Practice Bulletins
(D) GASB Implementation Guides

471. Which of the following regarding funds and fund accounting is correct?
  I. Fund accounting supports financial control by helping prevent overspending.
  II. A fund is a sum of money set aside to accomplish a specific goal.

  (A) I only
  (B) II only
  (C) both I and II
  (D) neither I nor II

472. All funds of a state or local government unit must be categorized as one of three separate classifications. Which of the following is NOT one of those classifications?

  (A) proprietary fund
  (B) fiduciary fund
  (C) governmental fund
  (D) permanent fund

473. Which of the following funds is a proprietary fund?

  (A) general fund
  (B) permanent fund
  (C) enterprise fund
  (D) special revenue fund

474. Which of the following correctly describes an internal service fund?

  (A) same basis of accounting as the general fund
  (B) a type of proprietary fund in which the services are open to the general public
  (C) a type of proprietary fund in which the services are open to other agencies of the local government rather than to the public
  (D) same basis of accounting as the debt service fund

Use the following facts to answer questions 475–477:

The following revenues were among those reported by Reading Township in Year 13:

Interest earned on investments held for employees' retirement benefits	$110,000
Property taxes available and measurable in Year 13	$6,100,000
Net rental revenue (after depreciation) from a parking garage owned by Reading Township	$47,000

475. Reading Township should account for how much revenue in governmental-type funds in Year 13?

   (A) $6,210,000
   (B) $6,100,000
   (C) $6,257,000
   (D) $47,000

476. How much revenue should Reading Township account for in proprietary-type funds in Year 13?

   (A) $47,000
   (B) $110,000
   (C) $157,000
   (D) -0-

477. How much revenue should Reading Township account for in fiduciary type funds in Year 13?

   (A) $6,100,000
   (B) $110,000
   (C) $47,000
   (D) -0-

478. The city of Wildwood is looking to rebuild Convention Hall. In Year 13, the state of New Jersey sent an unrestricted grant to the city for $2,000,000 that the city council plans to use in the construction. The remainder of the proceeds came from a 6% bond issuance in the amount of 10,000,000 issued at par on January 1 of Year 13. The bonds pay interest annually on June 30 and December 31. If the City of Wildwood accounts for the construction of City Hall in the capital projects fund, the City of Wildwood should credit other financing sources in Year 13 in the amount of

(A) $12,000,000
(B) $10,000,000
(C) $2,000,000
(D) -0-

479. Which of the following describes the basis of accounting used and measurement focus for all governmental-type funds?

(A) accrual basis of accounting, flow of financial resources focus
(B) modified accrual basis of accounting, flow of economic resources focus
(C) accrual basis of accounting, flow of economic resources focus
(D) modified accrual basis of accounting, flow of financial resources focus

480. The city of Morgan spent $50,000 on a new fire truck in Year 13. They also paid the 10 firemen their salaries of $60,000 each for Year 13. In addition they paid $12,000 to paint and maintain the firehouse during that year. Assume the Fire Department is accounted for as part of a governmental-type fund for the city of Morgan. How much represents expenditures for the Year 13 in the fund-based financial statements?

(A) $600,000
(B) $650,000
(C) $662,000
(D) $612,000

481. The City of Spanktown accounts for its public utility in an enterprise fund. On June 15, Year 13, the general fund for the City of Spanktown sent a check to the enterprise fund in the amount of $50,000. The general fund will debit "other financing uses" in Year 13 if the $50,000 sent to the enterprise fund was to

  I. pay the electric bill for City Hall
 II. cover a cash shortfall in the enterprise fund resulting from storm-related damage

(A) I only
(B) II only
(C) both I and II
(D) neither I nor II

Use the following facts to answer questions 482–483:

City of Spring Lake's Year 2 budget entry includes estimated revenues of $40,000,000, appropriations of $37,000,000, and an estimated transfer to capital projects fund of $600,000.

482. When Spring Lake's budget is adopted and recorded, the budgetary control account would include

(A) $3,000,000 credit balance
(B) $3,000,000 debit balance
(C) $2,400,000 credit balance
(D) $2,400,000 debit balance

483. When Spring Lake's budget is closed at the end of the fiscal year,

(A) appropriations is credited for $3,000,000
(B) estimated revenues is debited for $40,000,000
(C) appropriations is credited for $37,000,000
(D) estimated revenues is credited for $40,000,000

Use the following information to answer questions 484–486:

The City of East Hanover Township purchases a backup generator for the police department on February 3, Year 14, at an estimated cost of $40,000. The generator arrives on March 10, Year 14, with an invoice attached of $40,650. The vendor is paid in full by the township on April 5.

484. The journal entry to record the encumbrance on February 3 would include a

(A) debit to encumbrance for $40,000
(B) credit to encumbrance for $40,000
(C) debit to budgetary control for $40,000
(D) credit to budgetary control for $40,650

485. The journal entry to record the receipt of the backup generator on March 10 would include a

(A) debit to budgetary control for $40,650
(B) credit to encumbrance for $40,650
(C) credit to encumbrance for $40,000
(D) credit to budgetary control for $40,000

486. On April 5, the journal entry would include a $40,650

    (A) debit to expenditures
    (B) debit to vouchers payable
    (C) credit to vouchers payable
    (D) credit to budgetary control

487. The City of Saddle Brook levied property taxes of $6,000,000 for the current year and estimated that $250,000 would be uncollectible. The journal entry for the property tax levy in the general fund would include

    (A) credit to allowance for uncollectible property taxes—current $250,000
    (B) debit to property tax receivable $5,750,000
    (C) debit to allowance for uncollectible property taxes—current $250,000
    (D) credit to property tax revenue $6,000,000

488. The Township of Woodbridge prepares which of the following as part of its government-wide financial statements?
    I. statement of activities
    II. statement of net assets
    III. statement of cash flows

    (A) both I and II
    (B) both I and III
    (C) both II and III
    (D) I, II, and III

489. The Township of Smyrna should report the construction in progress for a senior center as an asset in the
    I. government-wide statement of net assets
    II. capital projects fund

    (A) I only
    (B) II only
    (C) both I and II
    (D) neither I nor II

490. On the government-wide financial statements for the City of White Plains, which of the following are normally shown as business-type activities rather than governmental activities on the statement of net assets?
  I. internal service funds
  II. enterprise funds
  (A) I only
  (B) II only
  (C) both I and II
  (D) neither I nor II

491. For a governmental entity, which of the following is an example of a derived revenue?
  I. sales tax
  II. income tax
  III. property tax
  (A) both I and II
  (B) both I and III
  (C) both II and III
  (D) I, II, and III

492. The Township of Edison is preparing general purpose financial statements for Year 13. The question has arisen as to whether the school system should be viewed as a primary government so that separate financial statements are appropriate. Which of the following would need to be shown for the school system to qualify as a separate primary government?
  (A) The school system's board is appointed by Edison's city council.
  (B) The school system serves the City of Edison exclusively.
  (C) The school system is NOT fiscally independent of the city.
  (D) The school system is a legally separate entity.

CHAPTER **18**

Not-for-Profit Entities

493. Not-for-profit (NFP) organizations include a wide array of organizations such as private colleges, hospitals, voluntary health and welfare organizations, and churches. Which of the following is the basis of accounting used for external reporting purposes for not-for-profit entities?

(A) modified accrual basis
(B) accrual basis
(C) modified cash basis
(D) cash basis

494. In the statement of financial position for a not-for-profit entity, how many categories of net assets (equity) appear?

(A) 2
(B) 3
(C) 4
(D) 5

495. How should the financial resources of a not-for-profit entity that are currently expendable at the discretion of the governing board and that have not been restricted externally be reported in the balance sheet of a not-for-profit?

(A) temporarily restricted for a specific use
(B) temporarily restricted until the passage of a certain amount of time
(C) restricted by board designation
(D) unrestricted

496. The Pisces Project is a nongovernmental not-for-profit that provides training and education to convicted felons who are near their release date. In Year 13 the Pisces Project received the following support:
  I. a cash contribution of $125,000 to be used at the discretion of the board of directors
  II. a promise to contribute $40,000 in Year 14 from a supporter who had made similar contributions in prior periods
  III. accounting services with a value of $35,000 that Pisces would have otherwise had to pay for
  IV. a building worth $300,000 with no stipulation as to use, which the Pisces board of directors plans to sell and use the proceeds for educational purposes

  How much would the Pisces Project classify as unrestricted support in Year 13?
  (A) $500,000
  (B) $420,000
  (C) $125,000
  (D) $460,000

Use the following facts to answer questions 497–499:

Spotted Owl Park, a private not-for-profit zoological society, received contributions temporarily restricted for research totaling $150,000 in Year 13. None of the contributions were spent on research in Year 13. In Year 14, $135,000 of the $150,000 was used to support the research activities of the society.

497. Which of the following is correct regarding the statement of activities for Spotted Owl Park in Year 13?
  (A) Temporarily restricted net assets decrease by $135,000.
  (B) Unrestricted net assets increase by $135,000.
  (C) Unrestricted net assets increase by $150,000.
  (D) Temporarily restricted net assets increase by $150,000.

498. Which of the following is correct regarding the statement of activities for Spotted Owl Park in Year 14?
  (A) Temporarily restricted net assets decrease by $135,000.
  (B) Unrestricted net assets increase by $150,000.
  (C) Unrestricted net assets decrease by $150,000.
  (D) Temporarily restricted net assets increase by $135,000.

499. Which of the following is NOT correct regarding Spotted Owl Park for Year 13 and Year 14?

(A) In Year 13, there is no impact on unrestricted net assets when the $150,000 is received.

(B) In Year 14, unrestricted net assets increase, then decrease to reflect the amount released from temporary restriction, $135,000.

(C) Total unrestricted net assets do not change in Year 13 or Year 14.

(D) In Year 13, unrestricted net assets increase by $135,000.

500. A private, not-for-profit organization prepares each of the following financial statements EXCEPT

(A) statement of activities

(B) statement of cash flows

(C) statement of restricted net assets

(D) statement of financial position

Bonus Questions

501. Dartam Center is a private not-for-profit educational organization in support of homeschooled kids. How should Dartam Center report contributions of $1,000,000 in cash in the statement of cash flows if the money is donor-restricted for 5 years and then can be spent at the discretion of the governing body?

(A) operating activity inflow

(B) investing activity inflow

(C) financing activity inflow

(D) either operating or investing inflow

502. Reporting expenses by function and by natural classification

(A) is required for most not-for-profits

(B) is not allowed for most not-for-profits

(C) is not allowed for voluntary health and welfare organizations

(D) is required for voluntary health and welfare organizations

503. For a not-for-profit entity, conditional pledges are considered unconditional when

I. the possibility that the condition will NOT be met is remote

II. the donor-imposed conditions have been met

(A) I only

(B) II only

(C) both I and II

(D) neither I nor II

504. In Year 9, Sonia Walton promised Orange College that she would provide 75% of the funds needed to construct a new parking deck if the not-for-profit could get the remaining 25% of the funds needed from other donors by April 1, Year 11. At December 31, Year 10, the board of directors had received donations from other donors for 20% of the cost of the new parking deck and believed that the probability of NOT getting the remaining 5% was remote. For the year ended December 31, Year 10, Walton's promise would

(A) be reported as an increase in permanently restricted net assets

(B) not be reported on the statement of activities since she has not made the contribution yet

(C) not be reported on the statement of activities since the college has not raised the full 25% yet

(D) be reported as an increase in temporarily restricted net assets

505. For a not-for-profit entity, *restricted* and *unrestricted* refer to

    I. the timing of revenue recognition

    II. the net asset classes

(A) I only

(B) II only

(C) both I and II

(D) neither I nor II

506. In July of Year 12, a storm damaged the roof of Homeless Shelters, a not-for-profit voluntary health and welfare organization. One supporter of Homeless Shelters, a one-time homeless man himself, now a trained professional roofer, repaired the roof at no charge. In the statement of activities for Year 12, the damage and repair of the roof should be reported as

(A) note disclosure only

(B) increase in net assets and contributions

(C) increase in both expenses and contributions

(D) nothing—not be reported at all

507. The Jersey Shore Free School is a calendar year, nongovernmental not-for-profit. On February 3 of Year 13, they received unconditional promises of $60,000 expected to be collected within 1 year. Based on past experience, the Jersey Shore Free School anticipates that 85% of unconditional pledges are actually received. By December 31, Year 13, $20,000 was actually received. What amount should Jersey Shore Free School record as contribution revenue in Year 13?

(A) $60,000

(B) $51,000

(C) $20,000

(D) -0-

508. PALS is a private not-for-profit to educate and benefit autistic children and their families. The functional expense categories used by PALS on the statement of activities are generally listed under the two main classifications of program expenses and which of the following?

(A) general and administrative expenses
(B) support services
(C) fund-raising
(D) membership development

509. Desert Samaritan Hospital, a not-for-profit medical facility, would include which of the following as "nonoperating" revenue in the statement of activities?

  I. recovery room fees after spinal surgery
  II. parking fees and cafeteria income
 III. donated medicines and supplies
 IV. unrestricted gifts

(A) both I and IV
(B) both II and III
(C) IV only
(D) II, III, and IV

510. For the spring semester Year 13, Stellar University, a nongovernmental not-for-profit university, assessed its students $5,000,000 for tuition and fees. The net amount realized was only $4,500,000 because refunds in the amount of $200,000 had to be given when certain low-enrollment classes had to be cancelled and scholarships were granted in the amount of $300,000. What amount should Stellar University report as gross revenue from tuition and fees?

(A) $5,000,000
(B) $4,800,000
(C) $4,500,000
(D) $4,700,000

ANSWERS

Chapter 1: Accounting Theory and Conceptual Understanding

1. (A) I is correct. The FASB statements of financial accounting standards are included in the Accounting Standards Codification. Prior to 2009, searching for generally accepted accounting principles (GAAP) was often difficult because GAAP existed in a variety of places. Since 2009, GAAP is contained in a single place known as the Codification. The Codification makes it easier to research US GAAP and find general and industry-specific accounting standards that are generally accepted. Since 2009, the FASB Accounting Standards Codification is the single source of authoritative nongovernmental US GAAP. Since the adoption of the Codification, accounting and reporting practices that are *not* found in the Codification are *not* generally accepted in the United States.

2. (C) I is correct. For financial information to be useful, it must be relevant. *Relevant* means that the information must be material and provide predictive and confirming value. For information to be relevant, it must be helpful to people making decisions about the entity. II is correct. For information to be useful, it must be faithfully represented, which means the information must be complete, without bias, and free from error. Although perfection is not achievable, for information to be faithfully represented these characteristics must be maximized. Relevance and faithful representation are considered the fundamental qualitative characteristics of financial reporting.

3. (C) I is correct. According to the FASB and IASB conceptual framework, for financial information to be relevant, it must have predictive value, that is, contain information used to predict future outcomes. For information to be relevant, it must be helpful to people making decisions about the entity. Therefore, relevance includes the qualitative characteristic of predictive value. II is correct. According to the FASB and IASB conceptual framework, for information to be relevant, it must have confirming value as well as predictive value. Confirming value is used to provide information about evaluations previously made. For information to be relevant, it must be helpful to people making decisions about the entity. Therefore, relevance includes the qualitative characteristic of confirming value.

4. (B) II is correct. According to the FASB and IASB conceptual framework, neutrality refers to the need for financial information to be free from bias in selection or presentation. For example, estimates made by management need to be without bias if financial information is to be considered faithfully represented. Therefore, neutrality is an ingredient of faithful representation.

5. (C) I is correct. According to the FASB and IASB conceptual framework, relevance is a fundamental characteristic of financial reporting. Financial information is considered relevant only if it's capable of making a difference in the decision-making process. *Relevant* means that the financial information must be material and provide predictive and confirming value. For information to be relevant, it must be helpful to people making decisions about the entity. II is correct. According to the FASB and IASB conceptual framework, faithful representation is also a fundamental characteristic of financial reporting. Financial information is faithfully represented when it's complete, without bias, and free from error. Although perfection is not achievable, completeness, neutrality, and freedom from error must be maximized if financial information is to be considered faithfully represented. For example, the independent auditor will test management estimates to determine if they are indeed neutral, or without bias. Only if the estimates are without bias can the financial information be viewed as faithfully represented.

6. (C) I is correct. According to the FASB and IASB conceptual framework, comparability is an enhancing, rather than a fundamental, characteristic of financial reporting. An enhancing qualitative characteristic of financial information is that financial information can be compared. Comparability enhances the user's experience with financial information by allowing current year to prior year comparisons. The user can compare one entity with another over the same time period. II is correct. According to the FASB and IASB conceptual framework, verifiability is an enhancing, rather than a fundamental, characteristic of financial reporting. Verifiability enhances the user's experience with financial information when different knowledgeable observers are able to reach consensus that a particular depiction is faithfully represented.

7. (A) According to the FASB and IASB conceptual framework, timeliness is a characteristic that enhances the usefulness of financial information. An example of timeliness is the fact that although there is an annual report, the investor wants more timely information. Quarterly reports, although they are unaudited, enhance the usefulness of financial information because they are more timely. According to the FASB and IASB conceptual framework, understandability is an enhancing qualitative characteristic of financial reporting. Information is understandable if it is classified, characterized, and presented clearly and concisely. Thus, both timeliness and understandability are enhancing (rather than fundamental) characteristics of useful financial reporting. When it comes to *enhancing* qualitative characteristics of useful financial information, remember that a VCUT could be very enhancing!

> *V*erify
> *C*ompare
> *U*nderstand
> *T*imeliness

8. (D) II is correct. Accounts receivable is generally measured at the net realizable value. Net realizable value of accounts receivable is equal to the gross amount of accounts receivable minus the ending balance of allowance for doubtful accounts. The net realizable value of accounts receivable represents the amount that the company expects to realize.

9. (B) II is correct. Under accrual accounting, revenue is recorded when earned, not when the cash is received. Receiving cash is not justification enough to book revenue under accrual accounting, unless the earnings process is complete. Often in accounting, revenue needs to be recorded even if the cash has not been received, because the earnings process often precedes the collecting of cash.

10. (A) I is correct. Accrual accounting adheres to the matching principle. Under the matching principle, revenues are recognized when the earnings process is complete and expenses are recognized in the same period as the related revenue. The matching principle is used for revenue recognition under accrual accounting to match the current costs with the current year revenues. The matching principle follows accrual accounting and all but ignores cash flow. Under accrual accounting, revenue and expense recognition do not automatically correspond to cash being exchanged.

11. (D) When selecting accounting principles in accordance with US GAAP, the method that is less likely to overstate assets and understate liabilities should be chosen according to the rule of conservatism. Therefore, whenever in doubt, the method that is least likely to overstate assets and net income should be chosen. The rule of conservatism in accounting is what requires the immediate recognition of losses, even contingent losses, while gains are generally not anticipated until realized.

12. (D) Comprehensive income is an element of the financial statements that includes all differences between beginning and ending equity other than transactions between a firm and its owners.

13. (C) I is correct. Under US GAAP, a material transaction that is "infrequent in occurrence" but not "unusual in nature" should be presented separately as a component of "income from continuing operations" when the transaction results in a gain. Under US GAAP, transactions that are unusual and infrequent are reported as extraordinary items. II is correct. Under US GAAP, a material transaction that is "infrequent in occurrence" but not "unusual in nature" should be presented separately as a component of "income from continuing operations" when the transaction results in a loss. Under US GAAP, transactions that are unusual and infrequent are reported as extraordinary items.

14. (B) $600,000 loss × (1 − the tax rate of 30%) = loss of $420,000. The Year 3 operating losses of the segment would be reported in the Year 3 income statement. Since the other transactions relating to the segment occurred in Year 4, the operating losses of the segment for Year 4 as well as the gain on disposal of the segment would be netted and reported in the Year 4 income statement, net of tax. These items would not be recorded in Year 3. Each amount should be reported in the period it occurs.

15. (C) In the year of sale (Year 4), the loss from operating the segment in the amount of $50,000 must be recognized as well as the gain from the actual sale of the division. The amount is calculated as follows:

Gain on sale	$900,000
Operating loss	− $50,000
	$850,000
	$850,000 × 0.7 = $595,000

The Year 4 operating loss and the gain on disposal would be netted and reported in the Year 4 income statement, after tax. Since the tax rate is 30%, the gain of $850,000 is reported net of tax as $595,000 because discontinued operations of a segment are reported in the income statement just below income from continuing operations and shown net of tax.

16. (D) Under IFRS, all four of these items would be included in income from continuing operations. Note that under US GAAP, items III and IV would be classified as extraordinary items, because expropriation of assets by a foreign government and a flood where floods are unusual and infrequent would be considered extraordinary. However, this question is about IFRS, and IFRS does not permit the reporting of extraordinary items. Therefore, all four items would be reported in the income statement as continuing operations under IFRS.

17. (C) I is correct. Change in depreciation method is treated as a change in estimate. If a company changed from double declining balance to straight line, this would qualify as a change in "accounting estimate," which affects only the current and subsequent periods. For a change in depreciation method, prior periods would *not* be restated, since no error is being corrected. For a change in depreciation method, retained earnings would *not* be adjusted, because no accounting principle is being changed. II is correct. Change in the useful life of an asset is treated as a change in estimate. If a company changed from estimating the useful life of an asset from 10 years down to 4 years, this would qualify as a change in "accounting estimate," which affects only the current and subsequent periods. For a change in the useful life of an asset, prior periods would *not* be restated, because no error is being corrected. For a change in the useful life of an asset, retained earnings would *not* be adjusted, because no accounting principle is being changed.

18. (A) I is correct. A change from FIFO inventory valuation to average cost is a change in accounting principle. An entity may change accounting principles if GAAP requires the change or, in this question, if the alternative accounting principle average cost more fairly presents the information. The entity will report this change in accounting principle by adjusting the beginning balance of retained earnings, net of tax, to show what the cumulative profit or loss would have been had the entity always used average cost rather than FIFO. If comparative financial statements are being shown, current and prior year, adjust the beginning retained earnings for the prior year, net of tax, and for the current year, use the new method for inventory.

19. (D) The cumulative effect adjustment is recognized by adjusting beginning retained earnings, net of tax. The difference between the pretax accounting income under the old method, $600,000, and the pretax accounting under the new method, $900,000, results in a higher profit of $300,000 prior to January 1, Year 8. With a tax rate of 30%, Ashbrook Corp will adjust the beginning balance of Year 8 retained earnings for $210,000.

20. (A) I is correct. A change in inventory methods from any other GAAP method to LIFO is handled as a change in accounting estimate rather than a change in accounting principle. A change to LIFO is considered "a change in principle inseparable from a change in estimate" and therefore handled prospectively as a change in estimate.

21. (C) I is correct. Correction of an error from a prior period is reported as a prior period adjustment, and as a result, an adjustment is made to the opening balance of retained earnings for the earliest period presented. II is correct. The cumulative effect of a change in accounting principle is shown as an adjustment to beginning retained earnings for the earliest period presented.

22. (B) II is correct. The correction of a failure to accrue bad debt expense is treated as a correction of an error, and thus as a prior period adjustment, it results in the amount of $30,000.

23. (C) I is correct. A change in companies included in consolidated financial statements is an example of a change in reporting entity. Financial statements of all prior periods presented should be restated when there is a change in companies included in consolidated financial statements from one year to the next. II is correct. When consolidated financial statements are issued in the current year and individual financial statements were issued in the prior year, this is an example of a change in reporting entity. Financial statements of all prior periods presented should be restated when consolidated financial statements are issued in the current year and individual financial statements were issued in the prior year.

24. (D) I is incorrect. A change in the amount of mineral expected to be recoverable from an underground mine is a change in accounting estimate. A change in accounting estimate is handled prospectively; current and future income statements are affected. No cumulative effect adjustment is made for a change in estimate, and no separate line item presentation is made on any financial statement. II is incorrect. A change in the expected useful life of a machine from 7 years to 4 years is a change in estimate. A change in accounting estimate is handled prospectively; current and future income statements are affected. No cumulative effect adjustment is made for a change in estimate, and no separate line item presentation is made on any financial statement.

25. (B) A change from the completed contract method to the percentage of completion method is treated as a change in accounting principle. The cumulative effect of a change in accounting principle equals the difference between retained earnings at the beginning of the period and what the retained earnings would have been if retained earnings were applied to all affected prior periods. Since comparative financial statements are not being shown, beginning retained earnings is adjusted. Therefore, retained earnings as of January 1, Year 9, is adjusted. Note: if comparative financial statements were shown, beginning retained earnings of the earliest period presented would be adjusted for the cumulative effect of the change. The other year presented would be handled using the new method.

26. (C) I and II are correct. Comprehensive income can be presented on a single financial statement with net income. Comprehensive income also may be shown separately on its own financial statement. Comprehensive income is an element of the financial statements that includes all differences between beginning and ending equity other than transactions between a firm and its owners.

27. (C) I and II are correct. Both US GAAP and IFRS require that a description of all significant policies be included as an integral part of the financial statements. To comply, most companies that report under US GAAP include a "summary of significant accounting policies" as the first or second footnote to the financial statements. Accounting policies commonly described as significant include basis of consolidation, depreciation methods, amortization of intangibles, inventory pricing, accounting for recognition of profit on long-term construction, and recognition of revenue from franchising or leasing operations.

28. (C) I is correct. The summary of significant accounting policies should identify and describe the policies, accounting principles, and methods used in preparing the financial statements. The "basis" of profit recognition on long-term construction contracts is an accounting policy and should be disclosed in the footnote known as the summary of significant accounting policies. II is correct. The summary of significant accounting policies should identify and describe the criteria used to measure items for financial statement reporting. The criteria for measuring cash equivalents is an accounting policy and should be disclosed in the footnote known as the summary of significant accounting policies.

29. (B) II is correct. IFRS requires disclosures of significant judgments and significant estimates.

30. (B) II is correct. Each interim financial statement must be marked "unaudited" so the users are put on alert that the statements were not audited. Interim financial reporting should be viewed as reporting for an integral part of an annual period.

31. (B) II is correct. IFRS requires in the footnotes a statement that the financial statements are presented in accordance with IFRS.

32. (D) I is incorrect. The dates of maturity for long-term debt are not an accounting policy. While this information is a required disclosure, it's a separate footnote and not included within the summary of significant accounting policies. II is incorrect. Subsequent events occurred after the balance sheet date, but they are important enough to disclose in a separate footnote because their impact on the company is material. Events are not accounting policies, and therefore subsequent events would not be included as part of the summary of significant accounting policies.

33. (D) I is incorrect. Interim reporting is *not* required by US GAAP or IFRS. Interim reporting is required by the US Securities and Exchange Commission (SEC) for publicly traded companies under the Federal Securities Act of 1934. A report comes out every quarter to provide timely information to the users, but the information is only reviewed, not audited, so reliability may be affected. Interim reporting emphasizes timeliness over reliability. Each statement must be marked "unaudited" so the users are put on notice. Interim financial reporting should be viewed as reporting for an integral part of an annual period. II is incorrect. Permanent inventory losses from market declines should be reflected in the interim period in which they occur. Market increases in subsequent interim periods should be recognized in the recovery interim period not to exceed the losses included in prior interim periods. Quarterly reporting requires the use of the same accounting methods as annual reporting.

34. (B) II is correct. A registered company that is considered a large accelerated filer must file Form 10-Q (quarterly report) within 40 days of the close of the entity's fiscal quarter. Registered companies that are considered accelerated filers but not "large" still must file their quarterly reports within 40 days. Other registrants not considered accelerated have 45 days to file their quarterly report. Quarterly reports and Form 10-Q contain unaudited financial statements.

35. (A) US registered companies required to file both the Form 10-K annual report and Form 10-Q quarterly reports must file those reports using US GAAP. Foreign entities registered with the SEC file Forms 20-F and 40-F. Forms 20-F and 40-F are similar but not identical to Form 10-K, as they require audited financial statements and disclosures of important financial information. A big difference is that forms 20-F and 40-F can be filed using US GAAP or IFRS.

36. (C) I is correct. Privately held companies are exempt from reporting EPS unless, of course, they have made a filing to become public. Publicly traded companies must report EPS on the face of the income statement. II is correct. Privately held companies are exempt from reporting segment information. Only publicly traded companies must report business segment information. For a publicly traded company, a segment is considered reportable if segment revenue represents 10% or more of the combined revenue of all operating segments. To determine whether the segment is reportable using the 10% test, sales to unaffiliated companies as well as intercompany sales are included. If a segment is deemed a reportable segment, separate disclosures are required for the amount of intercompany sales and unaffiliated sales. Using the 10% test, segment information is reported until sales representing 75% of total sales (to unaffiliated customers) have been disclosed. When 75% of sales to unaffiliated customers have been separately shown, at that point no additional reportable segments need to be identified.

37. (B) II is correct. Lead would not be a reportable segment for Year 13, because its combined revenue of $5,000 is less than 10% of total combined revenue for all segments. Revenue for all combined segments is $92,000, 10% would be $9,200. Since lead revenue was only $5,000, lead would *not* qualify as a reportable segment.

38. (D) For publicly traded companies, there must be enough segments reported so that at least 75% of unaffiliated revenue is shown by reportable segments. In Year 12, sales to external customers total $40,000,000, so unaffiliated revenue (external revenues reported by operating segments) must be at least $30,000,000.

39. (B) Under US GAAP, costs that are considered organization and startup costs should be expensed as incurred. Therefore, the legal fees of $50,000 to incorporate are charged to expense in Year 13. Underwriters' fees are not expensed. Underwriters' fees will directly reduce additional paid-in capital when the stock is issued. When the stock is sold for above par value, the underwriters' fees of $32,000 will reduce the additional paid-in capital. The purchase of land would not be expensed as organization costs, but should be capitalized as fixed assets.

40. (C) I is correct. Development stage enterprises must identify the financial statements as those of a development stage enterprise. II is correct. A development stage enterprise must disclose in the statement of stockholder's equity the number of shares of stock issued and dates of issuance. In addition, if consideration is received for the shares in a form other than cash, a description of the nature of the consideration received for the shares is required as well as the basis for the valuation of the noncash consideration received.

Chapter 2: Revenue and Expense Recognition

41. (B) I is correct. For revenue to be recognized under US GAAP, persuasive evidence of an arrangement or contract must exist. II is correct. For revenue to be recognized under US GAAP, goods must have been delivered or services must have been performed.

42. (C) I is correct. Under normal GAAP rules, revenue is not recognized until the earnings process is substantially complete. However, in a multiple deliverable arrangement, the company can recognize the revenue from each element if the delivered item has a value on a stand-alone basis. If the hardware and software installation has a value on a stand-alone basis, the revenue from the installation can be recognized upon delivery without having to wait until the contract is substantially complete. Although the customer support element of this contract carries over into Year 3 and is not complete until December 31 of Year 3, it is reasonable to believe that management of Advantage would want to recognize revenue at each deliverable element. Therefore, if the installation of the hardware and software and the training of the customer staff have a value on a stand-alone basis, Advantage would recognize that portion of revenue in Year 2 since that part of the contract has been completed. II is correct. Under normal GAAP rules, revenue is not recognized until the earnings process is substantially complete. However, in a multiple deliverable arrangement, the company can recognize the revenue from each element if the delivered item can be sold separately. If the hardware and software and the training of the staff can be sold separately, Advantage can recognize those elements of the multiple deliverable arrangement as they are completed.

43. (C) I is correct. A deferral of revenues will occur when cash is received but is not recognizable for financial statement purposes because it has not been earned. II is correct. Deferral typically results in the recognition of a liability when cash is received before the revenue is earned. A deferral results in a prepaid expense when cash is paid before the expense is incurred, such as prepaid insurance or prepaid rent.

44. (D) I is incorrect. A deferral includes cash collected in advance of services being rendered. The original journal entry includes a debit to cash and a credit to unearned revenue, a liability. At year end, an adjustment is needed to pick up the revenue earned since the time that the cash was collected up to the end of the year. The adjustment includes a debit to unearned revenue and a credit to earned revenue. II is incorrect. Cash paid up front for a 1-year insurance policy is a deferral of expense. The original entry is a debit to prepaid insurance and a credit to cash. The adjustment at year end includes a debit to insurance expense and a credit to prepaid insurance.

45. (A) A 1-year insurance policy with a cost of $3,000 expires at a rate of $250 per month. For Year 10, 5 months expired and need to be expensed: $250 × 5 months = $1,250 that has expired. When assets expire and lose their economic benefit, they are expensed. $3,000 − $1,250 expired = $1,750 still considered prepaid at year end. Journal Entry to record the adjustment at December 31, Year 10 is a debit to insurance expense and a credit to prepaid insurance for $1,250.

46. (B) When cash is received in advance, deferred revenue is recorded for the full amount received. The entry on November 1, Year 12, includes a debit to cash and credit to deferred revenue for $6,000. Deferred revenue is a liability account, not a revenue account.

47. (C) Both I and II are correct. When the certificates lapse, the company has no further liability and revenue is earned. Deferred revenue is decreased. The journal entry upon expiration would be a debit to deferred revenue and a credit to revenue. II is correct. When the certificates are redeemed, the revenue is earned and shown in the income statement. Deferred revenue is decreased. The journal entry upon expiration of the certificates would be a debit to deferred revenue and credit to revenue. Deferred revenue represents future income collected in advance. When the gift certificates are sold, deferred revenue is increased, not revenue.

48. (A) I is correct. A decrease in accounts receivable from the beginning of the year to the end of the year generally represents cash collections. As cash is collected, the accounts receivable balance decreases. As a result, cash basis revenue exceeds accrual basis revenue whenever accounts receivable decreases from beginning of the year to the end of the year.

49. (A) I is correct. When adjusting from cash basis revenue to accrual basis revenue, the ending balance of accounts receivable is added to cash basis revenue as additional accrual basis revenue when earned.

50. (C) A deferral impacts cash before impacting the income statement. With a deferral, cash is either coming in or going out, but there is no effect on the income statement until year end when an entry is needed to adjust from cash basis to accrual basis. An example of a deferral is cash paid for a 1-year insurance policy being recorded as prepaid insurance when purchased and adjusted to insurance expense at year end for the expired months. Notice that when the insurance policy is first acquired, only balance sheet accounts are affected. Although cash is being paid when the policy is first acquired, all is considered prepaid and an asset is debited (prepaid insurance). The credit is to cash for the amount paid. There is no income statement impact and no expense recorded at the time of purchase. The expense gets recorded as an adjusting entry at year end.

51. (A) I is correct. Unearned fees is a liability resulting from collecting money in advance. The ending balance of unearned fees represents cash received but not earned during the period.

52. (A) I is correct. Collecting cash in Year 1 for services that will be performed in Year 2 will increase cash basis revenue in Year 1 but not accrual basis revenue in Year 1.

53. (B) II is correct. Under the accrual basis, earning revenue in Year 1 would increase accrual basis revenue in Year 1, while cash basis revenue would have increased in Year 0.

54. (A) I is correct. Beginning unearned fees must be added to cash fees collected to arrive at accrual basis revenue so that what was unearned at the beginning of the year and actually earned during the period don't get subtracted when the ending balance of unearned fees gets subtracted. For example, assume cash of $100,000 is collected in advance during the year. Assume that the beginning balance of unearned fees is $5,000 and the ending balance of unearned fees is $15,000. To go from cash basis revenue to accrual, do the following:

Cash collected	$100,000
Ending balance of unearned fees	− $15,000
Beginning balance of unearned fees	+ $5,000
Accrual basis revenue for the year	$90,000

55. (C) The following can be used to convert cash basis revenue to accrual basis revenue beginning with cash fees collected:

Cash fees collected

\+ Ending accounts receivable
− Beginning accounts receivable
Accrual basis revenue

Cash fees collected

\+ Beginning unearned fees
− Ending unearned fees
Accrual basis revenue

Using the facts from the question:

Cash basis revenue	$100,000
Ending accounts receivable	+ $60,000
Beginning accounts receivable	− $40,000
Subtotal	$120,000
Beginning unearned fees	+ 0
Ending unearned fees	− $4,000
Accrual basis revenue	$116,000

56. (B)

Cash basis collections	$60,000
Rent receivable, ending	+ 8,200
Rent receivable, beginning	− 7,600
Unearned revenue	↓
Beginning	+ $28,000
Ending	−$21,000
Accrual basis rent revenue	$67,600

57. (B) The percentage of completion method is the generally accepted method to recognize profit from a long-term construction contract. The percentage of completion method recognizes profit from a long-term construction contract on the basis of costs incurred. Under the percentage of completion method, the costs incurred to date are the rationale for determining the profit to recognize. The costs incurred to date are divided by the total estimated costs to determine the percentage of completion. For Year 12 the profit to date is $100,000, which is determined as follows using the costs incurred:

Costs incurred to date $300,000 / $1,500,000 total estimated costs = 20%
20% complete × total estimated profit of $500,000 = current profit to date of
$100,000

Notice that the cash collected is not a basis for recognizing profit under the percentage of completion method.

58. (D) Under the percentage of completion method, each year the cost *to date* is compared to the estimated *total cost* to determine the degree of completion. This percentage is multiplied by the expected total profit to determine the *profit to date*. The costs incurred to date in Year 13 are up to $1,200,000. The $1,200,000 of costs incurred to date in Year 13 includes the $900,000 spent in Year 13 plus the $300,000 spent in Year 12. Because an additional $400,000 of cost is estimated to be spent beyond Year 13, total estimated costs under this contract have risen from the initial estimate of $1,500,000 to $1,600,000. Since total costs have increased, a lower profit than previously expected is now anticipated. Since the contract price is $2,000,000, the old profit estimate was $500,000 based on expected total costs of $1,500,000. The new profit estimate is $400,000 based on expected total costs of $1,600,000. To calculate profit in Year 13, the second year of the contract, the costs incurred to date will be divided into the total estimated costs as follows:

Costs incurred to date in Year 13 ($300,000 + $900,000)	$1,200,000
Total estimated costs ($300,000 + $900,000 + $400,000)	÷ $1,600,000
Percentage completed after Year 13	75%
75% × profit now expected of $400,000 = $300,000 cumulative profit	
Cumulative profit	$300,000
Less profit recognized in Year 12	− $100,000
Year 13 profit	$200,000

59. (C) I is correct. For a long-term construction contract being accounted for using the percentage of completion method, the construction in progress account is debited for construction costs incurred. When costs are incurred, the construction in progress account is debited and cash or accounts payable is credited. II is correct. For a long-term construction contract being accounted for using the percentage of completion method, the construction progress account is debited for profit recognized to date. When profit is recognized, the construction in progress account is debited and revenue is credited.

60. (D) In long-term construction projects, the contractor often will bill the customer to help finance the cost of construction. Such billings are recorded by the contractor on the balance sheet, but these billings do not impact the recognition of profit. The account "progress billings" is used to account for billings sent to customers during the contract. The journal entry when the bill is sent to the customer is a debit to accounts receivable and a credit to progress billings. When the customer pays, the debit is to cash and the credit to accounts receivable. The progress billings account is netted against the construction in progress account. If more billings have been sent out than costs incurred, the progress billings account is recorded as a liability. If construction costs incurred exceed billings, an asset is recorded.

61. (D) With regard to profit recognition from long-term construction contracts accounted for on the percentage of completion method, progress billings and cash collections have no impact on profit. Profit is recognized under the percentage of completion method in proportion to monies spent, not monies received. Under the percentage of completion method, the costs incurred to date are divided into total estimated costs to determine the percentage completed. That percentage is then multiplied by profit anticipated to arrive at profit recognized to date. Any profit previously recognized would then need to be subtracted to arrive at current year profit.

62. (C) Under the completed contract method, profit recognition is delayed until the project is substantially completed. However, in the event of a loss, conservatism says to recognize the loss in the year it becomes apparent.

63. (C) I is correct. A construction company must apply the percentage of completion method to account for long-term construction contract revenue if the buyer can fulfill its obligations and the contractor has the ability to estimate the degree of completion with reasonable accuracy. Since the state of Arizona is the buyer and should certainly be able to pay, Olney Corp would be expected to use the percentage of completion method. II is correct. A construction company must apply the percentage of completion method to account for long-term construction contract revenue if the buyer can fulfill its obligations and the contractor has the ability to complete the job. There were no uncertainties given in the facts regarding Olney's ability to complete the job. If on the exam the facts mentioned that this was the first time Olney Corp had ever built a highway and they were not sure they could finish, it would be an example of a possibility that would allow Olney Corp to choose between the completed contract method and percentage of completion.

64. (B) The installment sales method is allowable for certain sales of property at a gain. The installment method is used when cash is received in installments rather than one lump sum. If the company is unable to make a reasonable estimation of the cash to be collected, the installment sales method, rather than accrual accounting, must be applied. Under the installment method, recognition of profit is delayed and it is recognized only when cash is collected. The first step in connection with profit recognition under the installment method is the computation of the gross profit from the sale and the gross profit percentage. The final step is to multiply the cash collected by the gross profit percentage to determine the realized gross profit. The gross profit from the sale is $100,000 − $60,000 cost = $40,000 gross profit.

Gross profit	$40,000
Divided by sale price	÷ $100,000
Gross profit percentage	40%
Cash collected in Year 13	× $20,000
Gross profit realized in Year 13	$8,000

65. (A) Deferred gross profit from installment sales is the amount of cash not yet collected multiplied by the gross profit percentage. For Year 13, $20,000 of the $100,000 was collected, leaving a receivable balance of $80,000. The $80,000 represents the cash not yet collected. The profit on the $80,000 not yet collected is all deferred as of December 31, Year 13. Therefore, the deferred gross profit on December 31, Year 13, is calculated as

Accounts receivable balance from the installment sale	$80,000
Gross profit percentage	× 40%
Deferred gross profit	$32,000

Another way to determine deferred gross profit would be to simply subtract the amount of realized gross profit for Year 13, $8,000, from the total gross profit of $40,000.

Total gross profit from the installment sale	$40,000
Realized gross profit in Year 13	− $8,000
Deferred gross profit at December 31, Year 13	$32,000

66. (B) III is correct. The installment method is considered a cash basis rather than accrual basis method of revenue recognition. As cash is collected, revenue is recognized based on the gross profit percentage calculated on the sale.

67. (D) The cost recovery method is a cash basis method similar to the installment method but used when there is significant uncertainty as to whether cash will even be collected. The buyer, for example, might be on the verge of bankruptcy. The cost recovery method does not recognize a profit until an amount of cash is collected that equals the cost of the asset sold. Since $2,000 was collected in Year 13 but the asset cost $2,500, $500 of cost of goods sold have yet to be collected. So no profit is recognized in Year 13.

68. (B) In Year 14, $3,000 is collected, but the first $500 collected in Year 14 is still a recovery of cost. Therefore, under the cost recovery method, gross profit in Year 14 is reported as follows:

Cash collected in Year 14	$3,000
Remaining recovery of cost	− $500
Gross profit in Year 14	$2,500

69. (D) Had Russell Inc. used the installment method rather than cost recovery, Russell would have realized gross profit for Year 13 as follows:

Sales price	$5,000
Less cost	− $2,500
Total gross profit	$2,500
Gross profit on sale	50%
Cash collected in Year 13	× $2,000
Realized gross profit under the installment method	$1,000

70. (D) Payroll tax liability is equal to

$100,000 gross payroll × 0.14	$14,000
Plus employee withholding	+ $700
Total liability	$14,700

The employer is responsible for submitting the entire $14,700 to the government. Notice that the $14,700 payroll tax liability consists of both employer and employee taxes. The employee's share of the $14,700 is $7,700 computed as follows:

$100,000 × 0.07 employee FICA portion	$7,000
$700 employee federal income tax withholding	+ $700
Total employee portion of payroll tax	$7,700

The employer's share of the payroll tax is $7,000 computed as follows:

$100,000 × 0.07 employer's matching contribution to FICA = $7,000

71. (A) Payroll tax expense is equal to the employer's share of FICA: $100,000 × 0.07 = $7,000. The FICA that comes out of the employee's pay of $7,000 and the federal withholding tax of $700 that comes out of the employee's pay is not an expense to Stanley's Sportland Inc. As the employer, Stanley's Sportland Inc. is responsible and obligated to pay the entire

$14,700 to the government, but Stanley's Sportland Inc. expenses only $7,000 because that was their cost of having the employees working. The other $7,700 represents employee tax. What makes FICA tax difficult for many to understand is that the employer must match the employee contribution, but the employee doesn't see or even know that it's happening. The employee's paystub shows the employee FICA deduction, but the employee is often unaware that the employer is matching that contribution. This matching FICA contribution costs employers money over and above the salary being paid to employees. Since this matching FICA contribution gets paid from employer funds, the employer is entitled to an expense known as payroll tax expense. Thus payroll tax expense for July 31 is $7,000.

72. (A) Royalty revenue is recognized on the accrual basis, not the cash basis. The first check received on September 30, Year 4, for $10,000 is for the period January through June, Year 4, and should be included in Year 4 revenue. The second check received on March 31, Year 5, for $20,000 would also be for Year 4 revenue for the second half of Year 4 sales from July 1 through December 31, Year 4. The check received on September 30, Year 5, for $30,000 is for the sales from January 1, Year 5, to June 30, Year 5, so all $30,000 belongs in Year 5 revenue. The estimated sales for the second half of Year 5 in the amount of $180,000 × the 10% royalty = $18,000 more revenue for Year 5, even though it won't be received until March 31, Year 6. Therefore, total Year 5 revenue for royalties is $48,000. Remember that royalties are on the accrual basis, not cash basis.

73. (D) I is incorrect. Fees to acquire a patent and other intangible assets from third parties are capitalized and amortized over the shorter of the patent's remaining legal life or estimated life using the straight line method of amortization. Legal fees and registration fees associated with patents are also capitalized.

II is incorrect. Under US GAAP, costs incurred to internally develop a patent are expensed as research and development. US GAAP requires research and development costs to be expensed although certain costs like consulting fees, design costs, and registration fees associated with an internally generated patent are capitalized. Notice that the manner of acquisition of intangible assets is a factor in determining whether the intangible asset is capitalized or expensed. Intangible assets that are purchased from third parties are capitalized. Intangible assets that are internally developed are expensed as research and development.

74. (C) I is correct. Legal fees and other costs related to successful patent defense are capitalized. II is correct. Costs to unsuccessfully defend a patent should be expensed, and the patent should be tested for impairment since it may no longer have value.

75. (A) I is correct. All research and development costs are expensed as incurred under US GAAP. US GAAP requires that research and development costs are expensed.

76. (A) I is correct. Costs incurred for developing and maintaining goodwill are expensed.

77. (C) I is correct. Intangible assets with infinite lives such as acquired goodwill should be capitalized but *not* amortized, because under US GAAP assets with infinite lives such as goodwill are not amortized but tested for impairment. II is correct. Intangible assets with finite lives such as patents, franchises, and covenants not to compete should be capitalized and amortized. To amortize an intangible asset, it must have a finite life. US GAAP recognizes the fact that the value of intangible assets eventually disappear. Therefore, the cost of each type of intangible asset with a finite life is amortized over the period estimated to be benefited.

78. (B) II is correct. Under IFRS, intangible assets can be reported under either the cost or revaluation (fair value) model. Under IFRS, intangible assets are initially recognized at cost and then every reporting period the intangible is marked to market, and revalued to fair value at a future revaluation date. IFRS (not US GAAP) allows the reporting of intangible assets at fair value.

79. (A) Legal fees and other costs associated with registering a patent are capitalized. Research and development costs are expensed under US GAAP. If later on costs are spent to successfully defend the patent, those costs would be capitalized as well.

80. (D) I is incorrect. With regard to software that is to be used internally, all costs incurred up to the preliminary project state are expensed. Capitalize costs incurred after the "preliminary project state." Therefore, not all costs associated with the development of internal use software are expensed. II is incorrect. With regard to software that is to be sold, leased, or licensed before technological feasibility is established, computer software development costs are expensed as research and development. Once technological feasibility is established, computer software costs are capitalized; therefore, not all costs of computer software to be sold to customers are expensed.

81. (C) While the early costs associated with computer software development are expensed as research and development, once technological feasibility is established, computer software costs are capitalized. Therefore, the costs that would *not* be expensed as research and development would include the production and packaging costs for the first month's sales and the producing of product masters after technological feasibility has been established. The costs that would not be considered research and development would include

Production and packaging costs for the first month's sales	$72,000
Producing product masters after technological feasibility	+ $180,000
Total	$252,000

82. (D) Software development costs are expensed as research and development even if contracted out to a third party. The costs incurred in connection with preproduction prototypes are expensed as research and development. In addition, testing in search for new products is expensed as research and development under US GAAP. Quality control is not considered research and development, but would be capitalized rather than expensed. The amounts charged to research and development would include the following:

Research and development costs contracted out to third parties	$40,000
Design production and testing of preproduction prototypes	+ $120,000
Testing in search for new products	+ $25,000
Total research and development expense	$185,000

83. (B) The intangible asset franchise is initially recorded as a debit to franchise in the amount of $90,000. The cost will be amortized over 20 years on a straight line basis, $4,500 per year. Scotti reports the 4% of sales paid to Subway annually as an operating expense each year. On December 31, Year 13, the intangible asset franchise has a balance of:

Cost	$90,000
Less amortization	– $4,500
Carrying amount at December 31, Year 13	$85,500

84. (A) Step 1 is to compare the carrying value, $500,000, with the *undiscounted* cash flows of $498,000. Step 1 results in an impairment loss because the current carrying amount of $500,000 is higher than the undiscounted cash flows of $498,000. Step 2 takes place once impairment is imminent; the impairment loss is based on discounted cash flows (fair value):

Discounted or present value of future cash flows	$485,000
Carrying value of asset	– $500,000
Dollar amount of impairment loss	($15,000)

The dollar amount of the impairment is based on the discounted cash flows. Notice that both the undiscounted cash flows and the discounted cash flows need to be known. For an impairment loss to be determined and recorded, the undiscounted cash flows are used first to determine if there even is an impairment. Then if there is an impairment (based on comparing the undiscounted cash flows to the carrying amount), the discounted cash flows are used to determine the amount of impairment. Note that using the discounted cash flows to compare with the carrying amount will make the impairment loss larger than when the undiscounted cash flows were used.

85. (C) First step when testing for impairment involves the undiscounted cash flows that are expected from the trademark in the amount of $333,000 compared to the asset's carrying value of $320,000. In this comparison, no impairment is needed, because the undiscounted cash flows exceed the carrying amount.

86. (B) II is correct. No impairment is recorded if the undiscounted cash flows exceed the asset's carrying amount.

87. (C) I is correct. When testing an asset for impairment that is held for disposal as a part of a discontinued operation, the asset's carrying amount is first compared to the undiscounted cash flows to see if any impairment has occurred. II is correct. When testing an asset for impairment that is held for disposal as part of a discontinued operation, if an impairment has occurred, the discounted cash flows (fair value) is compared to the asset's carrying amount. The calculation of impairment loss on assets held for disposal is the same as the calculation of impairment loss on assets held for use.

88. (B) II is correct. Under US GAAP, when the asset is held for use, no restoration of impairment loss is permitted. Even if the asset regains its lost value, no entry is made if the asset is held for use.

89. (A) I is correct. Under US GAAP, no reversal of a fixed asset impairment loss is permitted when the asset is held for use. Under US GAAP, the reversal of impairment loss would be permitted only when the asset is held for sale.

Chapter 3: Marketable Securities

90. (C) I is correct. Under US GAAP, securities can be categorized as available for sale. Both debt and equity securities may be classified as available for sale if they do not meet the definition of either trading or held to maturity. III is correct. Under US GAAP, securities can be categorized as trading. Trading securities are those securities, both debt and equity, that are bought and held principally for the purpose of selling them in the near future. IV is correct. Under US GAAP, securities can be categorized as held to maturity. Investments in debt securities are classified as "held to maturity" only if the corporation has the positive intent and ability to hold these securities to maturity.

91. (B) I is correct. Both debt and equity securities may be classified as available for sale. If the equity securities are not purchased for a quick resale and if the debt securities are not to be held to maturity, they will be classified as available for sale. II is correct. Both debt and equity securities may be classified as trading. If the securities are purchased for immediate resale, they are classified as trading securities.

92. (A) I is correct. Held to maturity is a classification for debt securities only. Equity never matures, but debt securities mature and can be listed as held to maturity or available for sale. Investments in debt securities are classified as held to maturity only if the corporation has the positive intent and ability to hold these securities to maturity.

93. (B) The bonds will be marked to market and valued by Fords Inc. at $1,030,000. Although the bonds cost $800,000 and have a fair value of $1,000,000, the bonds are classified as trading securities because the facts indicate that the bonds are held for the purpose of selling them within the operating cycle. Therefore, the bonds are considered trading securities. Trading securities are reported at fair value on the balance sheet.

94. (B) II is correct. Losses on available-for-sale securities are reported in other comprehensive income. Unless the loss on available-for-sale securities is permanent, it should not be reported on the income statement.

95. (D) Since the loss on an available-for-sale security was considered temporary in Year 1, the security would be written down to fair value. The unrealized holding loss would be reported in other comprehensive income and not on the income statement.

96. (B) In Year 1, the security would have been written down to fair value. The unrealized holding loss would be reported in other comprehensive income. In Year 2, the unrealized holding loss would be removed from accumulated other comprehensive income and recognized in earnings as a realized loss on the Year 2 income statement, since the decline is classified as other than temporary in Year 2. This Year 2 entry has no effect on available-for-sale assets but decreases net income by the amount of the loss now considered permanent.

97. (B) I is correct. With regard to securities classified as available for sale, unrealized losses considered temporary are reported in other comprehensive income. III is correct. With regard to securities classified as available for sale, unrealized gains are reported in other comprehensive income rather than the income statement. II is incorrect. With regard to securities classified as available for sale, unrealized losses considered other than temporary are reported on the income statement.

98. (D) Loss on early extinguishment of bonds would be reported on the income statement, not comprehensive income, as either an extraordinary item or continuing operations, depending on the circumstances given in the question. Realized gains on available-for-sale securities are reported on the income statement. Unrealized losses on available-for-sale securities are reported in other comprehensive income.

99. (B) II is correct. The investment in investee is adjusted to fair value, marked to market at the end of the accounting period.

100. (D) I is incorrect. Under the cost method, the investment account is *not* reduced for cash dividends received by the investee unless the dividends are in excess of investee earnings. II is incorrect. Under the cost method, the investment account is *not* reduced for ordinary losses incurred by the investee. Under the cost method, the investment in investee account is reduced when shares of stock are sold, or cumulative dividends exceed cumulative earnings (a return of capital), or the investee incurs losses that substantially reduce net worth.

101. (D) I is incorrect. Cash dividend received under the equity method is not income, but it reduces the carrying value of investment account. II is incorrect. Stock dividends are never income under either the cost or equity method. Stock dividends received by the investee result in a memo entry only. No journal entry is made for the receipt of additional shares of stock under the equity (or cost) method. The new shares will serve to reduce the basis per share.

102. (B) As a 4% owner, Woodley would use the cost method to account for its investment in Jensen. Under the cost method, dividend income is equal to the number of shares times the cash dividend per share. At the time the cash dividend is paid, Woodley has 6,000 shares × $3 per share = $18,000.

103. (C) Under the equity method, adjustments to the investment account result from the differences between the price paid for the investment and the book value of the investee's net assets acquired. The premium paid for the investment is calculated as follows:

Total book value of the investee's net assets	$900,000
Percent acquired	× 40%
Book value of the 40% of the investee's net assets acquired	$360,000
Cost to acquire the 40% of the investee's net assets	− $400,000
Premium paid above book value for the 40% ownership	($40,000)

The $40,000 premium paid needs to be amortized based on what caused the premium in the first place. The facts indicate that there is undervalued equipment on the books of Clark Corp and that alone is the rationale for the premium paid of $40,000 for the investment. Therefore:

Undervalued equipment $100,000 × 40% acquired	$40,000
5-year life of equipment	÷ 5 years
Annual amortization for 5 years	$8,000

The $8,000 of amortization relating to the undervalued equipment needs to recorded each year for 5 years and will serve to reduce investee earnings of Clark Corp each year. Therefore, for the next 5 years, each time Clark Corp reports earnings, Rochelle Corp will recognize 40% of those earnings but then subtract $8,000 of amortization. The calculation of investee earnings net of amortization for Year 13 for Rochelle Corp is as follows:

Investee earnings $150,000 × 40% ownership	$60,000
Less annual amortization of undervalued equipment	−$8,000
Equity method investment income	$52,000

104. (A) I is correct. Singer would record the additional cost of goods sold associated with the undervalued beginning inventory by debiting investment income and crediting the investment in the Kaufman account.

Chapter 4: Stockholders' Equity

105. (D) I is incorrect. The issuer would credit, not debit, common stock for $10. When new stock is issued, common stock is credited for the par value of the shares. II is incorrect. The issuer would debit cash for $13, credit common stock for $10, and credit additional paid-in capital for $3. A corporation is not allowed to have a gain or loss on sale of its own stock.

106. (D) The land will be recorded at the fair market value (FMV) of the shares being surrendered by the company. If the FMV of these shares is not available, the FMV of the land will be used for reporting purposes. The journal entry includes a debit to land for $15,000, a credit to common stock for $10,000, and a credit to additional paid-in capital for $5,000.

107. (B) II is correct. The additional paid-in capital would increase on March 1, Year 6. The journal entry on February 1, Year 6, would include a debit to cash of $20 and a credit to common stock at par, $20. The journal entry on March 1, Year 6, would include a debit to legal fees of $60,000, a credit to common stock for $50,000, and a credit to additional paid-in capital of $10,000. I is incorrect. On February 1, Year 6, there is no increase to the additional paid-in capital account since the shares were issued at par on that date.

108. (C) I is correct. The credit to common stock would be for the 2,000 shares multiplied by the $5 par or $10,000. II is correct. The credit to additional paid-in capital would include the 2,000 shares multiplied by $95, $190,000. The $95 represents the excess of the current market value over par at the date of issuance. Notice that the value of the services is ignored since the stock has a ready market price. The value of the services would have been used for valuation if no other information was available.

109. (B) II is correct. The additional $12 per share ($12,000) that will be received is recorded as additional paid-in capital at the date of subscription. In addition, cash of $4,000 is recorded along with a subscription receivable of $18,000. The journal entry at the subscription date is a debit to cash for $4,000, a debit to subscription receivable for $18,000.

The credits are to common stock subscribed for $10,000 and additional paid-in capital for $12,000. I is incorrect. On the date of subscription, the additional paid-in capital account is increased in the amount of $12,000 not $4,000.

110. (C) I is correct. Preferred stock has no set rights other than the rights defined in the stock certificate. Preferred stock rights usually include a set dividend that takes precedence over the rights of the common stockholders dividend. Preferred stock may also contain rights to convert the preferred shares to common (convertible preferred) and may also contain rights to unpaid dividends in arrears (cumulative preferred). Preferred stock may also contain rights to participate with the common stockholder on dividends paid after both preferred and common receive a set dividend (participating preferred). II is correct. All common stock issued by companies incorporated within a state typically will have the same legal rights because the rights of common stockholders are established by the laws of that particular state.

111. (A) I is correct. *Cumulative* means that if the preferred stock dividend is not paid when due, the preferred dividend will have to be paid before holders of common stock can receive any dividend payment. If no dividend is ever paid to the owners of the common stock, then no dividend has to be paid to the preferred stockholders, even if the preferred stock dividend is cumulative.

112. (A) When the preferred stock is issued, the preferred stock is credited for par value of $500,000. The excess $10 over par is credited to additional paid-in capital from preferred stock. Therefore, $50,000 is credited to additional paid-in capital from preferred stock on February 1, Year 13. The journal entry on February 1 would include a debit to cash of $550,000 and a credit to preferred stock for $500,000 and a credit to APIC-preferred stock for the excess of $50,000 above par.

113. (D) On December 31, Year 14, when all the preferred shares are converted, preferred stock must be debited by $500,000 and additional paid-in capital preferred stock must be debited by $50,000. Total debits are $550,000. As for the credits, when the 5,000 shares of preferred stock are converted into 10,000 shares of common stock, the 10,000 shares of common stock need to be recorded with a par value of $10—$100,000. To balance the entry, the additional paid-in capital from common stock must credited for $450,000.

114. (B)

$4,000 × present value of annuity 4.18	$16,720
Cash down payment	+ $2,000
Installation cost	+ $1,000
Total	$19,720

115. (C) With regard to dividends paid by a corporation, retained earnings is debited on the date of declaration. The date of declaration is the date that the board of directors formally approves a dividend. The journal entry on the declaration date is a debit to retained earnings and credit to dividends payable. On the record date, no entry is needed, just a determination of who owns the stock. On the payment date, the dividends payable is reduced and cash is credited.

116. (C) I is correct. Cash dividends result in a reduction of retained earnings at the declaration date. II is correct. Property dividends result in a reduction of retained earnings for the market value of the property at the date of declaration.

117. (D) The journal entry on January 14, Year 13, to record the issuance of 20,000 shares is a debit to cash for $220,000 and a credit to common stock for the par value of $100,000, and the remainder of $120,000 is a credit to additional paid-in capital.

118. (A) Under the cost method of accounting for treasury stock transactions, treasury stock is debited for cost at the time the shares are acquired. The entry to record the repurchase of treasury stock is a debit to treasury stock and a credit to cash for $80,000.

119. (C) Under the cost method, the entry to reissue the treasury stock on December 5 would include a debit to cash in the amount of $95,000, a credit to treasury stock for cost of $80,000, and a credit to additional paid-in capital from treasury stock of $15,000. Reissuing treasury stock cannot increase retained earnings or net income. A corporation is not allowed to record a gain or loss from the sale or purchase of its own stock.

120. (D) The journal entry on January 2, Year 13, to record the issuance of 20,000 shares at $15 is a debit to cash for $300,000 and a credit to common stock for the par value of $200,000, and the remainder of $100,000 is a credit to additional paid-in capital. The $5 excess over par is credited at issuance to additional paid-in capital.

121. (A) Under the par value method of accounting for treasury stock, treasury stock is debited for the par value of the shares reacquired. Therefore, the debit to treasury stock is for 5,000 shares multiplied by $10 par, $50,000.

122. (C) Under the par value method of accounting for treasury stock transactions, when the treasury shares are repurchased, the original amount recorded as additional paid-in capital must be reduced. The 5,000 treasury shares were originally issued for $5 above par back in January of Year 13. This $5 per share above par must be eliminated from the books under the par value method. The 5,000 shares times the $5 per share original excess over par is debited to additional paid-in capital to remove that original APIC from the books, since those shares are no longer outstanding. The reduction of additional paid-in capital on June 7, Year 13, is calculated as follows:

Excess over par	$5
Shares reacquired	× 5,000
Reduction of additional paid-in capital	$25,000

123. (B) The journal entry on June 7, Year 13, would be as follows: Cash is credited for $90,000. The debits include treasury stock for $50,000, additional paid-in capital for $25,000, and the difference of $15,000 is a debit to retained earnings for $15,000. Notice that retained earnings can be debited, never credited, with regard to treasury stock transactions.

124. (D) Under the par value method of accounting for treasury stock transactions, the treasury shares are credited for the par value at the date of reissue. Therefore, on December 29, Year 13, treasury stock is credited for 5,000 shares multiplied by $10 par, $50,000.

125. (A) Under the par value method of accounting for treasury stock, the reissuance of the 5,000 treasury shares on December 29, Year 13, for $30 per share would involve an increase to cash for $150,000 and a credit to treasury stock for the par value of $50,000, and the excess would be a credit to additional paid-in capital in the amount of $100,000.

126. (C) Under the par value method of accounting for treasury stock transactions, the entry on January 2, Year 13, increased additional paid-in capital by $100,000. The second entry on June 7, Year 13, decreased additional paid-in capital by $25,000, dropping the balance to $75,000. The third entry on December 29, Year 13, increased additional paid-in capital by $100,000, bringing the ending balance up to $175,000.

127. (D) When accounting for stock dividends, the most important factor is the size of the stock dividend in proportion to the total number of shares outstanding before the dividend. When a corporation pays its dividend in shares of stock, it distributes additional shares of its own stock to investors of record as of a certain date. The stock dividend is accounted for as a small stock dividend if less than 20% of the total shares are being distributed. In a stock dividend accounted for as a small stock dividend, not enough shares are being issued to affect the market price of the stock. Therefore, in a small stock dividend, the company will debit retained earnings for the market value of the stock. Common stock is credited for the par value of the new shares distributed, and additional paid-in capital is credited for the difference. Conversely, if more than 25% of the total shares are distributed in the stock dividend, the stock dividend is accounted for as a large stock dividend, as it may be expected to reduce the market value of the stock. Therefore, a large stock dividend is recorded as a debit to retained earnings for the par value of the shares and a credit to common stock distributable on the declaration date. On the date of payment, the shares are issued and the common stock distributable account is debited and common stock is credited. No entry is made to additional paid-in capital for a large stock dividend.

128. (B) When recording the journal entry for the stock dividend, retained earnings is debited for the market value of the shares on the date of declaration, $18, because the stock dividend is considered small. The stock dividend is considered small because the total shares distributed, 10,000, is only 5% of the total shares prior to the stock dividend. The debit to retained earnings is $18 multiplied by 10,000 shares, $180,000.

129. (A) The journal entry to record the new shares issued as a result of a small stock dividend will include a debit to retained earnings and credit to common stock for the par value of the shares. The excess is credited to additional paid-in capital. Since common stock is always credited for par, when the journal entry to distribute the shares from a stock dividend is recorded, additional paid-in capital is credited for $80,000, calculated as follows:

Retained earnings	$180,000
Less credit to common stock	− $100,000
Additional paid-in capital	$80,000

130. (A) When more than 25% of the total shares prior to the dividend are distributed, the stock dividend qualifies as large. In a large stock dividend, retained earnings is debited for the par value of the shares, not the fair market value. The reason for debiting retained earnings for the par value of the shares is because the number of shares being distributed is large enough to affect the market price of the stock, similar to a stock split. As a result of debiting retained earnings at par, retained earnings is recorded as follows: $60,000 new shares distributed × $10 par = $600,000.

131. (C) The journal entry to record the declaration of the 30% stock dividend will include a debit to retained earnings and credit to common stock distributable for $600,000.

132. (D) Since retained earnings is debited for the par value of the shares, the full amount of $600,000 is first credited to common stock distributable and ultimately will be transferred to the common stock account. Nothing will affect additional paid-in capital, since the market price of the stock in the large stock dividend is being ignored.

133. (C) II is correct. In a cash dividend, retained earnings is reduced and cash is paid out, which serves to reduce both stockholders' equity and current assets.

134. (D) In connection with a stock split, there is no journal entry. Additional shares will be issued, but the reduction in par value will offset the new shares outstanding, so there is no effect on any accounts. The result of the 2:1 stock split will be that the original 10,000 shares of $20 par common stock were $200,000 and will remain at $200,000 after the split. After the split, 20,000 shares are outstanding with a $10 par; total is the same $200,000:

Before the split, 10,000 shares × $20 par = $200,000 stated capital.
After the split, 20,000 shares × $10 par = $200,000 stated capital.

135. (C) III is correct. A reverse stock split reduces the number of shares outstanding and increases the par value proportionately. The result of a reverse stock split is an increase in the market price of the stock. Companies will sometimes use the reverse stock split to reverse the embarrassment of an extremely low stock price as compared to its historical price.

136. (D) When stock options are issued to employees, the most relevant factor in determining the accounting treatment under US GAAP is whether the stock is being issued to employees as part of their compensation (compensatory stock options) or whether the stock options are not part of compensation (noncompensatory). Under a noncompensatory stock option plan, no journal entry is made for the stock options until the employees exercise their rights and purchase the shares. Noncompensatory stock options tend to allow employees to purchase shares at a small discount below market price. Conversely, compensatory stock options are valued at the time of issuance. Therefore, knowing whether the stock options are issued in lieu of salary is the most relevant factor of the given options in determining the accounting treatment under US GAAP.

137. (C) Under compensatory stock options, both US GAAP and IFRS agree that the expense is determined based on fair value when the options are granted. However, this expense is not booked on the grant date. Instead, under the matching principle the expense must be recognized over the vesting period that the person must work to earn the options.

138. (B) I and II are correct. When accounting for the expense related to compensatory stock options, the journal entry includes a debit to compensation expense and a credit to additional paid-in capital-stock options. The debit to compensation expense reduces net income; therefore, retained earnings as net income is closed out to retained earnings.

139. (D) When accounting for compensatory stock options, when the employees exercise their options and purchase the shares for an amount above par but below the market price, the journal entry will include a debit to cash for the amount received and another debit to close out the additional paid-in capital-stock options. The credits will include a credit to common stock for par and a credit to additional paid-in capital for the amount in excess of par.

140. (A) I is correct. Under US GAAP losses from write-down of assets under quasi-reorganization would affect retained earnings.

Chapter 5: Fixed Assets

141. (C) I is correct. The cost of shipping the machine to Lavroff's plant should be capitalized since the capitalized cost of the asset should include all costs that are reasonable and necessary to get the asset in the condition for its intended use. II is correct. The cost of readying the machine for its intended use should be capitalized since the cost of the machine should include all costs that are reasonable and necessary to get the asset in the condition or location for its intended use.

142. (D) When the buildings were revalued in Year 1, the $150,000 revaluation gain was booked to other comprehensive income as a revaluation surplus. Under IFRS, if a revalued asset becomes impaired, the impairment is recorded by first reducing any revaluation surplus to zero, with further impairment losses reported on the income statement. In this problem, the buildings were impaired on December 31, Year 2, because the $900,000 carrying value of the buildings exceeded the $720,000 recoverable amount. The $180,000 impairment loss is recorded by first reducing to zero the $150,000 revaluation surplus from the Year 1 revaluation and then recording the $30,000 remaining impairment loss on the income statement.

143. (B) The original acquisition price of the land was $80,000 in Year 3. At the end of Year 3, the carrying amount was revalued to $70,000. This would result in a loss on the income statement of $10,000. Under the revaluation model of IFRS, the reversal of a revaluation is recognized in profit or loss. For this reason, $10,000 represents an increase in profit. If a revaluation results in an increase in value, however, it should be credited to other comprehensive income. For this reason, the increase in value of $5,000 ($85,000 − $80,000) will be recognized as other comprehensive income.

144. (B) II is correct. Fixed assets can be revalued upward from the asset's carrying amount if the reporting framework is IFRS. Under IFRS, if an individual fixed asset is revalued, then the entire class of fixed assets to which that asset belongs must be revalued. Individual fixed assets cannot be revalued alone.

145. (A) I is correct. When replacing an asset in which the cost of the old asset is known, replace the old carrying value with the capitalized cost of the new asset.

146. (A) I is correct. When the cost of the old asset is unknown *and* the asset's life is extended rather than improved, reduce accumulated depreciation rather than capitalize the cost. Reducing accumulated depreciation will increase the book value of the asset class; remember, in the question, the carrying value of the specific asset was unknown.

147. (B) II is correct. When extraordinary repairs merely extend the life of an asset without increasing the usefulness, the preferred treatment is to reduce accumulated depreciation.

148. (D) I is correct. When acquiring land to be held as a future plant site, the cost of title insurance is capitalized, not charged to expense. II is correct. When acquiring land to be held as a future plant site, legal fees paid for recording ownership (recording the deed) are capitalized rather than expensed. III is correct. When acquiring land to be held as a future plant site, the cost of tearing down (razing) the old structure to clear the land for future development is capitalized rather than expensed. The amount to capitalize would be the cost to remove the old structure less any proceeds received from selling the scrap.

149. (B) II is correct. Excavating costs are not land costs but building costs. While sometimes it's enough to know whether a cost is capitalized or expensed, in this question the candidate needs to know where to capitalize the cost. Therefore, excavating costs (costs of digging a hole) is a building cost and should be capitalized to the new building and will eventually be depreciated as part of the building.

150. (C) I is correct. Land improvements are recorded as a separate asset from land and can include fence, water systems, sidewalks, landscaping, and paving. II is correct. While costs that are capitalized as part of the asset "land" cannot be depreciated, improvements to land such as sidewalks and fences are capitalized in the land improvements account and can be depreciated.

151. (D) III is correct. The cost of the installation of a septic system is a land improvement. The septic system can then be depreciated (the land itself cannot be depreciated).

152. (B) II is correct. The cost of a sewer system is charged to the land improvement account because Van Horn owns the sewer system on Parcel #381. A separate account called land improvement will be debited for the amount paid for the new sewer system.

153. (A) The corporation spent $100,000 for land and building. The land was recently appraised for $20,000, but the building was appraised for $120,000. Since only $100,000 is spent, pro rating is needed as follows:

Land	$20,000 / $140,000	14.28%
Building	$120,000 / $140,000	85.71%
Land	14.28% × $100,000	$14,280
Building	85.71 × 100,000	$85,710

154. (D) The $1,000,000 total cost ($800,000 cash + $200,000 mortgage) should be allocated to the building and the land separately. There is no other information with which to perform this allocation other than the property tax assessment. So 65% of the $1,000,000, or $650,000, is allocated to the building.

155. (C) I is correct. Under IFRS, property where the intent is to earn income on the property through renting it out should be classified as investment property. II is correct. Under IFRS, property where the intent is to sell the property and make income should be classified as investment property.

156. (B) Under IFRS, investment property is defined as land and buildings held by an entity to earn rentals or for capital appreciation. Therefore, the amount of total investment property is $4,000,000 land held for rental + $3,000,000 buildings held for capital appreciation = $7,000,000.

157. (C) I is correct. Under IFRS, if the entity elects the fair value method, no depreciation expense will be taken. II is correct. Gains and losses from fair value adjustments on assets classified as investment property are reported on the income statement. However, under IFRS, revaluation gains on fixed assets *not* classified as investment property are reported in other comprehensive income.

158. (A) I is correct. Under IFRS, gains from investment property resulting from fair value adjustments are reported on the income statement. Note that US GAAP does *not* have a separate classification for assets known as investment property.

159. (B) II is correct. Delays related to permit processing or inspections are ordinary delays and interest cost would be capitalized.

160. (A) I is correct. Interest costs incurred during the construction period of machinery to be used by a firm as a fixed asset should be capitalized as part of the cost of acquiring the fixed asset.

161. (D) I is incorrect. Do *not* capitalize interest on loans to construct inventory. II is incorrect. Do *not* capitalize interest on loans to buy inventory. Only capitalize interest if you are borrowing money to construct a building for use in the business, a factory, a warehouse, or an office building.

162. (D) I is incorrect. Do *not* capitalize interest (before or) after construction if the asset is built to use. Only capitalize the interest during construction. II is incorrect. Do *not* capitalize interest before or after construction if the asset is built to sell. Only capitalize interest during construction.

163. (B) If borrowings are not tied specifically to the construction of an asset, the weighted average interest rate for the other borrowings of the company should be used. The weighted average interest rate is calculated as follows:

($5,000,000 / $12,000,000) × 7%	2.9%
($7,000,000 / $12,000,000) × 10%	+ 5.8%
Weighted average interest rate	8.7%

If there was debt tied to the specific construction loan, the rate of that construction loan would be used.

164. (C) I is correct. Total interest cost for the period is a required disclosure. II is correct. The amount of capitalized interest for the period, if any, is a required disclosure.

165. (B) II is correct. The amount of capitalized interest is the lower of actual interest cost incurred or computed capitalized interest. Compute the capitalized interest by multiplying the appropriate interest rate by the weighted average accumulated expenditures. If the weighted average calculated amount does not exceed the total interest cost incurred, the amount calculated is capitalized.

166. (A) Capitalized interest equals the smaller of the total interest cost incurred versus interest computed on the weighted average amount of accumulated expenditures. In this case, total interest incurred is $62,000 from the construction loan plus $22,000 from other sources, a total of $84,000. The capitalized interest is limited to the lower of the $84,000 total interest cost incurred versus the $37,000 interest calculated based on the weighted average of accumulated expenditures.

167. (B) For straight line depreciation:

Step 1: Calculate depreciable base	$75,000 cost − $5,000 salvage = $70,000 depreciable base
Step 2: Divide	$70,000 / 7 years = $10,000 per year
Step 3: Multiply	annual depreciation × 9/12 = $7,500 (April 1 through December 31)

For US GAAP purposes, ignore the asset's useful life for tax purposes when given in the problem.

168. (B) If the asset is purchased in January, a full year of depreciation is taken. Using sum of the years' digits, an asset with a 5-year life, simply add $5 + 4 + 3 + 2 + 1 = 15$ years. In Year 1, $5/15 \times \$45,000 =$ depreciation expense for Year 1 of $15,000. Remember to deduct the salvage value from the cost when using SYD.

169. (D) Using sum of the years' digits, an asset with a 5-year life , add $5 + 4 + 3 + 2 + 1 = 15$ years. In Year 1, $5/15 \times \$45,000 =$ depreciation expense for Year 1 of $15,000. At the end of Year 1, the carrying value is $35,000. Cost minus accumulated depreciation equals carrying value. In Year 2, depreciation expense is $4/15 \times \$45,000$ or $12,000. $12,000 plus $15,000 = $27,000 total accumulated depreciation thus far in Year 2. Carrying value on December 31, Year 2, is calculated as follows:

Cost	$50,000
Accumulated depreciation	− $27,000
Carrying value	$23,000

170. (D) I is incorrect. When using straight line depreciation (or any other method), the carrying value of an asset is calculated by subtracting accumulated depreciation from the asset's historical cost, not from the asset's depreciable base: cost − accumulated depreciation = carrying or book value. II is incorrect. When using the sum of the years' digits depreciation (or any other method), carrying value of an asset is calculated by subtracting accumulated depreciation from the asset's historical cost, not from the asset's depreciable base: cost − accumulated depreciation = carrying or book value.

171. (D) Depreciable assets should not be depreciated below salvage value under any depreciation method. I is incorrect. Under the sum of the years' digits depreciation method, salvage value is subtracted in the first year to arrive at the asset's depreciable base. II is incorrect. Under the double declining balance method, the salvage value is *not* subtracted in the first year to arrive at depreciable base, but instead the asset is depreciated using the full cost as the depreciable base. The double declining balance method is unique because each year's depreciation expense serves to decline the asset's depreciable base. When the asset's depreciable base declines low enough to equal the salvage value, the salvage value limits the amount of depreciation taken in the *final* year. III is incorrect. Under the straight line method (similar in this regard to the sum of the years' digits depreciation method), salvage value is subtracted in the first year to arrive at the asset's depreciable base.

172. (B) The units of production method of depreciation is calculated based on usage rather than time. Total estimated usage is 200,000 miles. The rate of depreciation is $0.30 per mile and is calculated as follows:

cost of $70,000 − $10,000 salvage value = $60,000 depreciable base

depreciable base amount of $60,000 ÷ total estimated usage of 200,000 miles
= 0.30 per mile

Depreciation every year will therefore be 30 cents per mile driven under the units of production method. For Year 1, 12,000 miles were driven, so depreciation for Year 1 is calculated as follows:

12,000 miles driven × 0.30 = $3,600 of depreciation expense should be taken
for Year 1

Year 2 depreciation will be 0.30 times the number of miles driven in Year 2.

173. (A) I is correct. When calculating depletion, the asset's depletion base is the cost to purchase the property minus the estimated net residual value.

174. (D) I is incorrect. Under US GAAP, an impairment loss is reported as a component of income from continuing operations before income taxes unless the impairment loss is related to discontinued operations. In the event that the impairment loss is related to discontinued operations, the impairment loss would *not* be shown before tax but rather after tax. II is incorrect. Impairment losses reduce the carrying value of an asset due to a decline in the asset's fair value below book value, *not* due to a decline in book value below fair value. When an asset declines in value below carrying or book value, an impairment loss occurs and needs to be recorded in the income statement.

Chapter 6: Earnings per Share

175. (A) I is correct. A private entity that has yet to make such a filing is exempt from reporting EPS.

176. (D) I and II are incorrect. A company can report basic EPS and not have to report fully diluted EPS if they have common stock and no debt or equity securities that are convertible into common stock. If the company has options or debt securities that are convertible into common stock, they must report basic and fully diluted EPS.

177. (C) I is correct. Income available to common shareholders is determined by deducting dividends declared in the period on noncumulative preferred stock (regardless of whether they have been paid). II is correct. Income available to common stockholders is determined by deducting dividends accumulated in the period on cumulative preferred stock (regardless of whether they have been declared).

178. (B) The preferred stock dividend was not paid in Year 11. Therefore, the Year 11 preferred dividend needs to be subtracted from the $1,400,000. The preferred dividend is calculated as follows:

10,000 preferred shares × 5% = $500 × $100 par	$50,000
Net income	$1,400,000
Less preferred dividend	− $50,000
	$1,350,000
($1,350,000 / 60,000) shares of common stock outstanding	$22.5

179. (A) I is correct. When calculating the weighted average number of shares to be used in the EPS calculation, stock dividends and stock splits are treated as if they occurred at the beginning of the period, and those shares are counted as if they had been outstanding all year.

180. (B) II is correct. The preferred dividends should be subtracted to compute income available to common shareholders when calculating EPS.

181. (C) I is correct. When calculating basic EPS, include the convertible preferred shares that were converted during the period in the calculation of weighted average common shares outstanding and time-weight them based on the number of months that those shares were outstanding as common shares. II is correct. When calculating basic EPS, if convertible preferred shares are *not* converted into common shares during the period, ignore convertible preferred shares in the calculation of weighted average common shares outstanding.

182. (D) I is incorrect. If the preferred stock is cumulative, only the current year undeclared dividend is subtracted from net income to arrive at net income available for common shareholders. Dividends in arrears were subtracted from income in Year 1, the year that they first were an obligation of the company. II is incorrect. Only the current period dividends, and not the dividends in arrears from Year 1, on the cumulative preferred stock are added to the net loss. Dividends in arrears were subtracted from income in the year that they first were an obligation of the company.

183. (C) I is correct. When calculating EPS, income available to common shareholders is determined by deducting preferred dividends declared in the period on noncumulative preferred stock (regardless of whether they have been paid). II is correct. When calculating EPS, determine the income available to common shareholders by deducting the preferred dividends accumulated in the current period on cumulative preferred stock regardless of whether the preferred dividend has been declared.

184. (C) I is correct. In the event of a net loss for the period, declared dividends on non-cumulative preferred stock are added to the net loss even if the dividend was not yet paid. This is because dividends on noncumulative preferred stock are added to the net loss or subtracted from net income the moment they are declared. II is correct. In the event of a net loss for the period, current year dividends on cumulative preferred stock are added to the net loss regardless of whether the dividends have been declared, because the company is obligated to pay these dividends before distributions are made to common shareholders. Note that only the current year dividends not declared would be added to the net loss, not the dividends in arrears.

185. (B) II is correct. Stock options and other potential convertibles would be used to calculate fully diluted EPS.

186. (C) I is correct. If the debt is converted during the period, then it's not convertible any longer. So the shares have already been issued and should be time-weighted as part of basic EPS. II is correct. The starting point for fully diluted EPS is basic EPS, so debt already converted during the period would be included and time-weighted as part of basic and fully diluted EPS. Note that if the convertible debt were dilutive but *not* yet converted, only fully diluted EPS would be impacted. In this case, because the debt was converted, both basic and fully diluted EPS are impacted. The if-converted method of computing EPS data assumes conversion of convertible securities as of the beginning of the earliest period reported or at time of issuance if later.

187. (C) 65,000 shares of common stock is the weighted average for EPS. The year starts with 60,000 shares. The 10,000 shares issued on July 1, Year 13, must be time-weighted for the 6 months of the year (6/12) that they were outstanding. The calculation is as follows:

1/1/Year 13, outstanding all year	60,000
7/1/Year 13, 10,000 issued × 6/12	+ 5,000
Weighted average	65,000

188. (B) A 3% stock dividend equals 2,100 shares with a total of 72,100 shares outstanding after the distribution of the dividend. A stock dividend would be treated as if it had occurred at the beginning of the fiscal year. The net income figure given in the question was not relevant.

189. (C)

Beginning of year 10,000 shares × 12/12	10,000
2:1 stock split given full-year treatment	+ 10,000
Shares issued 10/1 (5,000 × 3/12)	+ 1,250
Weighted average common shares	21,250

190. (A) Since no additional common shares were issued in Year 13, weighted average number of shares outstanding equals the beginning balance of 360,000 shares. As for the numerator, net income available to common shareholders is $270,000 after subtracting the preferred dividend of $20,000 from the net income of $290,000. The additional preferred shares of 100,000 issued during Year 13 were not relevant.

Net income available to common shareholders
    ($290,000 − $20,000) $270,000
Weighted average number of shares outstanding   360,000
Earnings per common share ($270,000 / 360,000) $0.75

191. (A) I is correct. For basic EPS, income available to common shareholders is determined by deducting preferred dividends from net income to arrive at net income available to common stockholders.

192. (C)

Net income	$750,000
Less preferred dividends	− $30,000
Net income available to common stockholders	$720,000
Divided by weighted average common shares outstanding	÷ 100,000
Basic EPS	$7.2

193. (A) To calculate the numerator:

Add interest expense not incurred $1,000,000 × 0.09	$90,000
Less tax deduction eliminated 30%	− $27,000
Interest saved from conversion net of tax	$63,000
Net income	+ $750,000
Adjusted net income	$813,000

To calculate the denominator:

Adjusted common shares outstanding	100,000
Conversion of preferred shares	+ 20,000
Conversion of debt	+ 30,000
Adjusted shares outstanding	150,000
Fully diluted EPS $813,000 / 150,000 shares	$5.42

Chapter 7: Accounting for Income Taxes

194. (B) II is correct. Using the installment method for tax purposes allows the deferral of taxable income until cash is collected. When cash is collected under the installment method, some of the cash collected represents profit from the sale and is taxed each year as it's collected (cash basis). For US GAAP, under the accrual basis the income would already be on the financial statements in the year of sale, but the income would not be all taxed in the year of sale, thus creating a future tax liability.

195. (D) I is incorrect. Warranty expense results in deferred tax assets because with warranty expense, the expense is taken on the income statement first, when estimated, but warranty costs are not deductible on the tax return until paid in later years. II is incorrect. Bad debt expense results in a deferred tax asset rather than a deferred tax liability, because the expense for bad debts is taken on the income statement when first estimated, matching principle, in the year of sale. For tax purposes, however, the deduction cannot be taken until the debt is worthless.

196. (A) I is correct. Organization and start-up costs are an expense on the income statement in full in Year 1, but they are amortized over 180 months for tax purposes. Thus they result in a tax benefit later, in future years when they can be deducted.

197. (C) I is correct. For tax purposes, prepaid insurance would be deducted in full in the year in which the policy was paid, Year 13. For financial statement purposes, the entire cost associated with prepaying the policy is recorded as an asset when paid in Year 13 and charged to expense at the end of Year 13, but only for those months that have expired in Year 13. The remaining insurance expense for book purposes is taken in Year 14. Therefore, the cost associated with prepaying an insurance policy in Year 13 would result in a deferred tax liability at December 31, Year 13. II is correct. Rent receivable represents income earned but not yet received in cash. While all the increase in rent receivable during Year 13 will be an increase to financial statement income, taxable income will increase in the following years when the receivables are collected. For the tax return, this will result in more taxable income in years subsequent to Year 13. Therefore, an increase in rent receivable during Year 13 results in a deferred tax liability at December 31, Year 13.

198. (C) I is correct. Deferred income tax expense is equal to the change in deferred tax liability (or asset) on the balance sheet from the beginning of the year to the end of the year. II is correct. Current income tax expense is equal to the taxable income per the tax return multiplied by the current year tax rate. Current income tax payable represents the amount of taxes owed at the end of the current year. If no estimated tax payments were made, current income tax expense and the current income tax payable would be the same.

199. (C) Deferred income tax expense is equal to the change in deferred tax liability (or asset) on the balance sheet from the beginning of the year to the end of the year. Deferred taxes payable from one year to the next equals deferred tax expense.

200. (B) II is correct. Taxable income per the tax return multiplied by the tax rate equals the current year income tax expense.

201. (A) Taxable income is calculated as follows:

Pretax financial statement income	$400,000
Add warranty costs	+ $35,000
Subtract revenue taxed in later year	− $60,000
Taxable income	$375,000
Current year tax rate	30%

202. (B) The current portion of income tax expense is calculated by multiplying the taxable income of $375,000 calculated in the previous question times the current year tax rate of 30%. Therefore, the current year tax expense is

taxable income × current year tax rate = current year tax expense
$$\downarrow$$
$375,000 × 30% = $112,500

Note: The four estimated tax payments of $25,000 reduce the current income tax payable figure, but do not impact the current income tax expense. If the question had asked how much is the current income tax payable, the answer would have been $12,500, since the estimated payments reduce the current tax liability but not the current tax expense.

203. (B) Deferred income tax expense is a plug figure and is calculated as the difference between the deferred tax asset and the deferred tax liability. The deduction in the future for warranty costs of $35,000 creates a deferred tax asset of $14,000 based on a 40% tax rate. Notice that the tax rate for Year 14 is used. The revenue of $60,000 to be taxed in the future creates a deferred tax liability in the amount of $24,000 based on the enacted 40% future tax rate. Creating both the $14,000 deferred tax asset and the $24,000 deferred tax liability results in a $10,000 deferred tax expense for Aragona Corp at December 31, Year 13.

204. (C) Total income tax expense on the income statement for Year 13 would include the current income tax expense of $112,500 plus the deferred income tax expense of $10,000 for a total income tax expense of $122,500.

205. (D) The answer is -0- deferred income tax liability. The premium on the officer's life insurance (when the company is the beneficiary) as well as interest income on municipal bonds are permanent differences. Deferred taxes are not affected by permanent differences. Therefore, when the differences between financial statement income and taxable income are caused by permanent differences, deferred taxes will not result. Deferred taxes will be impacted only when the differences between financial statement income and taxable income are the result of temporary differences.

206. (B) The only permanent difference between book income and taxable income is the interest income on state of Florida bonds. Municipal bond interest income is not taxable but is included in the financial statements as income. Therefore, the difference will never reverse, making municipal bond interest a permanent difference. The excess tax depreciation of $8,000 is considered a deferred tax liability because it results in more tax later. The rent received in advance is taxable now, so it results in a deferred tax asset.

207. (D) Since the financial statement income is provided, taxable income will need to be determined. The $125,000 financial statement income includes municipal bond interest that will never be taxable, so the $18,000 is subtracted. The excess tax depreciation of $8,000 is subtracted from the $125,000 financial statement income because although depreciation was taken, the facts indicate that an additional $8,000 of depreciation can be taken this year on the tax return. The rent received in advance was not includable in the $125,000 financial statement income, because it has not been earned yet. But rent received in advance is taxable when received. Therefore, the $14,000 gets added to financial statement income to arrive at the taxable income for Year 13. Taxable income for Year 13 is computed as follows:

Financial statement income	$125,000
Add rent received in advance	+ $14,000
Subtract excess depreciation	– $8,000
Subtract municipal bond interest income	– $18,000
Taxable income	$113,000

208. (A) The current tax expense is computed by multiplying the current year's tax rate times the corporation's taxable income. Taxable income was determined in the prior question to be $113,000. Therefore, current year tax expense is calculated as follows: taxable income $113,000 × 35% tax rate = $39,550.

209. (D) The current tax payable is computed by multiplying the current year's tax rate times the corporation's taxable income and then subtracting the estimated tax payments made during the year. Taxable income and current income tax expense were determined in the prior question to be $113,000 and $39,550 respectively. Therefore, current year tax payable is calculated as follows:

Current income tax expense	$39,550
Subtract estimated tax payments	− $36,000
Current income tax payable at December 31, Year 13	$3,550

210. (D) At the end of Year 1, the deferred tax liability shown as a noncurrent deferred liability is based on the enacted tax rate (40%) expected to apply to annual income for Years 2, 3, and 4 (the years when the liability is expected to reverse).

211. (B) II is correct. For reporting purposes, all deferred income tax assets and liabilities should be classified according to the type of balance sheet account that originally created the deferral. If caused by a current account, the deferred income tax balance also is current; if caused by a noncurrent account, the deferred tax balance is noncurrent. Warranty obligations are part of the current operating cycle, so the deferred tax asset from warranty obligations is reported on the Year 1 balance sheet as current.

212. (A) I is correct. All current accounts (both deferred tax assets and deferred tax liabilities) are netted to form a single current figure to be reported, either reported as a net current deferred tax asset or reported as a net current deferred tax liability.

213. (B) II is correct. US GAAP provides for both the current and noncurrent treatment of deferred tax assets and liabilities.

214. (C) The estimate for bad debt expense and estimate for warranty expense are both temporary differences. Bad debt expense and warranty expense will both reverse in later years. For bad debt expense, the reversal will impact the tax return in a year that the receivable is worthless. For warranty expenses, the reversal will impact the tax return in a later year when money is spent for warranty costs. Life insurance proceeds are not taxable; therefore, life insurance proceeds are permanent differences between financial statement income and taxable income.

Chapter 8: Accounting for Leases and Pensions

215. (D) US GAAP and IFRS prefer that leases be accounted for as capital leases; therefore, if any one of the given criteria are met, the lease should be accounted for as a debit to an asset and a credit to a liability. The alternative, if none of the given criteria are met, is to account for the lease as an operating lease. But that would involve the lessee not recording a lease liability (or asset) on its books. Operating leases are a form of off-balance-sheet financing, and entities can use that to hide legal obligations such as monthly lease payments. Therefore, GAAP and IFRS prefer capital lease accounting for a lessee.

216. (B) Since there is no title transfer and no bargain purchase option, the lessee will only have use of the asset during the period of the lease. Thus 8 years is used for depreciation purposes in this question.

217. (B) The portion of the minimum lease payment in the 6th year applicable to the reduction of the net lease liability should be more than in the 5th year. A lease is a sophisticated loan, and all loans work essentially the same way. A typical loan payment includes both principal and interest. The principal portion of the loan payment reduces the obligation. The interest portion is the expense incurred to use other people's money. In a lease or loan payment, the interest portion of the payment is always higher in the early years compared to the principal portion, although the monthly payment never changes. Each lease payment is allocated between a reduction of the lease obligation and interest expense so as to produce a constant periodic rate of interest on the remaining balance of the liability. Since the interest will be computed based on a declining lease obligation balance, the interest component of each payment will also be declining. The result will be a relatively larger portion of the lease payment allocated to the reduction of the lease obligation in the later years of the lease term. In the early years of any loan repayment, much of the payment represents interest. Therefore, the portion of the minimum lease payment in the 6th year applicable to the reduction of the net lease liability should be more than in the 5th year.

218. (B) II is correct. If the lessor is either a manufacturer or dealer, the lessor would record the lease as a sales type lease rather than direct financing lease.

219. (A) The lease is "minor" because it will be classified as an operating lease (it fails all the tests for capital lease based on the given information). In minor sale-leasebacks, there is no deferral. Leaseback is considered minor because the lease life is less than 10% of its useful life. Therefore, all gain is recognized. Proceeds of $1,000,000 − $350,000 book value = $650,000 gain.

220. (D) There is no deferred gain, because under US GAAP, when the seller-lessee retains only a minor portion (present value of leaseback is 10% or less of fair value of the asset sold), any gain should be recognized immediately and none deferred.

221. (C) Since free rent is part of the lease arrangement, the tenant must calculate net cost for the entire lease term and divide it evenly over each period. The question involved a 5-year lease with the first 6 months free rent. Therefore, total rent to be paid is not $90,000 but rather $81,000. The net cost of $81,000 is divided over the 60 months, because US GAAP normally requires the same amount of rent expense each month regardless whether cash was paid that month. Although only $6,000 was collected in Year 13, an expense equal to all 12 months is recognized as follows:

$1,500 per month × 60 months	$90,000
Subtract 6 months free	− $9,000
Net cost for 5 years	$81,000
	↓
Divide by 60 months	$1,350 per month
	↓
$1,350 multiplied by 12 months	$16,200

222. (C) I is correct. If sales for the month were $800,000, rent expense for the month would be $16,000. If sales are $800,000 in a single month, $300,000 above base, the rent is $10,000 (base) plus 2% of the excess, $300,000. Total rent would be $16,000 for the month recognized in full. Notice that the additional $6,000 is recognized immediately as expense. II is correct. In months with no contingent rent, the base rent of $10,000 is recognized.

223. (D) The lease bonus should be recognized on the straight line basis over the 10-year lease term:

Lease bonus of $20,000 / 10 years	$2,000 per year
Excess sales of $100,000 result in additional rent expense	+ $5,000
Base rent	+ $80,000
Total rent expense	$87,000

224. (D) I is incorrect. If a lease contains a bargain purchase option, the lease would automatically be accounted for by the lessee as a capital lease rather than an operating lease. Therefore, if a lease contains a bargain purchase option, this is not evidence that the lease should be accounted for as an operating lease. II is incorrect. If the lease is for 8 years and the asset's life is 10 years, the lease would automatically be accounted for by the lessee as a capital lease. The rule is that if the lease life is equal to or greater than 75% of the asset's life, the lease should be capitalized. In this case, the lease life represents 80% of the asset's life; therefore, this is not evidence of an operating lease.

225. (A) I is correct. In an operating lease, no asset or liability is shown on the balance sheet; however, disclosures are required in footnotes. The full amount of remaining lease obligation is required.

226. (D) Since the lease is an operating lease, Bowman Inc., the lessee, must disclose in the footnotes the entire remaining balance of the lease obligation, but the amount does not appear anywhere on the balance sheet. For this reason, operating leases are some-times referred to as off-balance-sheet financing. Also in the footnotes Bowman must show a schedule disclosing the annual minimum lease payments for each of the next 5 years. The schedule would appear as follows:

Year 12	$23,000
Year 13	$23,000
Year 14	$23,000
Year 15	$23,000
Year 16	$23,000

227. (C) I is correct. The lessee must capitalize leasehold improvements even if the tenant is accounting for the lease as an operating lease. Leasehold improvements are then amortized over the shorter of the term of the lease or the life of the assets. Leasehold improvements are not expensed in the year incurred even if the lessee accounts for the lease as an operating lease. II is correct. The lessee would capitalize leasehold improvements if accounting for the lease as a capital lease (or operating lease). Leasehold improvements are then amortized over the shorter of the term of the lease or the life of the assets.

228. (A) I is correct. Leasehold improvements is capitalized even if the lessee reports the lease as an operating lease. The capitalized amount of leasehold improvements is $60,000 determined as follows:

Installation of drop ceilings	$20,000
Installation of new walls	+ $30,000
Installation of flooring and lighting	+ $10,000
Total leasehold improvements	$60,000

229. (B) II is correct. The $25,000 for last month's rent is recorded as an asset, prepaid rent. When rent is paid in advance, the asset prepaid rent should be debited and rent expense would represent the amount of cost incurred that has no future benefit. The $25,000 for last month's rent has a future benefit and thereby would not be expensed in Year 11.

230. (A) The total expense for Year 11 includes both the amortization of the leasehold improvements for Year 11 plus the lease payment. The security deposit of $63,000 and the last month's rent of $25,000 are recorded as assets. The total expense for Year 11 is determined as follows:

Leasehold improvements of $60,000 / 15 years = $4,000 multiplied by 1/12	$333
Lease payment for the month of December Year 11	+ $25,000
Total expense	$25,333

231. (D) The lease term began January 2, Year 13, on a lease valued at $371,600. Since the first lease payment was not made immediately, interest accrued on the entire balance for all of Year 13. Therefore, the calculation of interest expense is as follows:

present value of the initial lease obligation at January 2, Year 13 × interest rate

= interest expense for Year 13

$$\downarrow$$

$371,600 × 10% = $37,160

232. (C) The lease term began January 2, Year 13, on a lease valued at $371,600. Since the first lease payment was not made immediately, interest accrued on the entire balance for all of Year 13. Therefore, interest expense was calculated (prior question) to be $37,160. The remaining $62,840 of the $100,000 payment serves to reduce the liability balance down to $308,769, calculated as follows:

Balance at January 2, Year 13	$371,600
Principal reduction from payment on December 31, Year 13	− $62,840
Lease liability balance at December 31, Year 13	$308,760

233. (B) The lease term began January 2, Year 13, on a lease valued at $371,600. Since the first lease payment was made immediately, the initial payment of $100,000 reduces the principal amount by $100,000. All of the first payment applies to principal since no interest accrued yet. The principal balance becomes $271,600, and the calculation of interest expense at December 31, Year 13, is as follows:

Present value of the initial lease obligation at January 2, Year 13, $271,600 × interest rate

= interest expense for Year 13

$$\downarrow$$

$271,600 × 10% = $27,160

234. (A) The lease term began January 2, Year 13, on a lease valued at $371,600. Since the first lease payment of $100,000 was made immediately, no interest had accrued yet and all of the initial payment represented principal. The initial payment reduced the principal to $271,600. Therefore, interest expense was calculated (prior question) to be $27,160. The remaining $72,840 of the $100,000 payment serves to reduce the liability balance down to $198,760, calculated as follows:

Balance at January 2, Year 13	$271,600
Principal reduction from payment on December 31, Year 13	– $72,840
Lease liability balance at December 31, Year 13	$198,760

235. (A) The fair value of the equipment, $125,000, is equal to the present value of the future cash flows. Since the first payment is due immediately, annual payments equal $25,000, determined as follows:

Present value = annual rents × annuity due factor (5 years, 7%)

↓

$105,000 / 4.2 = $25,000 annual lease payments

236. (C) The fair value of the equipment is equal to the present value of the future cash flows determined as follows:

Present value = annual rents × annuity due factor (5 years, 7%)

↓

$105,000 / 4.2 = $25,000 annual lease payments

Total annual interest payments include principal and interest, so the interest portion is the amount received minus the present value of the principal given at $105,000.

$25,000 annual payment × 5 payments	$125,000
Subtract present value of equipment	– $105,000
Interest income over life of lease	$20,000

237. (B) In a lease that is accounted for by the lessor as a sales type lease there are two income statement components: interest income and profit on sale. Although the Golf Corp is not selling the equipment but rather leasing it, accounting for the lease as a sales type lease leads to recognition of profit from sale just as if the equipment was being sold. Profit from the sale is recognized as the excess of the present value of the selling price over its cost. The present value of the lease payments are used as the proceeds. If the present value of the lease payments were not given, the cash selling price would be used if that were given. On the CPA exam, one or the other will be given. The list price is irrelevant and is *not* to be used as a present value or fair value to determine the profit. In this question, the profit on sale is calculated as follows:

Present value of payments	$1,700,000
Subtract cost basis of equipment	– $1,100,000
Profit on sale of equipment	$600,000

238. (D) I is incorrect. The pay-as-you-go method expenses pension costs from the date the employee retires up until the date of the employee's death. The pay-as-you-go method does not properly match the expense for employee pension costs to the periods benefited.

With regard to pension expense, the Financial Accounting Standards Board (FASB) believes that the periods benefited are the years of service that the employee worked for the company. Therefore, those years of employee service should have expenses recorded for pension cost even though the employee is not collecting any retirement benefits in those working years. Since the pay-as-you-go method doesn't begin recognizing pension expense until the employee stops working, the pay-as-you-go method is not generally accepted under US GAAP. II is incorrect. Under the terminal funding method, similar to pay-as-you-go, the company does not record expense during the service period of the employee. Once the employee retires, the company incurs the expense all at once, usually by purchasing an annuity for the employee that is expected to furnish income to that employee over the next many years. The annuity is expensed as incurred and thus does a poor job of matching pension expense with the periods benefited. Therefore, the terminal funding method is not considered generally accepted under US GAAP.

239. (A) Under US GAAP, amortization of unrecognized prior service cost is calculated by assigning an equal amount of the cost to the future periods of service of each employee at the date of amendment to the plan. The average service life of the four employees is 8 years. Calculate the average service life as follows:

6 years + 8 years + 10 years = 24 years
↓
24 / 3 = 8-year average service life for the four employees
↓
$64,000 / 8 years = $8,000

240. (A) To calculate the $108,300 projected benefit obligation at year end, start with the beginning projected benefit obligation of $93,000 and add 10% interest of $9,300. Then add the service cost of $11,000 and subtract the pension benefits paid during the year of $5,000. The calculation appears as follows:

Beginning projected benefit obligation	$93,000
10% interest	$9,300
Service cost	+ $11,000
Pension benefits paid	− $5,000
Ending projected benefit obligation	$108,300

241. (D) Under US GAAP, all the components of net periodic pension cost must be aggregated and presented as one amount on the income statement. Therefore, the interest cost on the projected benefit obligation, the current service cost, the return on plan assets, the amortization of prior service cost, actuarial gains and losses, and amortization of existing net obligation are all combined and shown as one amount known as net periodic pension cost, pension expense, on the income statement. The separate components of net periodic pension cost is a required footnote disclosure. Other key pension disclosures include detailed description of the plan, including employee groups covered, the fair value of plan assets, and the funded status of the plan, either overfunded or underfunded.

242. (B) The actual return on plan assets is calculated as follows: $1,000,000 beginning fair value + $50,000 in contributions − benefits paid to retirees of $20,000 = $1,030,000.

If ending fair value of plan assets were $1,300,000, then $270,000 must have been the actual return on plan assets.

243. (A) The funded status of the pension plan at December 31, Year 7, is the fair value of the plan assets at the end of Year 7 minus the projected benefit obligation. $18,500,000 – $9,000,000 = $9,500,000. The pension plan is underfunded since the liability is greater than the fair value of the plan assets. This amount of underfunded status, $9,500,000, must be reported on the balance sheet at year end as a liability. If the pension plan status had been overfunded rather than underfunded, the overfunded amount would be reported on the balance sheet as an asset.

244. (D) When calculating the present value of future retirement payments, the projected benefit obligation (by definition) is a projection, an estimate of what future salaries may be. This inclusion of future salaries (in its calculation of benefit obligation) serves to increase the pension obligation compared to taking into account only past and current salary levels. Therefore, the projected benefit obligation is used for most pension calculations because of conservatism. The projected benefit obligation is the present value of future retirement payments attributed to the pension benefit formula to employee services rendered *prior* to a date, based on *current, past, and (an assumption about) future compensation levels.* The only difference between the accumulated benefit obligation and the projected benefit obligation is the assumption of future compensation levels.

245. (C) I is correct. Under US GAAP, interest cost included in the net pension cost recognized for a period by an employer sponsoring a defined benefit pension plan represents the increase in the projected benefit obligation due to the passage of time. The interest cost will probably need to be calculated by the candidate on the CPA exam. II is correct. The current service cost is the present value of all benefits earned in the current period. Current service cost represents the increase in the projected benefit obligation resulting from employee services in the current period. The actuary provides the current service cost. Current service cost will always be given on the CPA exam.

246. (D) The funded status of Century Corp's pension plan at December 31, Year 13, is the difference between the ending fair value of plan assets and the ending projected benefit obligation of $450,000. The ending fair value of plan assets is calculated as follows:

Beginning fair value	$350,000
Add contributions	+ $35,000
Add return on plan assets $350,000 × 12%	+ $42,000
Subtract benefits paid	– $40,000
Fair value at 12/31/13	$387,000

Ending projected benefit obligation of $450,000 – the ending fair value of plan assets of $387,000 = $63,000 underfunded. This underfunded status of $63,000 appears on the balance sheet at year end.

247. (C) The amount of unrecognized prior service cost that is amortized to pension expense in Year 13 = $240,000 / 15 years = $16,000 amortized to pension expense in Year 13.

Chapter 9: Partnerships, Sole Proprietorships, and Fair Value Accounting

248. (C) I is correct. Upon the formation of a partnership, tangible assets such as equipment would be recorded at fair value at the date of the investment. II is correct. Upon the formation of a partnership, tangible assets such as real estate would be recorded at fair market value at the date of the investment.

249. (C) Assets contributed by partners to a partnership are valued at fair value of the assets, net of any related liabilities. Zuckerman's land was worth $60,000 subject to a mortgage of $25,000, so Zuckerman's capital is $35,000 on November 13, Year 1.

250. (A) To add a new partner with an interest of one-fifth, use the following shortcut: Subtract 1 from 5, which equals 4. Take the 4 and divide it into the old partnership capital of $180,000. The result is $45,000. Therefore, Tim must contribute $45,000 to the partnership to receive an exact one-fifth interest. The $45,000 contributed by Tim will add to the $180,000 capital already there. The new total partnership capital will be $225,000 and Tim will receive one-fifth, or exactly, $45,000.

Tim's contribution for a one-fifth interest	$45,000
Partnership capital before Tim's admission	+ $180,000
Partnership capital after Tim's admission	$225,000
	↓
Tim's capital account (20% of $225,000)	$45,000

251. (B) II is correct. Under the goodwill method, the incoming partner's capital account is his or her actual contribution. Goodwill is then determined based on the incoming partner's contribution and shared by the existing partners only; therefore, the incoming partner's capital account is credited for the exact amount of the new partner's contribution.

252. (B) II is correct. The bonus method of accounting for Broskie's retirement increases (or decreases) the individual partners' capital accounts without changing total net assets of the partnership. Under the bonus method of accounting for retirement, any premium paid to the retiring partner is allocated to the remaining partners' capital accounts based on the profit and loss ratios of the remaining partners. Therefore, the bonus method of accounting for Broskie's retirement could increase partners' capital without increasing total assets of the partnership.

253. (D) If Chu will be admitted with 10% of total capital for an investment of $15,000 after revaluing partnership assets, then 10% of total capital equals $15,000. If 10% of total partnership capital equals $15,000, then total partnership capital must be equal to $150,000 and goodwill must be equal to $55,000, calculated as follows:

Total partnership capital equals $15,000 / 10%	$150,000
Subtract existing capital balances	
($45,000 + $35,000 + $15,000 = $95,000)	− $95,000
Goodwill to original partners	$55,000

254. (D)

	Desimone	Jeffrey	Profit
Capital	$140,000	$80,000	$5,000
Interest	+ 7,000	+ 4,000	− 11,000
	147,000	84,000	(6,000)
Loss allocation	− 3,000	− 3,000	(6,000)
Total	144,000	81,000	

255. (B) The salary is allocated first, which results in a loss that needs to be distributed. The loss gets allocated based on a loss ratio of 80% to Barry / 20% to Saralee.

	Barry	Saralee	Total
Earnings			$54,000
Salary	$40,000	30,000	− $70,000
Net loss to distribute			($16,000)
Distribution 80/20	− $12,800	− 3,200	($16,000)
Total	$27,200	$26,800	

256. (D) Rochelle's basis is equal to the cash contributed of $80,000. The fact that the partners agree to share profits 60/40 does not affect their partnership capital accounts at the date of formation.

257. (C) Bob's capital account is equal to the fair value of the land less the mortgage assumed by the partnership. Assets contributed by partners to a partnership are valued at the FMV of the assets net of any related liabilities.

Fair value of land	$70,000
Subtract mortgage	− $20,000
Basis to Bob	$50,000

258. (A)

Capital balances prior to Tatum's admission $50,000 + $30,000	$80,000
Fair value of Tatum's equipment investment	+ $25,000
New partnership capital balances	$105,000
	↓
Tatum's capital interest 30%	$31,500

259. (B) After Tatum's admission, the difference between the fair value of the equipment contributed by Tatum of $25,000 and the $31,500 credit to Tatum's capital account of

$6,500 is debited to Griffin and Owen's capital accounts based on the prior profit and loss ratio of 60:40.

Tatum's capital account credit	$31,500
Fair value of equipment contributed by Tatum	− $25,000
Bonus to Tatum	− $6,500
60% of $6,500 bonus allocated to Griffin	+ $3,900
Griffin's beginning capital	+ $50,000
Griffin's ending capital	$53,900

260. (C) Begin accounting for the liquidation by selling the other assets and realize cash of $360,000. A loss of $60,000 is recorded as the difference between the proceeds and carrying amount of the assets, $420,000. The $360,000 cash is first used to pay off the accrued taxes of $100,000. Cash of $260,000 remains. Before any cash can be distributed, the loss of $60,000 from the asset sale must be allocated based on profit and loss ratios of 70:30. Therefore, Rukke receives $42,000 of the loss and Murray receives $18,000 of the loss. Allocate the remaining cash to Rukke and Murray based on remaining capital balances.

Rukke capital prior to liquidation	$170,000
Subtract share of loss	− $42,000
Total cash paid to Rukke	$128,000

261. (B) The capital account for a sole proprietor begins with the initial investment of $3,000. Under the cash basis, the cash received for revenue in December of $10,000 increases capital and the withdrawal in December decreases capital. The expenses were not paid until January Year 13, so they have no effect on capital under the cash basis. Therefore, ending capital on the cash basis is $11,000 determined as follows:

Initial investment	$3,000
Add revenue	+ $10,000
Subtract withdrawal of	− $2,000
Ending capital on December 31 under the cash basis	$11,000

262. (A) The owner's initial investment of $3,000 and withdrawal of $2,000 do not affect the income statement. Therefore, on the accrual basis, net income is $3,000 calculated as follows:

Revenue earned in November	$10,000
Subtract expenses incurred in December	− $7,000
Accrual basis net income	$3,000

263. (C) On the cash basis, net income includes only the cash collected for revenue in December. Expenses were not paid until January, so net income in Year 13 under the cash basis is $10,000. The owner's initial investment of $3,000 and withdrawal of $2,000 do not affect the income statement.

264. (D) For a sole proprietorship, capital begins with the owner's initial investment of $3,000 and increases by the accrual basis net income of $3,000. The withdrawal of $2,000 does not affect the income statement but does result in a decrease in Chumley's capital account. Therefore, on the accrual basis, ending capital is calculated as follows:

Investment	$3,000
Accrual basis net income	+ $3,000*
Drawings	− $2,000
Ending capital accrual basis	$4,000
*Revenue earned in November	$10,000
Subtract expenses incurred in December	− $7,000
Accrual basis net income	$3,000

265. (C) I is correct. With regard to fair value measurement, US GAAP considers fair value as the price to sell an asset, which is sometimes known as "exit price." II is correct. With regard to fair value measurement, US GAAP considers fair value as the price to transfer a liability.

266. (A) I is correct. Fair value includes transportation costs if location is an attribute of an asset. If an asset has to be moved to be sold, fair value includes the cost of the transportation of the asset to the location in which it can be sold.

267. (D) In fair value measurement of financial assets, the most advantageous market is the market with the best price after considering transaction costs. Note: transaction costs are not included in final fair value. Only include transaction costs when determining the most advantageous market.

268. (C) I is correct. Transaction costs are considered when determining the most advantageous market. II is correct. Transaction costs are *not* included in the final fair value measurement.

269. (D) I is incorrect. A fair value measurement based on management assumptions only is a level 3 measurement and is acceptable when there are no level 1 or level 2 inputs or when undue cost or effort is required to obtain level 1 or level 2 inputs. II is incorrect. level 1 measurements are quoted prices in active markets for *identical* assets or liabilities only. Quoted prices in active markets for similar assets or liabilities are level 2 inputs.

270. (C) III is correct. Quoted market prices available from a business broker for a similar asset are considered to be a Level 2 input, not as reliable as those coming from a stock exchange for an identical asset.

271. (D) I is incorrect. Prices from observed transactions involving similar assets are Level 2 inputs. II is incorrect. Quoted stock prices in active stock markets are Level 1 inputs.

272. (A) I is correct. The market approach uses prices and other relevant information from identical or comparable market transactions to measure fair value.

Chapter 10: Current Liabilities and Contingencies

273. (C) Current liabilities are obligations with maturities within 1 year or one operating cycle, whichever is longer.

274. (B) II is correct. Under the matching principle, expenses are recognized when an entity's assets have no future economic benefit. The executive bonus of $25,000 to be paid in Year 6 was clearly earned in Year 5 and should be accrued as a current liability in Year 5.

275. (A) I is correct. Under the net method, if payment is made after the discount period, a purchase discount lost account is debited.

276. (C) Under the net method, the purchase is originally recorded net of the discount, so no actual account called "purchase discount" is ever recorded. Later, if payment is made within the discount period, no adjustment is made. If payment is made after the discount period, purchase discounts lost is debited. Under the gross method, accounts payable is recorded at the gross amount without regard to the discount.

277. (B) Under the gross method, record the purchase and payable at the gross amount, without regard to the discount. When invoices are paid within the discount period, a purchase discount is recorded.

278. (A) $10,000 base amount $\times$ 0.03 = $300; $300 $\times$ 3 employees = $900.

279. (C) Since the note calls for quarterly payments, the first step is to compute annual interest and then divide by 4. Annual interest on $1,000,000 note $\times$ 0.09 = $90,000 interest annually. Divide $90,000 annual interest by 4 quarters, and quarterly interest is $22,500. The payment itself is $264,200. The next step is to subtract the quarterly interest from the payment, and the difference is the principal reduction for the first payment. The principal reduction is $241,700. Therefore, the new liability after the first payment is $758,300.

280. (A) Normally, interest is imputed when no or an unreasonably low rate is stated. An exception exists for receivables and payables arising from transactions with customers or suppliers in the normal course of business when the trade terms do not exceed 1 year.

281. (B) II is correct. The note payable is reported on the balance sheet at the net of the note payable face value less the unamortized discount.

282. (B) II is correct. Loan origination fees deducted from the proceeds of the loan would be deferred and recognized over the life of the loan as additional interest revenue similar to the treatment of bond discount amortization.

283. (C) I is correct. Common debt covenants include limitations on how the borrowed money can be used. II is correct. Common debt covenants include minimum working capital requirements, so there is always cash available to pay bondholders.

284. (B) II is correct. Violation of a debt covenant results in technical default of the loan, and the lender could call the entire loan due and payable immediately. Normally the two sides get together to work out new terms and avoid default.

285. (C) Under the matching principle, a company should record a liability for warranty in the year of sale if the liability is both probable and can be reasonably estimated.

286. (D) First notice that service contracts are on the accrual basis, *not* the cash basis, so the entire 700 × $500 contracts may be collected in Year 1, but not all $350,000 of it is earned in Year 1. How much of the $350,000 is earned at December 31, Year 1, and how much is considered unearned or deferred? Since service contracts are on the accrual basis, you need to know when the revenue is earned, which the question provides: 30% is earned evenly in the first year and 70% is earned evenly in the second year. When service contracts are first sold, the entire proceeds are reported as unearned revenue liability. Then as the services are performed, revenue is recognized and deferral is reduced. Another important thing to notice is that not all repairs were made on the same day in Year 1. Because repairs are made evenly during the year, you can pick a date and say that all repairs were made that day, but that day you pick has to be in the middle of the year, not too early, not too late. This is because it says that repairs were made evenly throughout the year. July 1 is the middle of the year. Since 30% of the repairs are said to be made in the first year, you are allowed to say that all the repairs made in the first year were made "July 1," since repairs were made evenly during the year. Therefore, only half of the 30% of repairs will be in the current year. $350,000 collected × 30% × 1/2 = $52,500 earned revenue in Year 1; the balance of $297,500 is unearned.

287. (D) I is incorrect. Warranty expense must be estimated under US GAAP rules and is recognized in the year of sale under the matching principle. II is incorrect. Service contract revenue is recognized on the accrual basis, *not* when the contracts are first sold.

288. (A) Under IFRS, *probable* is defined as "more likely than not." *Possible* is defined as "may but probably will not occur."

289. (C) The question asked about a remote chance. *Remote* is defined as "slight" under US GAAP. Classification of contingencies, three levels under US GAAP:

    A. probable—likely to occur
    B. reasonably possible—more than remote but less than likely
    C. remote—slight chance of occurring

290. (B) II is correct. *Possible* is defined under IFRS as "may but probably will *not* occur."

291. (B) II is correct. Under US GAAP, provision for a loss contingency relating to pending or threatened litigation is recorded if the loss can be reasonably estimated.

292. (A) I is correct. In the event that a range of probable losses is given ($50,000 to $150,000), US GAAP requires that the best estimate of the loss be accrued.

293. (C) I and II are correct. IFRS and US GAAP agree that a contingent liability should be recorded when the loss is probable and can be reasonably estimated.

294. (A) I is correct. Under US GAAP, if no amount in the range is a better estimate than any other amount, the minimum amount in the range should be accrued, in this case $75,000, and a note describing the possibility of an additional $75,000 loss should be presented.

295. (B) A contingent liability that is probable and estimable must be recognized. If all amounts within a range of values are equally likely, then the lowest amount in the range is the measurement amount. The final settlement was unknown prior to the issuance of the financial statements, so a contingent liability of $400,000 should have been recorded.

296. (A) I is correct. A contingent liability must be disclosed in its financial statements if sold with recourse. Stabler Corp would need to disclose the contingency for the note at its face amount.

297. (C) I is correct. Under US GAAP, an example of a loss contingency that would be recorded if probable would include a note discounted with recourse. A note endorsed "with recourse" means the endorser is liable if the maker of the note does not pay. This contingent liability should be disclosed. The amount of the loss contingency would include the full maturity value of the note. II is correct. Under US GAAP, an example of a loss contingency that would be recorded if probable would include tax disputes with a state taxing agency. If a range of losses is known, the best estimate should be accrued. If no estimate is better than any other, the minimum loss in the range should be accrued.

298. (D) For a contingent loss to be accrued, the loss must be probable. This loss is only reasonably possible, so no loss is accrued but disclosed. The disclosure should include the range of between $150,000 and $300,000 and indicate that the best estimate is $220,000. No amount should be accrued for losses that are only "reasonably possible."

299. (A) I is correct. Under US GAAP, a gain contingency should be disclosed in the notes unless the likelihood of the gain being realized is remote. If there is a range, the full range of gain contingencies should be disclosed in the notes.

300. (D) Gain contingencies are not reported as revenue until realized. Since the out-of-court settlement had not been accepted by the date of the issuance of the Year 2 financial statements, the gain should not be reported in Year 2. However, there should be adequate disclosure in the notes to the financial statements.

301. (B) The likelihood of loss is reasonably possible and is disclosed on the financial statement notes, but it is not accrued on the financial statements, because it's not reasonably probable. The false claims lawsuit is a gain contingency, and gain contingencies are not recorded (conservatism), because to do so may cause recognition of revenue prior to its realization.

302. (C) As of February 22, Year 5, Triano Corp's financial statements have not been issued and the actual amount of the final settlement is known. Therefore the known amount should be accrued and disclosed in Triano Corp's December 31, Year 4, financial statements as a "subsequent event." This is a recognized subsequent event because it relates to litigation that originated in Year 4.

Chapter 11: Financial Instruments, Foreign Currency, Price Level Accounting, and Nonmonetary Exchanges

303. (C) I is correct. A derivative may be designated and qualify as a fair value hedge if there is formal documentation of the hedging relationship between the derivative and the hedged item. II is correct. A derivative may be designated and qualify as a fair value hedge if the hedged item is specifically identified.

304. (C) I is correct. The hedge must be expected to be highly effective in offsetting changes in the fair value of the hedged item, and the effectiveness is assessed at least every 3 months. II is correct. The hedged item presents exposure to changes in fair value that could affect income.

305. (C) I is correct. A perfect hedge results in no possibility of a gain on the derivative instrument because the gain would exactly offset the loss on the item or transaction being hedged. II is correct. A perfect hedge results in no possibility of a loss on the item being hedged, because in a perfect hedge, the loss on the item being hedged would be offset by the gain on the derivative instrument.

306. (D) I is incorrect. The risk that the other party to the instrument will not perform *must* be disclosed. II is incorrect. The risk that the other party to the instrument will not perform is known as concentration of credit risk, not market risk.

307. (B) II is correct. The risk of a significant number of unsecured accounts receivable with companies in the same industry is referred to as "concentration of credit risk."

308. (C) I is correct. Concentration of credit risk is the risk that a counterparty will partially or completely fail to perform per the terms of the contract. II is correct. Concentration of credit risk exists if a number of counterparties are engaged in similar activities and the industry in which they are involved experiences economic disaster, technological obsolescence, or ceases to exist.

309. (D) Fair value hedge *gains and losses* are recorded on the income statement. Conversely, *cash flow hedge* gains and losses, to the extent they are effective, are recorded as a component of other comprehensive income. Unrealized gains and losses on the effective portion of derivatives used as cash flow hedges are included in other comprehensive income until the future cash flows associated with the hedged item are realized.

310. (C) I is correct. Fair value hedge losses are recorded on the income statement, while cash flow hedge gains and losses, to the extent they are effective (which is assumed in this fact pattern), are recorded as a component of other comprehensive income. II is correct. Fair value hedge gains are recorded on the income statement. It is important for candidates to know that fair value hedges are not the same as cash flow hedges. Unrealized gains and losses on the effective portion of derivatives used as cash flow hedges are included in other comprehensive income until the future cash flows associated with the hedged item are realized.

311. (D) I and II are incorrect. Cash flow hedge gains and losses are not reported on the income statement. Only fair value hedge gains and losses should be reported within the income statement, not cash flow hedge gains and losses. Unrealized cash flow hedge gains and losses should be reported as a component of other comprehensive income. Unrealized gains and losses on the effective portion of derivatives used as cash flow hedges are included in other comprehensive income until the future cash flows associated with the hedged item are realized.

312. (A) I is correct. A contract that conveys to a second entity a right to receive future collections on accounts receivable or cash from a first entity is a financial instrument but not a derivative. A derivative is an instrument that derives its value from the value of some other instrument.

313. (A) I is correct. Gains or losses from remeasuring the foreign subsidiary's financial statements from the local currency to the functional currency should be included on the income statement in "income from continuing operations" of the parent company.

314. (C) Gains or losses from remeasuring the foreign subsidiary's financial statements from the local currency to the functional currency should be included on the income statement in "income from continuing operations" of the parent company.

315. (D) Conversion adjustments associated with translation of financial statements are displayed in accumulated other comprehensive income. As a result, the $36,000 translation gain is included in accumulated other comprehensive income.

316. (A) I is correct. A subsidiary's financial statements are usually maintained in its local currency. If the subsidiary's functional currency is its local currency, the subsidiary's financial statements are simply translated to the reporting currency. The resulting adjustment is reported as other comprehensive income.

317. (B) On October 5, the contract date, 20,000 Taiwan dollars equals $13,000 US dollars (20,000 units × the spot rate of $0.65). On December 31, the liability for Griffin Corp increases because it became more expensive ($0.80) to convert US dollars to Taiwan dollars. On December 31, the liability denominated in dollars rises to $16,000. Therefore, at year end the foreign currency transaction loss is the difference between the exchange rate at the contract date and the exchange rate at year end. The journal entry at year end would include a debit to foreign exchange transaction loss for $3,000 and a credit to accounts payable. The loss of $3,000 is determined as follows:

Original liability (20,000 × 0.65)	$13,000
Liability at 12/31/13 (20,000 × 0.8)	− $16,000
Loss on foreign currency	($3,000)

318. (C) I is correct. Accounts receivable is a monetary asset. Monetary assets include cash and receivables. II is correct. A contra account is classified as monetary or nonmonetary based upon the classification of the related account. Allowance for doubtful accounts is an example of a contra account and is considered monetary because the asset that its contra to, accounts receivable, is monetary.

319. (C) I is correct. Equipment is a nonmonetary asset. Nonmonetary assets fluctuate in value; they are not fixed like cash and receivables are. Nonmonetary assets include equipment, buildings, inventory, common and preferred stock investments, patents, and trademarks. II is correct. A contra account is classified as monetary or nonmonetary based upon the classification of the related account. Equipment is nonmonetary; therefore, accumulated depreciation-equipment is nonmonetary also. A contra account is classified as monetary or nonmonetary based upon the classification of the related account.

320. (B) Holding monetary assets in a period of inflation would result in a purchasing power decline because the dollars lose buying power during a period of rising prices. Holding monetary assets during periods of inflation will result in less purchasing power compared to when a person first started holding the cash.

321. (A) Under US GAAP, certain large publicly held companies may disclose information concerning the effect of changing prices. Historical cost/constant dollar disclosures ignore asset appreciation. Instead, the disclosures are based on historical cost but are adjusted for changes in the general purchasing power of the dollar due to inflation. Historical cost/constant dollar disclosures use a general price index to adjust historical cost based on the rate of inflation. Thus historical cost disclosures ignore appreciation of the asset over its original cost. Constant dollar disclosures adjust for inflation based on the consumer price index. Therefore, historical cost/constant dollar disclosures ignore asset appreciation but adjust for changes in the purchasing power of the dollar.

322. (D) Under US GAAP, certain large publicly held companies may disclose information concerning the effect of changing prices. Current cost/constant dollar disclosures involve adjustments for both purchasing power and appreciation. Current cost/constant dollar disclosures are based on current cost rather than historical cost and are adjusted for changes in the purchasing power of the dollar. Current cost/constant dollar may use specific price indexes or direct pricing to determine current cost and will use a general price index to measure general purchasing power effects. Therefore, current cost/constant dollar disclosures adjust for both purchasing power and inflation.

323. (B) Under US GAAP, a nonmonetary exchange is recognized at fair value of the assets exchanged unless fair value is not determinable.

324. (B) In nonmonetary exchanges that have commercial substance, gain is recognized for the difference in value between the fair value and book value of the asset given up. Since the exchange has commercial substance, Drexel's gain is calculated as follows:

Fair value of the asset given up	$60,000
Book value of the asset given up	− $52,000
Gain on nonmonetary exchange	$8,000

325. (C) When a nonmonetary transaction has commercial substance, gains and losses are recognized immediately based on the difference between the asset's fair value and book value at the time of exchange. Since the exchange has commercial substance, the entire gain is recognized by Hayley Corp despite the payment of $5,000 in cash to Dylan Corp. For Hayley Corp, gain on the asset given up is calculated as follows:

Fair value	$95,000
Subtract book value (cost $130,000 – accumulated depreciation $75,000)	– $55,000
Gain	$40,000

326. (D) I is incorrect. Under US GAAP, losses on nonmonetary exchanges are recognized immediately even if the transaction lacks commercial substance, the rule of conservatism. II is incorrect. Under US GAAP, losses on nonmonetary exchanges are recognized immediately whether or not the exchange has commercial substance, the rule of conservatism. An exchange is said to have commercial substance if the amount and timing of future cash flows change as a result of the exchange.

327. (B) II is correct. Under US GAAP, nonmonetary exchanges that lack commercial substance could possibly result in a portion of the gain being deferred. If the exchange is said to lack commercial substance *and* the amount of cash received in the transaction is less than 25% of the total consideration received, then a proportional amount of the gain is recognized.

328. (D) Since the cash flows will significantly change, the exchange has commercial substance; therefore, the fair value method is used to calculate gain or loss. The fair value of the equipment is $380,000 less the equipment's book value of $400,000, which equals a loss of $20,000. The payment of cash of $5,000 does not enter into the calculation of gain or loss.

329. (C) Under US GAAP, the equipment's fair value of $380,000 plus the cash paid of $5,000 equals the basis of the new warehouse $385,000. Exchanges that have commercial substance use the fair value method.

330. (A) I is correct. Under IFRS, nonmonetary exchanges are characterized as exchanges of similar assets and exchanges of dissimilar assets. Under IFRS, exchanges of dissimilar assets are treated in the same manner as exchanges having commercial substance under US GAAP. Exchanges of dissimilar assets under IFRS are regarded as exchanges that generate revenue. Exchanges of similar assets under IFRS are not regarded as exchanges that generate revenue and no gains are recognized.

Chapter 12: Bonds and Troubled Debt Restructuring

331. (B) If the market rate of interest (6%) is higher than the stated or coupon rate (5%), the bonds will sell at a discount. A comparison of coupon rate and market rate is always done on the issue date to determine what the bonds will sell for.

332. (D) I is incorrect. The market rate would have to be below 5% for Anna Inc. bonds to sell at a premium, above par. II is incorrect. Whether the bonds pay interest annually or semiannually will not determine discount or premium.

333. (A) With regard to a $1,000 bond issued at a premium of 102 on January 1, Year 10, that pays interest semiannually on June 30 and December 31, the stated interest rate is used to calculate the amount of interest payment. If the stated interest rate was 8%, the amount of interest payment would be $1,000 times 8%, or $80 per year. Since the bond pays interest twice per year, the investor would receive $40 on June 30 and $40 on December 31 for a total of $80 per year.

334. (A) $500,000 × 0.98 = $490,000 bond proceeds plus accrued interest of $12,500 = $502,500. Accrued interest is calculated as follows: $500,000 × 10% = $50,000 interest for one year divided by 12 months equals interest each month of $4,166.67. Accrued interest must be collected for May 1 to Aug 1. Multiply 3 by $4,166.67 = $12,500.

Since the amount of interest, $25,000, is legally obligated to be paid every 6 months, accrued interest is calculated from the previous interest date of May 1 to the bond issue date of August 1. Since the amount of interest, $25,000, is legally obligated on November 1, Blue must pay $12,500 for 3 months of interest (from May 1 to August 1). That way, Blue may receive 6 months' interest of $25,000 on November 1 and come out even, since Blue held the bonds for only 3 months prior to the November 1 interest date.

335. (B) Under the straight line method of amortizing the discount, the same amount is amortized each period. The amount of cash paid for interest is added to the amortization, and the total of the two represents the interest expense for the period. The interest expense is a plug figure and is determined last. Also, under the straight line method, the interest expense and the amortization do not vary from period to period. The same amount is amortized each period. The amount of amortization is added to the carrying value of the bonds and increases the carrying amount of the bonds, but it does not affect the interest expense or amortization of future periods. Finally, under the straight line method, the bonds carrying value increases by the same amount each period. By the maturity date, the carrying amount will equal the par value.

336. (C) Under the effective interest method, the interest expense is determined first and the amortization is a plug figure. The interest expense is determined by multiplying the carrying amount of the bonds at the beginning of the period multiplied by the market rate of interest. The amount of *cash interest paid* is then subtracted from the interest expense, and the difference is the amount of discount amortization for the period. The amount of amortization is then added to the carrying value of the bonds and increases the carrying value of the bonds. The increase in the carrying value of the bonds will increase the interest expense in the following period. Also under the effective interest method, the bonds carrying value increases by a different amount each period. By the maturity date, the carrying amount will equal the par value. Note that when bonds are issued at a discount, interest expense is always greater than cash interest paid.

337. (D) Under the effective interest method, the amount of interest expense is determined by multiplying the carrying amount of the bonds at the beginning of the period by the effective rate of interest. $468,500 × 10% = $46,850 *but* the bonds were outstanding for only 6 months from July 1, Year 1, to December 31, Year 1. Therefore, the interest expense for Year 1 is for the 6 months, or half of the $46,850: $23,425. Interest expense is recognized for the period from bond issuance, July 1 through the end of the year, December 31.

338. (A) Under the effective interest method, the interest expense is determined first. The interest expense was computed in the previous question as $23,425. The interest payable at December 31, Year 1, is $20,000 resulting in a discount amortization of $3,425. Under the effective interest method, the amortization is a plug figure and determined last. The $3,425 is then added to the carrying amount at the beginning of the period, which was $468,500. Therefore, the carrying amount of December 31, Year 1, is $471,925.

339. (C) At December 31, interest would be accrued from September 1 through December 31. At year end, accrued interest needs to be recorded from the most recent payment date to the end of the year.

340. (A) Accrued interest at September 30, Year 5, is the interest owed at year end since the June 30, Year 5, interest payment. Accrued interest is calculated as $200,000 × 11% × 3/12 = $5,500. The period of time from June 30 through September 30, 3 months needs to be accrued on the September 30 balance sheet. The journal entry at September 30 (end of year) would include a debit to interest expense of $5,500 and a credit to interest payable of $5,500.

341. (D) II is correct. Serial bonds mature on different dates rather than all maturing on the same day. Serial bonds are prenumbered bonds that the issuer may call and redeem a portion by serial number. III is correct. Debentures are unsecured bonds issued by a corporation. Debentures are unsecured because they are not secured by any specific assets of the corporation in the event of default.

342. (C) $9,333 is calculated as follows: $800,000 × 7% = $56,000; $56,000 × 1/2 = $28,000; $28,000 × 2/6 = $9,333. Since $28,000 of interest is legally obligated to be paid on the next interest payment date of December 1, Year 13, accrued interest is calculated for 2 months, from the previous interest date of June 1 to the bond issue date of August 1. Since the amount of interest, $28,000, is legally obligated to be paid by Tucker on December 1, Tucker collects 2 months of interest on August 1 (from June 1 to August 1) so that Tucker may pay 6 months' interest on December 1 and come out even, because Tucker issued the bonds only 4 months prior to the December 1 interest date.

343. (B) $4,667 is calculated as follows: Accrued interest at December 31, Year 13, is the amount of interest owed since the last payment date on December 1. Accrued interest at December 31, Year 13, is calculated as follows: $800,000 × 0.07 = $56,000 × 1/12 = $4,667. The journal entry would include a debit to interest expense of $4,667 and a credit to interest payable for $4,667.

344. (B) Interest expense is calculated from the date the bonds were issued. Interest would be calculated from August 1 through December 31, 5 months: $800,000 \times 0.07 = \$56,000$; $\$56,000 \times 5/12 = \$23,333$.

345. (D) The entry to record the bond premium would be a debit to cash of $1,020,000, a credit to bonds payable for $1,000,000, and a credit to bond premium for $20,000.

346. (B) Amortization of a bond premium always results in more cash interest than interest expense. This is because when bonds are originally issued at a premium, the issuer gets to keep the premium but only has to pay back the par. In this case, the company raises $1,020,000, keeps the excess $20,000, and only has to pay back the $1,000,000. This serves to reduce overall borrowing cost. The entry to record the amortization of the premium will include two debits, one to amortize the premium and the other to record the interest expense. The credit will be to cash for the total of the two. Therefore, interest expense will always be less than cash paid when bonds are sold for a premium due to the amortization of the premium each period. Conversely, when bonds are sold for a discount, interest expense will always be greater than cash paid.

347. (C) I is correct. Under US GAAP, no value is assigned to the conversion feature of convertible bonds, because the conversion feature cannot be sold separately from the bonds. Under US GAAP, the theory is that the entire amount should be allocated to the bonds because the conversion feature has no value on a stand-alone basis. II is correct. Under IFRS, both a liability and an equity component should be recognized when convertible bonds are issued. IFRS recognizes the bond as a liability and the conversion feature as an equity component. Under IFRS, the bond liability is valued at fair value with the difference between the actual proceeds received and the fair value of the bond liability being recorded as a component of equity.

348. (C) All costs associated with the issuance of a bond are capitalized as a deferred charge and amortized over the outstanding term of the bonds. Capitalized costs of a bond issuance include commissions paid to an underwriter, legal fees, registration fees, printing, and engraving.

349. (B) II is correct. A conversion feature that is separate from a security should be accounted for separately, and a value should be assigned to it at the time of issuance of the bonds. Detachable warrants are option contracts that are issued with and are detachable from the bond. The warrant gives the bondholder the right to buy stock, within a certain time period. If the warrants are detachable, then the fair value of the warrants is credited to APIC-Warrants at the time the bonds are issued. Since the bonds were issued at par, the remainder of the bond proceeds would be credited to bonds payable. Because they are detachable, the warrants are traded separately and are considered to be a separate financial instrument.

350. (D) Stockholders' equity is increased by the value of the warrants. There are 500 bonds with 20 warrants worth $5 each: $500 \times 20 \times \$5 = \$50,000$.

351. (C) I is correct. While the entire balance in the sinking fund account is generally considered to be a noncurrent asset, sinking fund accounts that are considered to offset current bond liabilities can be included within current assets. II is correct. A bond sinking fund is basically an appropriation of retained earnings to indicate to the shareholders that certain retained earnings are being accumulated for the purposes of repaying debt.

352. (B) II is correct. Concessions made by the creditor normally include reduced interest rates.

353. (C) I is correct. With regard to troubled debt restructuring, creditors typically will extend maturity dates to minimize the risk of bad debt write-off. II is correct. With regard to troubled debt restructuring, creditors typically will reduce accrued interest to minimize the risk of bad debt write-off. Reducing or eliminating accrued interest would result in a fresh start for the debtor, and is a good faith gesture by the creditor.

354. (A) When assets are transferred in a troubled debt restructuring, the asset (land) is adjusted to fair value and an ordinary gain or loss is recorded.

Carrying amount	$140,000
Fair value of land	− $80,000
Ordinary loss	($60,000)

355. (D) When assets are transferred in a troubled debt restructuring, the asset (land) is first adjusted to fair value and an ordinary gain or loss is recorded. The $60,000 loss was recorded in the prior question. Then the gain or loss on restructuring is recorded as the difference between the debt and fair value of asset transferred. Liability $165,000 − the fair value of land (80,000) = debt forgiven gain $85,000. The gain is extraordinary, since it meets the criteria (listed in the facts) as unusual and infrequent.

Chapter 13: Working Capital Components

356. (B) The gross method means recording the sale at the gross amount without taking the cash discount into consideration. The journal entry would include a debit to accounts receivable and a credit to sales of $49,000. The $49,000 is determined as follows:

List price	$70,000
Subtract 30% trade discount	− $21,000
Balance	$49,000

357. (C) If the buyer pays within the discount period, the debit to sales discounts taken would be for $980: Accounts receivable $49,000 × 0.02 = $980. Journal entry would be a debit to cash for $48,020, a debit to sales discounts taken for $980, and a credit to accounts receivable for $49,000.

358. (C) If the customer pays after the discount period, the entry would be a debit to cash for $49,000 and a credit to accounts receivable for $49,000.
Notice that accounts receivable is debited for $49,000 whether the buyer pays within 10 days or after 10 days. The speed of the collection only affects how much cash is collected;

accounts receivable needs to be removed for the entire amount that it was set up for, in this case $49,000.

359. (B) II is correct. The allowance method is consistent with US GAAP because it provides for matching of current year credit sales with the estimated uncollectible expenses from those sales.

360. (C) Working capital can be defined as current assets minus current liabilities. Working capital is a measure of solvency. Working capital is an assessment of an entity's ability to pay debts as they become due.

361. (D) Current assets are assets that are reasonably expected to convert into cash, be sold, or be consumed within 1 year or one operating cycle, whichever is longer. Current assets include cash, accounts receivable, trading securities, inventories, and prepaid expenses.

362. (A) I is correct. Under US GAAP, if a current liability is expected to be refinanced on a long-term basis, the liability may be reclassified as long term on the balance sheet. For the entity to reclassify the liability as long term under US GAAP, the company must have both the intent and ability to refinance. The actual refinancing may be done after year end, and the liability may still be reclassified to long term. If the current liability has not been refinanced prior to the issuance of the financial statements, the liability would likely be listed on the balance sheet as current, unless the entity has a signed noncancelable agreement with a solvent lender to refinance the short-term debt on a long-term basis. If such an agreement with a lender is in place prior to the issuance of the financial statements, the liability may be presented as long term even though it has not been refinanced yet.

363. (A) I is correct. Besides cash, demand deposits, and money market accounts, highly liquid investments that are readily convertible into cash can be shown on the balance sheet as cash or cash equivalent if the investments have a maturity of 90 days or less from the date the investment is acquired.

364. (D) Compensating balances are not included as cash or cash equivalents if the deposit is legally restricted. Compensating balances may be included as a cash or cash equivalent if the deposit is not restricted. Compensating balances are often required by lenders so that a debtor can borrow from the institution, but the debtor must leave some amount behind as collateral as a compensating balance. If the amount left behind is legally restricted, then it cannot be included as a cash equivalent. Instead, it would be reported separately as a current asset but not part of cash or cash equivalents.

365. (B) II is correct. A US Treasury bill in the amount of $1,000 purchased December 1, Year 13, that matures February 15, Year 14, has an original maturity of 90 days or less; therefore, it is included in cash or cash equivalents on December 31, Year 13.

366. (C) The $1,800 check written to Snell Corporation is still cash that legally belongs to Early Corporation on December 31, Year 13. Although the check was dated December 31, Year 13, it was not mailed out until Year 14. No adjustment should be made regarding the $1,800 check written out to Snell Corporation. The $500 check that was returned for insufficient funds should be subtracted out of the cash balance on December 31, Year 13. As of December 31, Year 13, not only did the check bounce but there was no way of knowing on that date if it would ever clear. Therefore, $15,000 − $500 = an adjusted cash balance of $14,500.

367. (D) I is incorrect. Factoring without recourse transfers the risk of uncollectible receivables to the buyer. Factoring with recourse leaves the risk of uncollectible receivables with the seller. II is incorrect. Factoring receivables without recourse is a sale of receivables, not a loan. If A had assigned or pledged the receivables in exchange for the $250,000, that would be, in effect, a loan for A rather than a sale of receivables.

368. (D) Under the percentage of credit sales approach, uncollectible accounts expense would be debited and allowance for uncollectible accounts would be credited for $160,000 (2% × $8,000,000). For accounts written off, allowance for uncollectible accounts would be debited and accounts receivable would be credited for $315,000. The December 31, Year 6, allowance for uncollectible accounts balance would be $95,000 ($250,000 + $160,000 − $315,000).

369. (C) III is correct. An entry to write off an account receivable under the allowance method (accrual basis) involves a debit to the allowance account and a credit to accounts receivable. The effect of that entry is a decrease in allowance for doubtful accounts and a decrease in accounts receivable.

370. (B) II is correct. In Year 13 when Costas Corp recovers 40% of the receivable from the bankruptcy trustee, this results in two journal entries. The first entry reverses the write-off of 40% of the amount previously written off ($15,000). Accounts receivable would be debited for $6,000 and allowance for doubtful accounts would be credited for $6,000, resulting in an increase to both the allowance account and to accounts receivable. The simultaneous increase in $6,000 results in an increase to cash and a decrease to accounts receivable in the amount of $6,000. The net effect of the recovery is an increase in cash, increase in allowance, no effect on net income, and no effect on accounts receivable, since accounts receivable first goes up for the reversal and then down by the amount of cash recovered.

371. (A) Face amount of note, $400,000 × 10% interest = $40,000. Maturity value of the note is therefore equal to $440,000. This means that if Hondo held the note to maturity, he would receive $440,000 from the customer.

372. (D) $411,400 is computed as follows:

Maturity value of note	$440,000
Discount by bank: 13% × $440,000 = $57,200 × 6 months	
held by bank	− $28,600
Proceeds received by Hondo from the bank	$411,400

373. (A) The results of the aging schedule will determine the ending balance in the allowance account. The aging schedule results in a balance of $4,600 determined as follows: $50,000 × 0.03 = $1,500; plus $10,000 × 0.06 = $600; plus $2,500 = $4,600. Therefore, the ending balance in the allowance for doubtful accounts equals $4,600 credit. Notice that when using the aging schedule approach, what results is the ending balance of the allowance for doubtful accounts. This is known as a balance sheet approach. Under this approach, any prior balance in the allowance account is ignored for purposes of determining the ending balance in the allowance account. For this reason, the $700 credit balance is not taken into consideration for determining the ending balance in the allowance account.

374. (B) The ending balance in the allowance account of $4,600, minus the previous balance in the allowance account of $700 credit results in the need for an adjustment to the allowance account of $3,900 credit. The journal entry involved in bringing the allowance account from $700 credit up to $4,600 credit involves a debit to bad debt expense of $3,900 and a credit to the allowance for doubtful accounts of $3,900.

375. (B) Even if the prior balance in the allowance account had a balance of $500 debit rather than $700 credit, the allowance account would still need to have an ending balance of $4,600. The results of the aging schedule will always determine the ending balance in the allowance account. Once again, when using the aging schedule approach, what results is the ending balance of the allowance for doubtful accounts. Under this approach, any prior balance in the allowance account is ignored for purposes of determining the ending balance in the allowance account. Thus the $500 debit balance is ignored, and the ending balance of the allowance account is still $4,600 determined as follows: $50,000 × 0.03 = $1,500; plus $10,000 × 0.06 = $600; plus $2,500 = $4,600.

376. (C) If the prior balance in the allowance account had a balance of $500 debit rather than $700 credit, the allowance account would still need to have an ending balance of $4,600. To get the allowance account to $4,600, the prior balance of $500 debit would result in the need for an adjustment to the allowance account for $5,100. The adjustment would involve a debit to bad debt expense for $5,100 and a credit to the allowance account in the amount of $5,100.

377. (B) II is correct. The results of the aging schedule will always determine the ending balance in the allowance account. When using the aging schedule approach, what results is the ending balance of the allowance for doubtful accounts. Under this approach, any prior balance in the allowance account is ignored for purposes of determining the ending balance in the allowance account.

378. (A) $5,000 is calculated as follows: Using the balance sheet approach, accounts receivable of $2,000,000 × 0.04 = $80,000, which represents the ending balance in the allowance account. $75,000 represents the prior balance in the allowance account. Therefore, the adjustment to the allowance account would be a credit of $5,000. The journal entry would be to debit bad debt expense and credit allowance for doubtful accounts for $5,000. Notice that the credit sales are ignored since Miller uses the balance sheet approach to estimating bad debt expense.

379. (B) Under the income statement approach to estimating bad debt expense, the income statement accounts are used to estimate the bad debt expense without any regard for balance sheet accounts. Using the income statement accounts, the net credit sales of $1,800,000 is multiplied by 2% and the bad debt expense for Year 13 is $36,000. The journal entry is a debit to bad debt expense for $36,000 and a credit to the allowance for doubtful accounts in the amount of $36,000.

380. (A) I is correct. At year end, when using the income statement approach to estimating bad debt expense, the previous balance in the allowance account is ignored for the purposes of determining bad debt expense. Under the income statement approach, bad debt expense is calculated based on a percentage of net sales. The result is the amount of bad debt expense for the year without regard to any prior balance in the allowance account.

381. (C) The beginning balance of $55,000 less the amount written off of $15,000 brings the allowance account down to $40,000. Since the ending balance is given at $45,000, an adjustment for $5,000 is needed at year end. This adjustment increases the allowance account and increases bad debt expense in the amount of $5,000.

382. (A) Under US GAAP, if a company intends to refinance a short-term obligation and has the ability to do so, the liability can be recorded as long term rather than current. The requirements are that the entity has a signed commitment from a solvent financial institution to refinance the debt or the debt is refinanced prior to the date the financial statements are issued. Since both conditions have been met, the obligation should be recorded as a long-term liability rather than short term.

383. (A) $500,000 accounts payable + $150,000 current portion of mortgage = $650,000. The bank loan was refinanced long term prior to the financial statements being issued.

384. (C) I is correct. Cash in checking accounts are included in cash and cash equivalents. If any bank accounts are overdrawn, they should be netted and offset by the accounts with positive balances. II is correct. Petty cash is included in cash and cash equivalents. Petty cash includes cash on hand.

385. (D) I is incorrect. A check from a customer dated after the balance sheet date should not be part of unrestricted cash. Cash is defined as unrestricted cash. A postdated check is *not* unrestricted. In fact, there is no guarantee that the postdated check will even clear the bank. II is incorrect. A check dated after the balance sheet date should not be a part of cash equivalents. A cash equivalent is a short-term highly liquid investment that is near maturity (within 3 months) at the time of purchase.

386. (C) I is correct. The numerator for the quick ratio includes cash, net receivables, and marketable securities. II is correct. The numerator for the quick ratio includes cash, net receivables, and marketable securities.

387. (C) I is correct. Total current liabilities is used as the denominator in determining the current ratio. The current ratio is expressed as current assets divided by current liabilities. II is correct. Total current liabilities is used as the denominator in determining the quick ratio. The quick ratio is expressed as cash plus marketable securities plus net receivables divided by current liabilities.

388. (A) I is correct. Factoring involves a company converting their receivables into cash by assigning them to a factor, in this case without recourse. When a company factors receivables without recourse in exchange for cash, title to the receivables is transferred to the factor and the transaction is treated as a sale of receivables. Factoring without recourse means the sale is final and the factor assumes the risk of any losses. Without recourse refers to the fact that if customers do not pay, the factor has no recourse against the entity who sold the receivables. For this reason, the factor often charges fees up front to allow for returns and uncollectible accounts.

389. (D) When a company factors receivables without recourse in exchange for cash, title to the receivables is transferred to the factor and the transaction is treated as a sale of receivables. Without recourse refers to the fact that if customers do not pay, the factor has no recourse against the entity who sold the receivables. For this reason, the factor often charges fees up front to allow for returns and uncollectible accounts. Of the $100,000 factored, 15% is charged as an allowance for returns, $15,000. Another 5% commission is taken off the $100,000. $5,000 + $15,000 = $20,000 deducted. Total received by Barnes Corp is therefore $80,000.

Chapter 14: Accounting for Business Combinations

390. (B) When 100% of the subsidiary is acquired, goodwill is equal to the cash paid of $960,000 minus the fair value of the net assets of the subsidiary. $940,000 assets − $240,000 liabilities = fair value of the net assets of $700,000. $960,000 − $700,000 = $260,000 goodwill.

391. (A) I is correct. When a subsidiary is acquired with an acquisition cost that is less than the fair value of the underlying assets, the balance sheet is adjusted to fair value, which creates a negative balance in the acquisition account. If there are any identifiable intangible assets, they are recognized at fair value and this would increase the negative balance in the investment account. The total negative balance in the investment account is recorded as a gain.

392. (B) II is correct. Consulting fees as well as finder's fees associated with combining two or more corporations are expensed as incurred. If a corporation hires Goldman Sachs to consult or find them a company for takeover, the direct costs paid to Goldman Sachs are expensed as incurred.

393. (D) The net income of the subsidiary will only be included in consolidated net income from the date of acquisition. Therefore, for Year 13, 25% of Flower's net income until September 30 would be reported by Heart. From October 1 to the end of the year, 95% of Flower's income belongs to Heart.

394. (D) The implied value of B Corporation is based on the purchase price of $500,000 and the percentage acquired by Corporation A, 80%. The amount paid by Corporation A of $500,000 divided by the percentage acquired, 80%, equals $625,000. If Corporation A is willing to pay $500,000 for an 80% ownership of B Corporation, the implied value of B Corporation must be $625,000. $625,000 × 80% = $500,000. Notice that although the fair value of B Corporation's net assets were $350,000, the implied fair value of B Corporation is $625,000 based on the amount paid by Corporation A and the percentage acquired by Corporation A.

395. (B) $625,000 − $350,000 = $275,000. When less than 100% of the subsidiary is acquired, goodwill is calculated as the excess of the implied fair value of the subsidiary based on purchase price, $625,000, minus the fair value of the net assets acquired, $350,000. Notice that regardless of the amount acquired, 100% of the net assets, $350,000, are adjusted to fair value and the difference is reported as goodwill.

396. (B) The implied value of Steel Corp based on the purchase price can be calculated based on the purchase price of $800,000 divided by the ownership percentage acquired of 80%. Therefore, the implied fair value of Steel Corp based on purchase price is $1,000,000.

397. (C) The first step would be to calculate the implied value of the subsidiary based on purchase price. The cost of $800,000 divided by the percentage acquired, 80%, equals $1,000,000. The implied fair value of Steel Corp is therefore $1,000,000, and although Platinum acquired only 80%, 100% of the net assets are adjusted to fair value, and the difference between the total fair value of $1,000,000 and the fair value of the net assets is reported as goodwill. $1,000,000 is the implied fair value of Steel Corp minus 100% of the fair value of the net assets acquired, $700,000, which equals $300,000 excess. This $300,000 excess is first allocated to any acquired intangible assets at fair value and then to goodwill. Since there are no acquired intangibles, goodwill equals $300,000.

398. (D) All majority owned subsidiaries should be consolidated—domestic, foreign, similar, dissimilar—under one management (economic entity assumption). Consolidated financial statements should be prepared when a parent subsidiary relationship has been formed. Owning more than 50% of the voting stock is the threshold for control of another corporation when it comes to consolidated financial statements. Filing of consolidated financial statements would be mandatory for Salas and all subsidiaries of which Salas owns more than 50% of the voting stock.

399. (B) On the acquisition date, the fair value of Sienna Corp is calculated as follows: $2,800,000 / 0.80 = $3,500,000. The implied fair value of Sienna Corp based on purchase price is therefore $3,500,000.

400. (B) On the acquisition date, the fair value of Sienna Corp is calculated as follows: $2,800,000 / 0.80 = $3,500,000. The implied fair value of Sienna Corp based on purchase price is therefore $3,500,000. The $750,000 difference between the fair value of the subsidiary of $3,500,000 and the $2,750,000 book value of the net assets acquired must be allocated first by adjusting 100% of Sienna's net assets to fair value. The $750,000 difference minus the $100,000 land adjustment minus the $50,000 furniture and fixtures adjustment leaves $600,000. The next step is to allocate $525,000 of the remaining $600,000 to the unpatented technology. This leaves a balance for goodwill in the amount of $75,000.

401. (C) As part of the eliminating entry on the consolidated work papers, the fair value of any portion of the subsidiary that is *not* acquired by the parent must be reported as noncontrolling interest in the equity section of the consolidated financial statements, separate from the parent's equity. On the acquisition date, the fair value of Sienna Corp is calculated as follows: $2,800,000 / 0.80 = $3,500,000. The implied fair value of Sienna Corp is therefore $3,500,000. $700,000 is the noncontrolling interest (equity account with normal credit balance) calculated as 20% of the fair value of $3,500,000.

402. (B) Since Peyton Corp acquired 90% of Shore but not 100%, a noncontrolling inter-est account will need to be created. To calculate the noncontrolling interest at the date of acquisition, the first step is to determine the total fair value of the net assets of the subsid-iary. As part of the eliminating entry on the consolidated work papers, the fair value of any portion of the subsidiary that is *not* acquired by the parent must be reported as noncontrol-ling interest in the equity section of the consolidated financial statements, separate from the parent's equity. Although Peyton is acquiring only 90%, 100% of the net assets needs to be adjusted to fair value. $180,000 / 0.9 = $200,000. $200,000 is the total fair value of all the net assets of Shore. $200,000 fair value multipled by 10% not acquired equals the noncontrolling interest of $20,000 at January 1, Year 13. Under the acquisition method, 100% of the subsidiary's net assets are adjusted to fair value regardless of percentage of stock acquired by the parent. Therefore, the noncontrolling interest at the beginning of Year 1, $20,000, represents the percentage of the fair value of the net assets of Shore that were *not* acquired by Peyton Corp.

403. (C) Since Peyton Corp acquired 90% of Shore but not 100%, the noncontrolling interest amount starts out at $20,000 but then will increase by 10% of the net income earned by Shore Inc. and will decrease by 10% of the dividends paid by Shore Inc. $20,000 + $1,800 − $400 = $21,400.

404. (C) Consolidated equity is equal to the parent company's equity plus the fair value of any noncontrolling interest. The subsidiary company's equity accounts are eliminated.

405. (A) The debit to investment in subsidiary is equal to the market price of the stock issued on the closing date, not the average selling price or the market price on the announce-ment date. The acquisition price is calculated on the date the acquisition is finalized: 20,000 shares × $40 per share = $800,000.

406. (B) The journal entry to record the investment in subsidiary would include a debit to investment in subsidiary of $800,000, a credit to common stock for $200,000, and a credit to additional paid-in capital for $600,000.

407. (D)

Fair value of net assets (assets minus liabilities)	$450,000
Acquisition price	− $375,000
Excess of fair value over acquisition price	$75,000
Intangible asset acquired	+ $165,000
Gain	$240,000

When Plato acquired the assets with a net fair value of $450,000 upon paying only $375,000, that resulted in a bargain of $75,000. The deal got even better for Plato when they determined that an intangible asset was also being acquired with a fair value of $165,000. The total excess of fair value acquired, $615,000, minus the acquisition price of $375,000 equals a gain of $240,000.

408. (C) In a business combination accounted for as an acquisition, legal and consulting fees are expensed. Thus $80,000 is expensed immediately. The registration costs of $15,000 will serve to reduce the additional paid-in capital account.

409. (D) In a business combination accounted for as an acquisition, the registration costs of $15,000 will serve to reduce the additional paid-in capital account. When the stock is issued to acquire the subsidiary, common stock is credited for the par value of $100,000. The additional $13 per share, or $1,300,000, would have been recorded as additional paid-in capital but for the stock issuance costs of $15,000, which serve to reduce additional paid-in capital to $1,285,000.

410. (C) In the journal entry to record the acquisition, cash is credited for $95,000, common stock is credited for $100,000, and additional paid-in capital is credited for $1,285,000. The credits add up to $1,480,000. The only other debit besides the investment account is a debit to legal and consulting expense in the amount of $95,000. Thus the debit to the investment in subsidiary account is (plugged) $1,385,000.

411. (B) II is correct. Consolidated common stock will consist of Pie Corp's common stock only. Therefore, consolidated common stock will be $140,000.

412. (D) I is incorrect. A dividend paid by the subsidiary to its parent would simply be a transfer of cash from one company to another. There would be no effect on consolidated retained earnings. The parent would simply pick up 80% of the subsidiary's earnings. 80% of the dividend would be eliminated in consolidation. II is incorrect. The other 20% of the dividend would serve to reduce the noncontrolling interest on the consolidated balance sheet, because under the equity method the noncontrolling interest is decreased by its share of subsidiary dividends and increased by its share of subsidiary earnings.

413. (A) The acquisition method requires that 100% of the subsidiary's assets be adjusted to fair value (regardless of the percentage acquired). For that reason, consolidated property plant and equipment should be reported at $250,000 for Seltzer Corp plus $1,200,000 for Potomac Corp, total of $1,450,000. Under US GAAP, property plant and equipment (of the parent) is not written up above book value even if fair value is higher.

414. (D) Assets and liabilities acquired in a business combination must be valued at their fair value. When a parent acquires a subsidiary with an acquisition cost that is less than the fair value of the net assets acquired, the excess is recognized as a gain by the acquirer at the time of acquisition. Calculation of gain:

Fair value of the net assets acquired	$400,000
Less cost to acquire subsidiary	− $250,000*
Gain	$150,000

---

*25,000 shares × $10 per share

Chapter 15: Statement of Cash Flows

415. (A) Under US GAAP, there are three sections to the statement of cash flows. The three sections are cash flows from operating activities, cash flows from investing activities, and cash flows from financing activities. I is correct. Under US GAAP, a statement of cash flows operating activities section prepared under the direct method requires disclosures, including a reconciliation of net income to net cash flow from operating activities. This reconciliation of net income to net cash flow from operating activities is essentially the cash flows from operating activities prepared under the indirect method. Companies choose the indirect method of presenting the statement of cash flows from operating activities (rather than the direct method) because if they use the direct method, they still have to show the reconciliation from net income to net cash flows from operating activities, which is essentially presenting the indirect method anyway.

416. (D) I is incorrect. Under US GAAP, a statement of cash flows prepared under the direct method requires reconciliation, but the reconciliation is from net income (not retained earnings) to net cash flow from operating activities. The direct method is prepared showing the major sources and uses of cash starting with cash received from customers. II is incorrect. Under US GAAP, a statement of cash flows prepared under the indirect method does not require a disclosure from retained earnings to cash flows from operating activities. A statement of cash flows prepared using the indirect method begins with net income and then reconciles net income to cash flows from operating activities, avoiding the need for any reconciliation.

417. (A) I is correct. The direct method shows the exact sources and uses of cash, cash collected from customers, cash paid to suppliers, cash received for interest, and cash paid for income taxes.

418. (D) I is incorrect. Borrowing cash would be shown in the financing section of the statement of cash flows, not the investing section. II is incorrect. Repaying amounts borrowed would be shown in the financing section of the statement of cash flows, not the investing section. Note that repaying interest on the amounts borrowed would be shown in the operating section, but this question specifically referenced repaying the amounts borrowed.

419. (C) I is correct. Making loans to others is an investing activity and would be shown in the investing activities section of a statement of cash flows. II is correct. Collecting loans that were previously made to others is an investing activity and would be shown in the investing activity section of a statement of cash flows.

420. (D) I and II are incorrect. Cash flow per share is *not* a required disclosure when preparing the statement of cash flows using the direct or the indirect method. Cash flow per share is not a required disclosure in financial statements and should not even be disclosed. To disclose cash flow per share would imply that cash flow per share is somehow indicative of an entity's performance such as earnings per share.

421. (D) I and II are incorrect. Regardless whether the direct or indirect method is used, the cash provided by operating activities will be the same, only the presentation is different.

422. (A) I is correct. The primary purpose of the statement of cash flows is to provide relevant information about the cash receipts and cash disbursements of an enterprise during an accounting period.

423. (B)

Net income	$190,000
Increase in accounts receivable	− $7,000
Increase in allowance for doubtful accounts	+ $500
Decrease in prepaid insurance	+ $3,000
Increase in payroll taxes payable	+ $2,600
Net cash provided by operating activities	$189,100

Net income is $190,000. The increase in accounts receivable means that accrual net income is higher than cash basis net income, so subtract $7,000 from net income to arrive at cash flows from operating activities. Whenever current assets go up, subtract the increase from net income. The allowance account works the opposite way of accounts receivable, since it's a contra asset. Add the increase in the allowance account of $500 to net income. The decrease in prepaid insurance is added to net income, so add $3,000. Whenever current assets decrease, add the decrease to net income. Finally, payroll taxes payable increased by $2,600. Anytime a current liability increases, add the increase to net income.

424. (B) II is correct. The entire amount of cash proceeds from the sale of equipment (including the loss) should be shown in the investing section of the statement of cash flows. Cash flows related to fixed asset sales (and purchases) are shown in the investing section. The loss on sale of equipment reduced net income but should not be included in operating cash flows, so it must be added to net income to compute cash flows from operating activities.

425. (B) II is correct. Financing activities include the cash effects of transactions obtaining resources from owners and providing them with a return on their investment.

426. (D)

Payment for early extinguishment of debt is a financing cash outflow of	− $425,000
Payment of Year 13 dividend is a financing cash outflow of	− $50,000
Proceeds from the sale of treasury stock is a financing inflow of	+ $20,000
Net cash used by financing activities	($455,000)

427. (C) Under IFRS, dividends paid may be reported as an operating cash outflow or a financing cash outflow. Under IFRS, dividends are reported as a financing outflow, unless paying dividends is part of the company's core business, in which case dividends are reported as operating outflow. Under US GAAP, dividends paid are reported as a financing outflow on the statement of cash flows.

428. (A) Under IFRS, paying interest is reported as a financing outflow unless paying interest is part of core operations. Banks, for example, will report interest paid as an operating outflow on the statement of cash flows, since paying interest to customers on deposited funds is part of a bank's core operations. Under US GAAP, interest paid is reported as an operating outflow on the statement of cash flows.

429. (B) II is correct. Under IFRS, paying interest and dividends may be reported as financing outflows or operating outflows. Most likely the payment of interest and dividends will be reported as a financing outflow under IFRS, unless the payment is consistent with core operations. In such a case, the payment of interest and dividends will be reported in operating activities. Under IFRS, classifying dividends paid as a financing outflow rather than operating outflow would improve an entity's operating cash flow to total debt ratio.

430. (B) II is correct. Under IFRS, dividends received may be reported as an investing or operating activity on the statement of cash flows.

431. (A) I is correct. Interest received may only be reported as an operating activity on the statement of cash flows under US GAAP.

432. (C) I is correct. Under US GAAP, dividends received and interest paid must be reported as operating activities. II is correct. Under IFRS, dividends received are reported either as an operating activity or investing activity. Interest paid under IFRS is reported as an operating activity or financing activity.

433. (C) Under US GAAP, cash payments made to reduce debt principal are financing outflow. The interest portion would be reported as an operating outflow.

434. (A) I is correct. Bond discount amortization makes interest expense higher and therefore makes net income lower. Bond discount amortization reduces net income, but because it's a noncash expense, the amount of bond discount amortization gets added back to net income under the indirect method.

435. (C) Amortization of bond premium reduces interest expense and makes net income higher. But because no cash is received, the amortization of the premium should be subtracted from net income to arrive at net cash provided by operating activities under the indirect method. So in this question, $18,000 would be subtracted from net income to arrive at cash flows from operating activities.

436. (D) The decrease in inventory represents a cash inflow of $100,000. The decrease in accounts payable represents a cash outflow of $20,000. The net cash inflow is $80,000. Reducing cost of goods sold, $350,000, by the amount of net cash inflow of $80,000 would result in cash paid to suppliers of $270,000.

437. (D) The decrease in inventory from $300,000 to $250,000 represents a cash inflow of $50,000. The decrease in accounts payable represents a cash outflow of $100,000. The net cash outflow is $50,000. Therefore, the $50,000 net cash outflow is added to cost of goods sold to get $1,050,000 as cash paid to suppliers under the direct method.

438. (B) An increase in accounts receivable of $8,000 represents less cash collected than revenue recorded. Therefore, cash basis revenue is less than accrual basis revenue by $8,000, because under the cash basis, revenue is not recorded until the $8,000 cash is received. The decrease in unearned fees represents the amount earned during the period but is collected in a prior period. Therefore, cash basis revenue would be less than accrual basis revenue by $6,000. If accrual basis revenue is $200,000, then cash basis revenue must $186,000.

439. (A)

Beginning cash balance	$20,000
Net cash provided by operating activities	+ $320,000
Net cash used by investing activities	− $402,000
Net cash provided by financing activities	+ $262,000
Ending cash balance	$200,000

The loss on sale of the fixed asset was already included as part of cash flows from investing activities and does not get considered separately.

440. (B) Net cash from investing activities should include the total proceeds received from the sale of investment, $25,000, minus the common stock purchase of $13,000, for a total of $12,000. The dividends and interest income are both considered cash flows from operating activities.

441. (B) II is correct. Financing activities include the cash effects of transactions obtaining resources from owners and providing them with a return on their investment.

Chapter 16: Inventory Valuation Methods

442. (B) If prices are falling, the inventory valuation method that would produce the highest net income would be the method that has the lowest cost of goods sold. Under LIFO, the more recently purchased, cheaper items are being expensed first; therefore, LIFO would show the highest net income when prices are falling.

443. (A) I is correct. In a period of rising prices, cost of goods sold would be higher under LIFO as compared to FIFO. Under LIFO, the more recent purchases are expensed through cost of goods sold, and those are the higher priced items in a period of inflation.

444. (D) Under US GAAP, inventory is valued at the lower of cost or market. Market is defined under US GAAP as the median value between the market ceiling of $16,850, the market floor of $16,545, and the replacement cost of $16,490. Whichever value is in the middle of those three is the market. The median figure for market would therefore be the floor of $16,545. Since cost of $16,730 is higher than market, inventory under US GAAP should be valued at the lower of cost or market in the amount of $16,545.

445. (A) Under IFRS, inventory is valued at the lower of cost or net realizable value. Net realizable value is equal to the net selling price minus the costs to complete and dispose. Cost is $16,730, and net realizable value is $16,850. Net realizable value under IFRS is the same as market ceiling under US GAAP, $16,850. Therefore, under IFRS, inventory will be valued at $16,730, the lower of cost or net realizable value.

446. (A) Cost of goods sold is calculated as follows:

Beginning inventory	$41,875
Purchases	+ $112,800
Purchase returns	− $20,200
Freight in	+ $24,360
Total available for sale	$158,835
Ending inventory	−$32,109
Cost of goods sold	$126,726

447. (A) I is correct. In a period of rising prices, LIFO can be advantageous on a tax return to show lower ending inventory and therefore lower net income. However, if LIFO is used for tax purposes, it must also be used for financial statement purposes under the LIFO conformity rule under US GAAP.

448. (B) Cost of goods available for sale under FIFO is the total of the beginning inventory plus the purchases. The first step to doing inventory valuation is to get the cost of goods available. Prior to any units being sold, the cost of goods available for sale amounts to $113,200, calculated as follows:

Beginning inventory 10,000 units at $1	$10,000
Purchase on 2/10/13 11,200 units at $3	+ $33,600
Purchase on 12/30/13 11,600 units at $6	+ 69,600
32,800 units	$113,200
Total cost of goods available for sale	$113,200

Note that cost of goods available for sale would be identical regardless of using LIFO, FIFO, or average cost. Cost of goods available for sale would be identical using perpetual or periodic.

449. (A) Under FIFO, cost of goods sold consists of the oldest units. In this question, prices are rising so the oldest units sold are the cheap units. Of the 32,800 units available, 11,800 were sold. Of the 11,800 units sold, the first 10,000 come from beginning inventory at a cost of $1. The other 1,800 units sold come from the oldest purchase, in this case 2/10/13 at a cost of $3. Therefore, cost of goods sold under FIFO, assuming a periodic system for the 11,800 units sold, would be calculated as follows:

10,000 units sold at $1	$10,000
1,800 units sold at $3	+ $5,400
Cost of goods sold	$15,400

450. (D) Ending inventory consists of the 21,000 units not sold. Under FIFO, ending inventory will consist of the most recent purchases, since the oldest is sold first. Therefore, of the 21,000 units *not* sold and still in ending inventory, the first 11,600 were from the $6 purchase. The other units not sold, 9,400, are priced at $3. Ending inventory at FIFO:

11,600 units at $6	$69,600
9,400 units at $3	+ $28,200
Ending inventory	$97,800

Another way to determine the ending inventory under FIFO involves subtracting cost of goods sold from cost of goods available for sale. Using information already determined in the prior questions, cost of goods available for sale is $113,200 minus cost of goods sold of $15,400. Ending inventory must therefore be $97,800.

Cost of goods available for sale (from prior question)	$113,200
Minus cost of goods sold (from prior question)	− $15,400
Ending inventory	$97,800

451. (A)

Beginning inventory, 10,000 units at $1	$10,000
Purchase on 2/10/13, 11,200 units at $3	+ $33,600
Purchase on 12/30/13, 11,600 units at $6	+ $69,600
Total available for sale	$113,200

Note that cost of goods available for sale would be identical regardless of using LIFO, FIFO, or average cost. Cost of goods available for sale would be identical using perpetual or periodic.

452. (B) Under periodic LIFO, cost of goods sold consists of the most recently purchased items without regard for whether they were even on hand at the time of sale. Therefore, the most recent purchase at December 30, Year 13, is expensed first, followed by the next most recent purchase on 2/10/13. Under periodic LIFO, cost of goods sold for the 11,800 units sold is calculated as follows:

11,600 units sold that cost $6	$69,600
200 units sold that cost $3	+ $600
Total cost of goods sold	$70,200

453. (B) Ending inventory under periodic LIFO consists of the oldest units, since the first in are also the first out. Therefore, ending inventory under periodic LIFO is made up of the oldest 21,000 units. The 21,000 units are accounted for as follows: 10,000 units of beginning inventory and 11,000 units from the purchase on 2/10/13. Under periodic LIFO, the oldest 21,000 units are accounted for as follows:

From beginning inventory, 10,000 units at $1	$10,000
From the purchase on 2/10/13, 11,000 units at $3	$33,000

Another way to determine ending inventory is to subtract cost of goods sold from the cost of goods available for sale. Ending inventory can be calculated as follows:

Beginning inventory, 10,000 units at $1	$10,000
Purchase on 2/10/13, 11,200 units at $3	+ $33,600
Purchase on 12/30/13, 11,600 units at $6	+ $69,600
Total available for sale	$113,200
Less cost of goods sold (determined in the prior question)	− $70,200
Ending inventory	$43,000

454. (C) Under perpetual LIFO, ending inventory consists of the oldest units, as the most recent purchases are charged to cost of goods sold. The sale on 3/20/13 could not have come from the most recent purchase on 12/30, since the 11,600 units purchased on 12/30 had not been acquired as of 3/20/13 and therefore could not have been sold yet. As a result, the units sold on 3/20/13 had to have consisted of the next most recent purchase on 2/10/13. Thus the 11,800 units sold consisted of the following:

Purchase on 2/10/13, 11,200 units at $3	$33,600
Beginning inventory, 600 units at $1	+ $600
Total cost of goods sold	$34,200

455. (B) Ending inventory under perpetual LIFO consists of the oldest units, since the purchases made just before the sale were charged to cost of goods sold. Therefore, under perpetual LIFO, the 9,400 units of beginning inventory that were not sold are still on hand at year end, for a total of $9,400. In addition, the entire end of year purchase of 11,600 units at $6, $69,600, would still be on hand under perpetual LIFO, since it could not have been sold on 3/20/13 as it had not been acquired yet. Therefore, ending inventory under perpetual LIFO could be calculated as follows:

Beginning inventory units not sold on 3/20/13, 9,400 units at $1	$9,400
Purchase on 12/30/13	+ $69,600
Total ending inventory	$79,000

An easier way to determine ending inventory under perpetual LIFO is to subtract cost of goods sold (already calculated in the prior question) from cost of goods available for sale as follows:

Beginning inventory, 10,000 units at $1	$10,000
Purchase on 2/10/13, 11,200 units at $3	+ $33,600
Purchase on 12/30/13, 11,600 units at $6	+ $69,600
Total available for sale	$113,200
Less cost of goods sold (calculated in the prior question)	− $34,200
Ending inventory	$79,000

It is important to note that calculation of cost of goods available for sale is the same regardless of periodic or perpetual, LIFO or FIFO.

456. (A) The first step in determining average cost per unit is to determine cost of goods available for sale.

Beginning inventory, 10,000 units at $1	$10,000
Purchase on January 14, 4,000 units at $3	+ $12,000
Purchase December 22, 6,000 units at $6	+ $36,000
Cost of goods available for sale = 20,000 total units	$58,000
Average cost per unit = $58,000 / 20,000 units	$2.90

457. (D) When determining cost of goods sold using the weighted average method, the average cost per unit is multiplied by the number of units sold. In this question, cost of goods sold under the weighted average method is calculated as follows: average cost per unit $2.90 × 8,000 units sold = $23,200.

458. (B) When determining ending inventory under weighted average, the first step is to determine the average cost per unit, $2.90 (see prior answer). Once the average cost per unit is determined, the next step is to multiply the ending inventory units of 12,000 by the average cost per unit of $2.90.

Average cost per unit $2.90

Units in ending inventory   12,000 (20,000 units available minus 8,000 units sold)

Ending inventory $34,800

Another way to determine ending inventory under weighted average would be to subtract the cost of goods sold figure from the total available for sale in dollars.

Total available for sale $58,000

Less cost of goods sold   − $23,200 (calculated in previous question)

Ending inventory $34,800

459. (D) I is incorrect. Under FOB shipping point, the seller's last point of responsibility is the place of shipment, as the seller, Shula Corp, no longer owns the goods sold to Langer Corp on December 31. II is incorrect. Under FOB destination, the seller's last point of responsibility is the tendering of the goods at their destination, which had not occurred yet as of December 31, Year 13. Therefore, as the buyer, Shula Corp, does not have title yet at year end in regard to the goods purchased from Mandich Corp.

460. (A) The consignor of goods must include consigned goods (in the hands of consignees) as his or her own inventory at year end. The final cost of consigned inventory on the consignor's books should include cost of inventory plus warehousing costs plus shipping costs to consignees.

461. (C) I is correct. An understatement of beginning inventory of $1,000 causes an understatement of total available for sale of $1,000. With beginning inventory given incorrectly at $13,000 and with purchases of $5,000, total available for sale would be $18,000 instead of the correct amount of $19,000. Total available for sale minus ending inventory equals cost of goods sold; therefore, the understatement of beginning inventory also leads to an understatement of cost of goods sold for $1,000. II is correct. Since cost of goods available for sale minus ending inventory equals cost of goods sold, an overstatement of ending inventory also leads to an understatement of cost of goods sold. If ending inventory is overstated by $2,000, then cost of goods sold is understated by $2,000. The net effect of the two errors is an overstatement of cost of goods sold by $3,000, determined as follows:

Incorrectly Stated

Beginning inventory	$13,000
Purchases	+ $5,000
Total available for sale	$18,000
Ending inventory	− $10,000
Cost of goods sold	$8,000 incorrectly stated

Correctly Stated

Beginning inventory	$14,000
Purchases	+ $5,000
Total available for sale	$19,000
Ending inventory	− $8,000
Cost of goods sold	$11,000 correctly stated

Net effect of the two errors on cost of goods sold is $3,000 understatement.

462. (C) *Perpetual* describes an inventory system where quantity is updated for each purchase and sale as they occur. Under a perpetual inventory system, the actual cost of goods sold is determined and recorded for each sale. At year end, inventory per the perpetual records can be compared to a physical count and inventory shortages can be identified. Perpetual inventory is more expensive to install and maintain, but the advantages often outweigh the limitations.

463. (C) When determining cost of goods sold under average cost, the first step is to determine cost of goods available for sale in units. This is determined by taking the beginning inventory in units and adding the inventory purchases. Therefore, before any units are sold, total available for sale in units is 16,000 units determined as follows:

Beginning inventory	5,000 units
1/9 purchase	+ 5,000 units
1/19 purchase	+ 6,000 units
Total units available for sale	16,000 units

The next step is to determine total available for sale in dollars. This is determined by taking beginning inventory in dollars and adding the dollar amount of each purchase:

Beginning inventory 5,000 units at $4	$20,000
1/9 purchased 5,000 units at $6	+ $30,000
1/19 purchased 6,000 units at $7	+ $42,000
Total available for sale in dollars	$92,000

The next step is to divide the total available for sale in dollars by the total available for sale in units as follows: $92,000 / 16,000 units = average cost of $5.75 per unit. The final step is to take the $5.75 and multiply by number of units sold to determine cost of goods sold under average cost. Since 9,000 units were sold and the average cost per unit was $5.75, cost of goods sold is $51,750 under average cost.

464. (C) In determining ending inventory under average cost, the first step is to determine cost of goods available for sale in units. This is determined by taking the beginning inventory in units and adding the inventory purchases. Therefore, before any units are sold, total available for sale in units is 16,000 units determined as follows:

Beginning inventory	5,000 units
1/9 purchase	+ 5,000 units
1/19 purchase	+ 6,000 units
Total units available for sale	16,000 units

The next step is to determine total available for sale in dollars. This is determined by taking beginning inventory in dollars and adding the dollar amount of each purchase:

Beginning inventory 5,000 units at $4	$20,000
1/9 purchased 5,000 units at $6	+ $30,000
1/19 purchased 6,000 units at $7	+ $42,000
Total available for sale in dollars	$92,000

The next step is to divide the total available for sale in dollars by the total available for sale in units as follows: $92,000 / 16,000 units = average cost of $5.75 per unit. The final step is to take the average cost of $5.75 and multiply by number of units *not* sold to determine cost of ending inventory. Since 7,000 units were *not* sold and the average cost per unit was $5.75, ending inventory is $40,250 under average cost.

465. (D) As the name implies, the moving average inventory method requires that a new weighted average be computed after each purchase of inventory. Ending inventory is priced at the latest weighted average cost.

	Units	Unit Cost	Total Cost
Balance 1/1	1,200	$1	$1,200
Purchase 1/11	800	$3	$2,400
Balance	2,000	$1.80	$3,600
Sold 1/19	1,000	$1.80	$1,800
Balance	1,000	$1.80	$1,800
Purchase 1/30	600	$5	$3,000
Balance	1,600	$3.00	$4,800

466. (B) Under the moving average method, Sanchez Corp would price the next units sold at $3.00 per unit, the new weighted average.

467. (A) With an estimated gross profit of 20%, cost of goods sold must be 80% of sales. Cost of goods sold is therefore $160,000 and can be added to the ending inventory of $10,000 to calculate the total available for sale at $170,000. With the total available for sale now known at $170,000, purchases can be backed into as follows:

Ending inventory	$10,000
Add cost of goods sold	+ $160,000
Total available for sale	$170,000
Minus beginning inventory	– $25,000
Purchases	$145,000

This calculation is used when purchases are not known. Sometimes the exam makes you work backward. If purchases were given, cost of goods sold would have been calculated the normal way as follows:

Beginning inventory	$25,000
Purchases	+ $145,000
Total available for sale	$170,000
Minus ending inventory	– $10,000
Cost of goods sold	$160,000

Chapter 17: Fund Accounting and Government-Wide Financial Statements

468. (D) As part of the fund-based financial statements of the general fund, a balance sheet is prepared on the modified accrual basis as well as a statement of revenue, expenditures, and changes in fund balance. No statement of cash flows is prepared for the general fund as part of the fund-based financial statements.

469. (B) II is correct. With regard to the dual objective of governmental reporting, the idea that government should be accountable to its public by demonstrating that resources allocated for a specific purpose are used for that purpose is described as fiscal accountability. A government attempts to demonstrate fiscal accountability with the use of fund accounting. Fund accounting is how a government attempts to show that it used legally restricted monies for the purpose intended. Through fiscal accountability, the government attempts to demonstrate that the government's actions have complied with public decisions concerning the raising and spending of public funds in the short term, usually one budgetary period. I is incorrect. Operational accountability is one of the dual objectives to government reporting standards but does *not* relate to the idea that government should be accountable to its public by demonstrating that resources allocated for a specific purpose are used for that purpose. Instead, operational accountability deals with the extent to which the government has met its objectives using all resources available and the extent to which it can continue to meet its objectives for the future. Operational accountability deals with the financial statement objectives of timeliness, consistency, and comparability. With operational accountability, the government entity seeks to demonstrate its accountability for the entity taken as a whole. Therefore, fiscal, not operational, accountability relates to the government being accountable to its public for the money being spent as designated. Note: state and local government units gather and report financial information through the use of fund accounting. At the end of the fiscal year, funds prepare financial statements *and* the government as a whole prepares financial statements. This results in two sets of financial reporting.

470. (B) The GASB establishes accounting and reporting standards for governments. GASB statements and interpretations are the most authoritative source of government accounting standards. The GASB is the equivalent of the FASB, and its statements and interpretations are considered the most authoritative.

471. (C) I is correct. Fund accounting supports financial control by helping prevent overspending and making sure that legally restricted and designated monies are spent as intended. Fund accounting makes it easier to monitor compliance with legal restrictions and spending limits. By using fund accounting, the governing body attempts to demonstrate fiscal accountability. II is correct. A fund is a sum of money set aside to accomplish a specific goal. The purpose of fund accounting is to isolate the recording of each activity or group of activities. With fund accounting used by governmental units, resources are segregated for the purpose of carrying on specific activities and attaining certain objectives. Therefore, a self-balancing set of accounts is established for the fire department, the community pool, the subway system, and so on. Each of these sets of accounts is known as a fund.

472. (D) All funds of a state or local government unit must be categorized as one of three separate classifications: proprietary, fiduciary, and governmental type funds. Permanent funds are a type of governmental fund.

473. (C) An enterprise fund is one of the proprietary funds. Proprietary funds include activities of a government that have a user charge (such as a bus system or a municipal airport). If an activity has a user charge (or at least a user charge that is a reasonably significant amount), the activity is recorded and reported by the government within the proprietary funds. A proprietary fund such as an enterprise fund uses fund accounting but also uses accrual accounting, almost like a for-profit business. A fund set up as a proprietary fund has an actual profit motive. Net income is a measurement focus of a proprietary fund. Other than the fact that they use fund accounting and for-profit companies do not, proprietary funds are accounted for much like a for-profit business using the full accrual method of accounting. Under accrual accounting, all assets and liabilities appear on the balance sheet for proprietary funds. This is different than accounting for governmental type funds, which follow modified accrual accounting. Under modified accrual accounting, only current assets and current liabilities appear on the balance sheet for governmental funds in the fund-based financial statements.

474. (C) An internal service fund is a type of proprietary fund in which the services are provided to other agencies of the local government for a fee on a cost reimbursement basis, but the internal service fund typically does not offer those same services to the public. An example of an internal service fund would be a motor pool to store township cars. Proprietary funds use the full accrual basis of accounting and the economic resource focus, as opposed to the financial resource focus. All assets and liabilities are included in the fund-based financial statements of an internal service fund, not just the current assets and current liabilities.

475. (B) Property tax revenue is accounted for in a governmental-type fund, the general fund. Property taxes are recorded in the period in which they are available and measurable. Available under modified accrual accounting means that the property taxes are collectible within the current period or 60 days after year end. *Measurable* simply means "quantifiable in monetary terms."

476. (A) Since the parking garage revenue is shown net of depreciation, that must mean that the parking garage is being accounted for in a proprietary fund and not a governmental fund. Proprietary funds carry all their own assets and liabilities and record depreciation. Governmental funds carry only current assets and current liabilities in their fund-based financial statements. Governmental funds do not record depreciation, since no property plant and equipment exist on the balance sheet. Therefore, the $47,000 of garage rental income must be accounted for in a proprietary fund.

477. (B) Fiduciary funds include assets that the government must monitor and then give to a third party. Only the interest income on employee retirement benefits of $110,000 qualifies as a fiduciary fund, since the money is not available to the government.

478. (B) Money received for the construction of government-owned assets is recorded in the capital projects fund. Of the $12,000,000 raised, a $2,000,000 unrestricted grant from the state of New Jersey represents revenue for the City of Wildwood. The journal entry would include a debit to cash and a credit to revenue in the amount of $2,000,000. The $10,000,000 from the bond issuance is accounted for as other financing sources. The journal entry to record the bond issue is a debit to cash and credit to other financing sources for $10,000,000 on January 1, Year 13, when the bonds are issued. Notice that the account "other financing sources" is credited and not "bonds payable," since the City of Wildwood is going to account for the construction using a capital projects fund. A capital projects fund is a governmental-type fund and uses the modified accrual basis of accounting, and the measurement focus is on current financial resources. As such, the capital projects fund cannot carry long-term debt on the fund-based financial statements. Therefore, the journal entry in the capital projects fund for the City of Wildwood would include a credit to other financing sources. The new convention center will not even appear on the balance sheet in the fund-based financial statements of the capital projects fund, because only current assets and current liabilities can be shown. Convention hall will appear only on the government-wide financial statements. In the capital projects fund, all costs of construction will be shown as expenditures.

479. (D) For all governmental-type funds, including the general fund, capital projects fund, special revenue fund, debt service fund, and permanent funds, the basis of accounting is modified accrual and the measurement focus is the flow of financial resources. The modified accrual basis refers to recognizing revenue when available and measurable. The financial resource focus refers to carrying only the current assets and current liabilities in the fund-based financial statements. The flow of financial resources answers the question, "Where did the monies come from and where did they go?" Net income is not a measurement focus of governmental-type funds.

480. (C) For governmental-type funds, expenditures include capital outlay for large acquisitions as well as expense type costs. Since no property plant and equipment get included on the fund-based financial statements, all the given costs will be recorded as expenditures. Notice that the term *expenditures* is used rather than *expenses* for all governmental type funds when they incur these costs. The term *expense* would be used rather than the term *expenditure* if the fund was a proprietary or fiduciary type fund.

481. (B) II is correct. If the enterprise fund is short of cash and needs $50,000 from the general fund to stay afloat after a storm damages equipment, the $50,000 transfer of cash by the general fund to the enterprise fund is recorded by the general fund as a credit to cash and a debit to other financing uses. Although not an expenditure, transfers from one fund to another fund represent the use of financial resources. While the general fund records this as an "other financing use" the enterprise fund records the receipt of the cash transfer as a credit to "other financing sources" and a debit to cash.

482. (C) Only a governmental-type fund like the general fund would record budget entries into the books at the start of the fiscal year. The entry to record the budget includes a debit to estimated revenues of $40,000,000, and a credit to estimated expenditures (known as appropriations) in the amount of $37,000,000. The expected transfer of $600,000 to the capital projects fund is credited in the budget entry to show that this amount is already assigned or committed. The remaining amount, $2,400,000, is credited to budgetary control, which basically represents budgetary equity at the time the budget is adopted. A credit to budgetary control indicates an expectation that enough revenues will cover expenditures. The estimated revenues could be an estimate of property tax revenues from homeowners. If conditions change, this may affect the government's ability to collect the property taxes. For example, the economy could turn and citizens could lose jobs. A loss of jobs could lead to homeowners going into default and eventual foreclosure, and if so, less property tax revenue would be collected. Although the budget entry is just an estimate, it's still required of every governmental-type fund at the start of the fiscal year because of accountability and control.

483. (D) After the budgetary accounts are recorded at the beginning of the year, no other entries are made to estimated revenues or to appropriations during the year. Budgeted accounts are closed against the budget accounts at year end. For example, to close estimated revenues, credit estimated revenues, and to close appropriations, debit appropriations. The budget closing entry is for the same accounts and same amounts as the budget opening entry, but the debits and credits are reversed. Therefore, in the budget closing entry, estimated revenues is credited in the amount of $40,000,000, appropriations is debited for $37,000,000, other financing uses are debited for $600,000, and budgetary control is debited for $2,400,000.

484. (A) To avoid overspending, purchase orders are recorded as encumbrances when a commitment is made. The assumption is that the encumbrances plus expenditures cannot exceed appropriations. Government accounting systems must reflect not only the expenditures but also the obligations to spend (purchase orders). Encumbrances represent obligations to spend. The encumbrance is debited on February 3 in the amount of $40,000 for control purposes to prevent overspending of appropriations. The credit is to budgetary control. The encumbrance is *not* an expenditure nor is the budgetary control account a liability. The budgetary control account acts as a constraint that reduces available fund balance.

485. (C) On March 10 when the backup generator arrives, the commitment becomes a liability. The original encumbrance is removed and replaced by the actual expenditure. Two journal entries are needed on March 10. The first entry reverses the encumbrance by the actual amount encumbered, $40,000. The first entry is a debit to budgetary control and a credit to encumbrance for $40,000. The second journal entry would involve a debit to expenditures in the amount of $40,650 and a credit to vouchers payable for the same amount.

486. (B) On April 5 when the invoice is paid, the journal entry would include a debit to vouchers payable for $40,650 and a credit to cash of 40,650. The expenditure was booked when the generator and invoice arrived on March 10. When the bill is paid, the liability is reduced and the cash is paid.

487. (A) The journal entry to record property taxes receivable and revenue occurs when the property tax levy takes place. The amount estimated to be uncollectible is $250,000 and that allowance reduces the amount of revenue recognized to the measurable and available amount of $5,750,000. Along with the $250,000 credit to the allowance, the journal entry to record the property tax levy includes a debit to accounts receivable for the full amount levied of $6,000,000. The difference of $5,750,000 is a credit to property tax revenue at the time of levy.

488. (A) I is correct. The government-wide statement of activities is like the income statement for the township. The government-wide statement of activities is prepared using the accrual basis, and the measurement focus is on the flow of economic resources. II is correct. The government-wide statement of net assets is much like a balance sheet. The government-wide statement of net assets is prepared on the accrual basis, and the measurement focus is on the flow of economic resources. Both fixed assets and long-term debt are reported in the government-wide statement of net assets. Infrastructure assets, like roads and bridges, tunnels, and storm sewers are included also. The government-wide statement of net assets reports all assets and liabilities of the primary government except the fiduciary funds. Fiduciary activities are *not* reported in the government-wide financial statements (GWFS) since the net assets of fiduciary funds do not belong to the government. Reporting fiduciary funds in the GWFS would be misleading.

489. (A) I is correct. Assets like a senior center would appear in the government-wide statement of net assets prepared on the accrual basis. The construction in progress prior to completion would also be reported as an asset until the project is complete.

490. (B) II is correct. On the government-wide statement of net assets, enterprise funds are shown as business-type activities, since enterprise funds conduct business activities on behalf of the government and serve the needs of the general public for a fee.

491. (A) I and II are correct. Sales tax and income tax are examples of derived revenue for a governmental entity. Derived revenue is where the underlying event is being taxed.

492. (D) For the school system to qualify as a separate primary government, several criteria must be established including the fact that the school system is a legally separate entity from the city. For a school system to qualify as a separate primary government and file its own financial statements, the following conditions need to be met: the school board would have to be a legally separate entity from the city, have a separately elected governing board (not city council members), and be fiscally independent of other state and local governments. If these criteria can be established, then the school board qualifies as a special purpose local government and would need to report its own government-wide financial statements. Note: a component unit of a primary government such as a school system is blended into the primary government if the board of directors of the component unit is basically the same as the board of the primary government. Also, if the component unit serves the primary government almost exclusively and the debts of the component unit are to be repaid by the primary government, then the component unit should be blended with the primary government on the government-wide statement of activities. In addition, if the component unit is *not* a separate legal entity, then once again, the component unit is blended with the primary government. When the criteria for blending is *not* met and the component unit does not qualify as a separate primary government either, then the activities of the component unit would have to be shown in its own column on the government-wide statement of activities, discrete presentation.

Chapter 18: Not-for-Profit Entities

493. (B) Not-for-profit (NFP) organizations include a wide array of organizations such as private colleges, hospitals, charities, voluntary health and welfare organizations, and churches. Not-for-profit entities use accrual accounting, similar but not identical to for-profit accounting. Accrual accounting is used by all not-for-profit organizations for external reporting purposes. For all not-for-profits, revenue is recognized when earned, and expenses (not expenditures) are recognized as incurred. Resources are received primarily from providers that do not expect repayment or economic returns. Although the operating purpose is other than to provide goods or services at a profit, accrual accounting is nevertheless used. Without a single indicator of performance, the measurement focus of reporting for nonprofits is on the organization "taken as a whole." Accrual accounting is used to determine whether management is performing well in its role as custodian of resources. The Financial Accounting Standards Board (FASB) is the primary source of literature regarding not-for-profit accounting.

494. (B) In the statement of financial position for a not-for-profit, there are three categories of net assets (equity). The categories of net assets are based on whether any restriction has been placed on the net assets by an external donor. The three categories of net assets for a not-for-profit are as follows: unrestricted net assets (governing body can use for any purpose), temporarily restricted net assets (time restriction or use restriction exists), and permanently restricted net assets (only the income can be used, principal must be retained).

495. (D) Financial resources of a not-for-profit entity that are currently expendable at the discretion of the governing board and that have not been restricted externally should be reported in the balance sheet of a not-for-profit entity as unrestricted net assets. When assets are contributed to a not-for-profit, always look to the donor. A building received by a not-for-profit would be shown as unrestricted if the donor placed no restrictions on its use, thus allowing the governing body of the not-for-profit to do whatever it wishes with the structure. If restrictions were placed on the building's use by the external donor, the building would be shown as restricted, either temporarily restricted or permanently restricted based upon the donor's instructions. Assets that are donated to the not-for-profit without an external restriction but later become restricted by the governing board must still be shown as unrestricted. Regardless of the type of asset, if no external restriction exists, the asset is shown in the financial statements as unrestricted. Board-designated restrictions are not the same as donor-imposed restrictions. All board-designated assets are to be shown as unrestricted.

496. (D) Unrestricted support amounts to $460,000 in Year 13. The $125,000 cash contribution is considered unrestricted support, since it can be used at the board of director's discretion and no restrictions were imposed by external donors. Services of $35,000 that are donated would be included as unrestricted support to the extent that they represent skilled services that the not-for-profit would otherwise have to pay for. Since the facts suggest the services were accounting related and that they would otherwise have to pay, all $35,000 of the accounting services are considered unrestricted. Finally, the building worth $300,000 is shown as unrestricted. A building received by a not-for-profit would be shown as unrestricted if the donor placed no restrictions on its use, thus allowing the governing body of the not-for-profit to do whatever it wishes with the structure. If restrictions were placed on the building's use by the external donor, the building would be shown as restricted, either temporarily restricted or permanently restricted based upon the donor's instructions. Assets, such as a building, that are donated to the not-for-profit without an external restriction, but later become restricted by the governing board, must still be shown as unrestricted. Regardless of the type of asset, if no external restriction exists, the asset is shown in the financial statements as unrestricted. Board-designated restrictions are not the same as donor-imposed restrictions. All board-designated assets are to be shown as unrestricted.

497. (D) In Year 13 the contributions are received of $150,000, but they have strings attached. The donor restricted the $150,000, indicating that it can only be used for research. In Year 13 none of the $150,000 was used yet; therefore, in Year 13 all the $150,000 is considered temporarily restricted revenue on the statement of activities (income statement).

498. (A) In Year 13 the contributions received were $150,000, but they had strings attached. The donor (temporarily) restricted the $150,000, indicating that it can only be used for research. By the end of Year 13, none of the $150,000 was used yet; so in Year 13 all of the $150,000 was considered temporarily restricted revenue on the statement of activities (income statement). In Year 14, $135,000 of the temporarily restricted net assets were spent on research. This involves a reclassification of net assets from temporarily restricted to unrestricted. The reclassification involves reducing temporarily restricted net assets by $135,000 and simultaneously increasing unrestricted net assets for the same amount. Just as the unrestricted net assets are going to increase by $135,000, they will also decrease by $135,000 to reflect the spending of the $135,000 that has been released from restriction. If a temporarily restricted net asset is released from restriction, it reflects a decrease in temporarily restricted net assets by the amount released, in this case, $135,000.

499. (D) In Year 13 unrestricted net assets increase by $150,000, not $135,000. In Year 13 the contributions received were $150,000, but the donor restricted the $150,000, indicating that it can be used only for research. By the end of Year 13, none of the $150,000 was used yet; so in Year 13 all of the $150,000 was considered temporarily restricted revenue on the statement of activities (income statement). In Year 14, $135,000 of the temporarily restricted net assets was spent on research. This involves a reclassification of net assets from temporarily restricted to unrestricted. The reclassification involves reducing temporarily restricted net assets by $135,000 and simultaneously increasing unrestricted net assets for $135,000. Just as the unrestricted net assets are going to increase by $135,000, unrestricted net assets will also decrease by $135,000 to reflect the spending of the $135,000 that has been released from restriction.

500. (C) A private, not-for-profit organization prepares all of the given except a statement of restricted net assets. Instead, the not-for-profit prepares a statement of financial position. The statement of financial position (balance sheet) is prepared under accrual accounting, but since there are no owners of a not-for-profit, there is no owner's equity. Instead, the statement of financial position presents: assets − liabilities = the organization's net assets taken as a whole. Instead of having owner's equity, a private not-for-profit must classify all of its net assets into one of three categories on the statement of financial position: unrestricted net assets, temporarily restricted net assets, and permanently restricted net assets. Therefore, a private not-for-profit organization does prepare a statement of financial position.

Bonus Questions

501. (C) Contributions of cash that are donor-restricted for 5 years represent temporarily restricted net assets. Proceeds received from restricted contributions are included in the financing section of the statement of cash flows whether permanently or temporarily restricted. Also included as financing inflows are cash flows related to borrowing. Interest and dividend income restricted to reinvestment are classified as financing inflows as well.

502. (D) Reporting expenses by function and by natural classification are very different ways to report expenses. Reporting by natural classification refers to listing each expense: salary expense, rent expense, and depreciation expense. For-profit companies show expenses by natural classification. Not-for-profits can also show expenses by natural classification but must show a statement of functional expenses either on the face of the financial statements or as a separate disclosure. Showing expenses by function refers to listing each program of the not-for-profit and showing the income and the expense from each program. While not-for-profits are encouraged to report expenses by function on the face of the financial statements, they can choose to present expenses by natural classification instead of by function. If not-for-profits don't present expenses by function on the face of the financial statements, they must do so in a separate disclosure and include a statement of functional expenses. That being the general rule, an exception exists for voluntary health and welfare organizations. The reason that voluntary health and welfare organizations must report expenses by function in the statement of activities *and* report expenses by natural classification is because voluntary health and welfare organizations typically raise large amounts of money through contributions. Donors are interested in knowing how their money is being utilized, therefore voluntary health and welfare organizations must present expenses both by function and by natural classification.

503. (C) I is correct. Conditional pledges are considered unconditional (earned) when the possibility that the condition will *not* be met is remote. The exam question will indicate whether the possibility that the condition will not be met is remote. II is correct. Conditional pledges are considered unconditional (earned) when donor-imposed conditions have been substantially met. For example, if the donor places a condition on the pledge, such as a matching contribution, then the donor-imposed conditions expire when the matching funds are received by the not-for-profit. Until that point the promise is said to be unconditional, unless the possibility that the matching contributions won't be received is remote.

504. (D) A conditional promise is considered unconditional if the possibility that the condition will not be met is remote. Since the college believed that the possibility of not receiving the remaining 5% was remote on December 31, Year 10, Walton's promise is treated as unconditional and revenue is recorded. The revenue is considered temporarily restricted since it must be used for the new parking deck. Although the promise is unconditional, the money is temporarily restricted.

505. (B) II is correct. *Restricted* and *unrestricted* are net asset concepts. When assets are donated to a not-for-profit, they often have strings attached by the donor. Only if the asset has no strings attached can the assets be designated as unrestricted when received.

506. (C) The general rule regarding services donated to a not-for-profit is that no entry is made unless the services require specialized skill donated by experts in their field, such as doctors, lawyers, CPAs, and professional contractors like electricians, roofers, and craftsmen, that would need to be purchased if not donated. Donated professional services such as the preceding are *not* capitalized but are recorded as *both* expense and revenue on the statement of activities. Thus homeless shelters would increase both expenditures and contributions in Year 12. The journal entry would involve a debit to expense and a credit to nonoperating revenue. Had the roof been repaired by a group of amateur volunteers without specialized roofing skills, Homeless Shelters would not have made any entry in the statement of activities.

507. (B) A not-for-profit entity such as the Jersey Shore Free School would recognize contribution revenue based on the net realizable value of the pledges receivable at the time the pledges are made. Therefore, the contribution revenue should be recognized on February 3, Year 13, as follows:

Unconditional pledges	$60,000
(Multiplied by uncollectible percentage	×15%)
Allowance for doubtful accounts	− $9,000
Net realizable value	$51,000

The journal entry to record the pledge on February 3 would include a debit to pledge receivable for $60,000. The credits would be to allowance for doubtful accounts in the amount of $9,000, and $51,000 is credited to contribution revenue. Notice that the actual amount received in Year 13 of $20,000 does not enter into the calculation of contribution revenue.

508. (B) The functional expense categories used by not-for-profit organizations are generally listed under the two main classifications of program expenses and *support services.* Included in the main classification of support services are three subcategories: general and administrative expenses, membership development, and fund-raising. While program expenses directly relate to the mission of the not-for-profit such as a teacher's salary, support services include all other costs involved in maintaining a not-for-profit.

509. (C) IV is correct. Revenues for a not-for-profit hospital arise from activities associated with the providing of health care services, since the providing of health care constitutes the ongoing major or central operations of providers of health care services. There are three categories of revenue for a not-for-profit hospital: patient service revenue, other operating revenue, and nonoperating revenue. Unrestricted gifts to a not-for-profit hospital would be considered nonoperating revenue. Nonoperating revenues would represent incidental earnings unrelated to the central operations of the hospital. Unrestricted gifts would represent nonoperating revenue but would nevertheless be reported as revenue. Therefore, unrestricted gifts would be reported by a not-for-profit hospital as nonoperating revenue.

510. (B) For not-for-profit colleges and universities, gross revenues for tuition are reported net of refunds for cancelled classes. The scholarships are presented as an expense rather than netted against tuition on the statement of activities. Therefore, tuition should be reported at $4,800,000 for the spring semester, Year 13, calculated as follows:

Gross tuition revenue assessed	$5,000,000
Less refunds for cancelled classes	− $200,000
Gross tuition revenue	$4,800,000

The journal entry would be a debit to cash for $4,500,000, a debit to expenses-scholarships for $300,000, and a credit to revenue-tuition and fees for $4,800,000.

CPSIA information can be obtained
at www.ICGtesting.com
Printed in the USA
FSHW020817080121
77504FS